5-

a long the riverrun

RICHARD ELLMANN

a long the riverrun

SELECTED ESSAYS

VINTAGE BOOKS

A DIVISION OF RANDOM HOUSE, INC.   NEW YORK

First Vintage Books Edition, March 1990

Copyright © 1988 by The Estate of Richard Ellmann

All rights reserved under International and Pan-American Copyright Conventions. Published in the United States by Vintage Books, a division of Random House, Inc., New York, and simultaneously in Canada by Random House of Canada Limited, Toronto. Originally published, in Great Britain, by Hamish Hamilton Ltd., London, in 1988 and in the United States of America by Alfred A. Knopf, Inc., New York, in 1989.

Library of Congress Cataloging-in-Publication Data
Ellmann, Richard, 1918—
    A long the riverrun: selected essays / Richard Ellmann. —
1st Vintage Books ed.
        p.   cm.
    "Originally published in Great Britain by Hamish
Hamilton, Ltd., London. Originally published in the United
States of America by Alfred A. Knopf, Inc., New York, in
1989"—T.p. verso.
    ISBN 0-679-72828-7
    1. English literature—History and criticism.   2. American
literature—History and criticism.   I. Title.
[PR99.E66 1990]
820.9—dc20   89-40516
                                                                    CIP

Manufactured in the United States of America
10 9 8 7 6 5 4 3 2 1

Contents

Contents

Publisher's Note

RICHARD ELLMANN died on May 13, 1987, a few months before his biography of Oscar Wilde was published to great acclaim and many expressions of regret that he did not live to see its success. Before that, however, Ellmann had already made plans for his next book, a collection of essays. He had outlined its contents and begun assembling typescripts and off-prints of the pieces that were to be included. It is that collection now published here.

In both date and subject matter the essays are wide-ranging—two go back some thirty years, others only a few years—and have been drawn from many published sources: journals, pamphlets, reviews, a small number from earlier books. One piece—'Becoming Exiles'—has not appeared in print before. And while this latter essay is the only one in the book to deal particularly with James Joyce, Richard Ellmann so distinguished himself as our leading Joycean critic and biographer that to title this collection with a phrase taken from Joyce's masterpiece seems entirely appropriate: *a long the riverrun* are the words that link the end of *Finnegans Wake* with its beginning.

The publishers gratefully acknowledge the assistance of Richard Ellmann's widow, Mary, and his daughters, Lucy and Maud, in the preparation of this volume. Thanks are also especially due to Catharine Carver for her editorial help.

ONE

If we must suffer, it is better to create the world in which we suffer, and this is what heroes do spontaneously, artists do consciously, and all men do in their degree.

—'Yeats Without Analogue'

The Uses of Decadence:
Wilde, Yeats, Joyce

VICTORIAN melancholy disclosed its uneasiness in the concept of decadence. The word began to be used in England about 1850, as if the distentions of empire necessarily entailed spiritual decline and fall. 'Decadent' was not a word that Ruskin or Arnold found congenial: Ruskin preferred 'corruption' and Arnold 'philistinism' and 'barbarism'. But decadence, with implications of the fading day, season and century, had an unfamiliar ring and gradually came to seem the right word. As if to confirm its rightness, the principal guardians of the Victorian age in statecraft and in literature ailed and then died symbolically as well as literally. Most were gone by the time the Nineties started. 'The woods decay, the woods decay and fall.'

What distinguished decadence from corruption or philistinism was that it could be discussed with relish as well as with concern. Gautier, whose writings were in vogue in England as well as in France, declared in his preface to Baudelaire's *Les Fleurs du Mal* in 1868 that the decadent spirit was in harmony with the contemporary crisis. He interpreted decadence as the extreme point of maturity of a civilization. Paul Verlaine could accordingly announce in 1883 with *Schadenfreude* rather than discomfiture, '*Je suis l'Empire à la fin de la Décadence.*' Dying cultures make the best cultures. A few months after Verlaine's poem came Huysmans's novel, *A Rebours*, to give decadence the force of a program. His decadent nobleman (decadents are always male and preferably noble; female decadents are called by other names) has no normal tastes. A determined quester for unheard-of pleasures, he collapses at last in neurasthenia, but of the most glamorous kind. This powerful work outlasted all other decadent prose because it established a new type – the sampler, who keeps changing his drink, who moves from one inordinate and esoteric fancy to another. *A Rebours* became at once a favorite book of Whistler, Wilde, George Moore, Arthur Symons. Wilde and Moore wrote books that in part derived from it, and something of the book's effect rubbed off on Wilde's life as well. The cult of the green

3

carnation, for instance, probably stemmed from Des Esseintes' peculiar notion that, while artificial flowers were to be preferred to natural ones, best of all would be natural flowers that looked like artificial ones. (A florist in the Burlington Arcade dyed white carnations green every day.) What was also valuable about *A Rebours* was that it criticized decadence even while touting it. The intricate schemes of Des Esseintes to amuse himself with new sensations are checked as much by Huysmans's sardonic irony as by their inherent futility, and Huysmans, while never indifferent to his hero, avoids identification with him.

A Rebours was read with more solemnity than it was written with, and remained for a time the Bible of decadence. Devotees of that movement were as determined in their advocacy as its bourgeois adversaries in their rejection. They flourished, however, for only a few years in Paris, during the Eighties. By the time English writers took an interest in decadence it had already lost its lustre, or what they labeled (in a mistranslation of Baudelaire) 'its phosphorescence of putrescence'. In England nobody called himself a decadent, though it was a fine epithet to ascribe to someone else. Ten years after Verlaine's poem Arthur Symons published his article in *Harper's* on 'The Decadent Movement in Literature'. Symons expressed a wry fondness for decadence as 'a new and interesting and beautiful disease', but within a few years he acknowledged that the decadent movement had been 'an interlude, a half-mock interlude'. He was persuaded later to call the movement symbolist rather than decadent, a change of title which had already taken place in Paris ten years earlier. The element of mockery was overt in Oscar Wilde's references to decadence in the late 1880s. He spoke of a new club called 'The Tired Hedonists' who he said 'wore faded roses in their buttonholes' and 'had a sort of cult for Domitian'. The essay in which he evoked this fantasy movement was 'The Decay of Lying', the title itself a mockery of decadence.

The fact that in England decadence never gained the status of a literary movement did not keep people from taking sides about it. It was a subject of debate, it affected the course of literature, it did everything but exist. What opponents of decadence meant by the word was principally its parent movement, aestheticism. The battle lines had been drawn early in the century in two books. One was Gautier's *Mademoiselle de Maupin* (1837), the other Kierkegaard's *Either/Or* (1843). Gautier provided a heroine with bisexual tastes; in his preface he scorned morality, social utility, and nature as points of reference for art. Art was amoral, useless and unnatural. Kierkegaard took up aesthetic man, as opposed to ethical man, and anatomized

4

the way in which aesthetic man sought to be absorbed in a mood, a mood which must necessarily be only a fragment of himself. For fear of losing the mood, he cannot afford to reflect, nor can he attempt to be more than what he for that mood-moment is. He moves from sensation to sensation, much in the manner that Pater was later to extol; Kierkegaard seems to be refuting Pater before Pater wrote.

During the century both aestheticism and anti-aestheticism gathered force. In Joyce's *Stephen Hero* the president of the college warns Stephen, 'Estheticism often begins well but ends in the vilest abominations....' The term could still be used without reproach, however. In 1868 Pater described the Pre-Raphaelites under the honorific title of the 'aesthetic movement'. But the counter-movement had its weapons of ridicule. In 1881 Gilbert's *Patience* presented an aesthete – Bunthorne – as effeminate and narcissistic. Up to now no memorable type of decadent aestheticism had been evolved in English literature to match Huysmans's character Des Esseintes, but Pater tried to establish one with his *Marius the Epicurean*, published two years after *A Rebours*. Marius is also a sampler, attracted to a series of cults like a series of sensations; one of them is a new Cyrenaicism, which as Pater explains 'from time to time breaks beyond the limits of the actual moral order, perhaps not without some pleasurable excitement in so bold a venture'. As his double negative indicates, Pater was a cautious man. His Marius is cautious too, and cannot be said to succumb to Cyrenaicism or to Christianity either; he seeks the impassioned realization of experience, but in so sobersided a way as to deprive aestheticism of its unwholesomeness. (For true decadent aestheticism a gamey whiff of the Borgias is required.) Pater situated his story in imperial Rome during the reign of Marcus Aurelius, and so left it open for someone else to provide a more modern and English instance. This was exactly what Wilde tried to furnish in *The Picture of Dorian Gray*, first published four years after *Marius* and part of the same cycle of novels.

The familiar ways of attacking decadent aestheticism were to quarrel with its supposed morbidity and pretentiousness, its narcissism, its excesses in technique and language, its concern with mere sensation, its artificiality and abnormality. Most of these criticisms could easily be turned against those who made them. Wilde said that if one looked for examples of decay, one would find them among the sincere, the honest, the earnest. In *Ecce Homo* Nietzsche declares, 'Agreed that I am a decadent, I am also the reverse.' By his lights 'morality itself' was 'a symptom of decadence'. It was a revenge upon life, an attempt to 'unself man' (*Ecce Homo*). In *Stephen Hero* Joyce acknowledged that at moments Stephen showed signs of decadence, then added, 'But we cannot but see a process to life through corruption.' One man's decadence was another man's renaissance.

Mallarmé saw in the dying century 'the fluttering of the veil of the temple', as if some infinite revelation were in store (*'Crise des vers'*). So Yeats in 1896 wrote an essay under the title of 'The Autumn of the Flesh', and said in Ninetyish rhythm, 'I see, indeed, in the arts of every country those faint lights and faint colours and faint outlines and faint energies which many call "the decadence" and which I, because I believe that the arts lie dreaming of things to come, prefer to call the autumn of the flesh.' The best season is autumn, and the best time of day is of course the Celtic twilight, which also heralded a victory of moonlit spirit over sunlit matter. Wilde, less mystically, offered the heraldic figure of the new man, the 'do-nothing', a creature who emerges only after five in the afternoon, what used to be called 'the lounge lizard'. In a period when Victorians were infernally busy in misdoing everything, what really needed to be recognized was what he called 'the importance of doing absolutely nothing'. Under cover of indolence, which others were free to call decadence if they liked, Wilde proposed to transform society.

The debate about decadence achieved such resonance that any account of the Nineties must take notice of it. C. E. M. Bowra reports in his *Memoirs* that Yeats wrote to him, 'The 'nineties was in reality a period of very great vigour, thought and passion were breaking free from tradition.' The allegation that they were decaying prompted writers to disprove the charge. In so doing, they had to rethink problems of art, language, nature, life, religion, myth. Wilde is the supreme example. He had adopted aestheticism while still at Trinity College, Dublin, and in the early 1880s he went to America to present the doctrine under the title of 'The English Renaissance'. At the time he was between two versions of aestheticism. One, deriving from Gautier, and supported by Whistler, extolled art for its absolute uselessness and its élitism, and denied that it had any but a per-functory connection with life and nature. The other held that art could remake the world. In America Wilde spent most of his time extolling beauty, but he also urged that artistic principles might beautify houses and dress as well as life generally. This meant that it was not useless, nor necessarily élitist.

Wilde preached renaissance for a whole year to the Americans, then returned and went to Paris. He found himself there *en pleine décadence*. Parisian decadence made his inveterate proselytizing for undefined beauty seem somewhat out of date. Soon after returning to England, Wilde made clear in a review that he did not at all

6

accept that art was for art's sake. That slogan referred only to what
the artist feels when he is composing, and had nothing to do with
the general motive of art. Towards the end of the Eighties Wilde
propounded such a general motive of art in 'The Decay of Lying'.
In this he turned Aristotle on his head by saying that art does not
imitate nature, nature imitates art. It was a paradox that no one
had been able to state so succinctly before, though it had certainly
been implied by the Romantics. The effect was not to divorce art
from life, as Whistler and Gautier would do, but to bring the two
together again, though with the priorities changed. The difference
between Wilde and the Romantics was not in estimating the value
of art, but in putting so much emphasis as Wilde did on artifice.
When he said, 'A sunset is no doubt a beautiful thing, but perhaps
its chief use is to illustrate quotations from the poets', he was suggesting that artists were not only the Shelleyan unacknowledged
legislators, but the quickeners of perception. Nature as we know it
is built up out of imaginative fictions. Strip as we will, we will never
be naked. People fall in love because poets have talked up that
sentiment. They limp because Byron limped, they dress up because
Beau Brummell did, Wilde's point here being that people are not
only affected by the works of art that are written down, but by the
works of art that are lived.

This view of art was not at all élitist, it was democratic and
inescapable. Wilde set himself against the contempt that Whistler
expressed for art critics, which derived from Gautier's comment,
'There was no art criticism under Julius II'. Wilde's contrary view
was, 'The Greeks were a nation of art critics', and he would have
said the same of the Italians of the Renaissance. For criticism was
one way in which expression could recognize its cultural antecedents.
In his other great essay, 'The Critic as Artist', he explained that if
it were not for criticism art would merely repeat itself. But since all
fine imaginative work is self-conscious and deliberate, the role of
criticism is to subvert what has just been done, by confronting it with
what was done before and elsewhere. The critical faculty brings to
bear 'the concentrated experience of the race' as opposed to momentary consolidations arrived at by individual artists. Art is a great
subverter, but always in danger of forgetting to subvert. Criticism
prevents art from forgetting, prevents it from sinking into conformity.
The image of subversion leads Wilde to see the artist and the critic
within the artist as in some sense criminal. He disrupts, he destroys
as he creates. In pursuing ever ampler and as yet unaccepted versions
of the world, the artist is always breaking bonds.

The effect is to challenge all effigies, all that is established, such as the established virtues. Chastity is a virtue that, as Renan says, nature cares little for, and art, according to Wilde, correspondingly little. Charity creates a false sense of obligation, since the rich have no right to their wealth any more than the poor to their poverty. As for self-sacrifice, Wilde says that only a thoroughly secular age like our own deifies it, for self-sacrifice is a survival of the self-mutilation of the savage and part of the old worship of pain. (This was not his final word on the subject.) It involves exactly that contraction of impulse, that narrowing in, which art sets itself to overcome. Wilde examines, or rather cross-examines, all the accepted virtues. So he takes up the virtue of presence of mind. He had a story to illustrate this. Once in a crowded theatre, the audience saw smoke rising from the wings. They panicked and ran for the exits. But a leading actor, a man with presence of mind, went to the proscenium and called out, 'Ladies and gentlemen, there is nothing to worry about. This tiny disturbance is of no consequence. The real danger to you is your own panic. The best thing for you to do is to go back to your seats.' They all turned and went back to their seats, and ... were burned to a crisp.

The virtues are all to be tested afresh, then, and in fact all things require testing. The artist, equipped with a critical eye that constantly enforces a larger context – as, for example, of Greece and Rome as well as Christianity, has this task to perform. We speak of the artistic imagination, but what we mean is this eye for 'the concentrated experience of the race' which keeps the new from solidifying. Writ large, this shift in perception brings a new dispensation – Wilde speaks of it as the 'new Hellenism' as in youth he had spoken of it as the Renaissance. Does it matter whether we call it decadent or resurgent? He thinks not, and simply says, 'When that day dawns, or sunset reddens', as if either phrase would do so long as we recognize that the world will be changed.

Without having read Nietzsche, Wilde had arrived at something of the same view of things. In their different ways, both were constructing a new man, what Wallace Stevens called a 'major man'. Wilde did not share Nietzsche's elaborate view of the genealogy of morals, by which Christianity overturned the pagan virtues and put a morality of slavery in their places; but he did see hypocrisy all about him, masquerading as seriousness. His conception of the major man was of the artist who dared to 'harrow the house of the dead'. Nietzsche would have agreed.

In making the artist an advance man rather than a camp-follower of his society, Wilde implied that the artist is by necessity as well as choice a deviant. His sense of his own sexual deviation helped

8

him to find justification for this view. (Later writers such as D. H. Lawrence also made an alliance between their sexual and their artistic needs.) In Wilde's time the word 'homosexual' was not in use, but there was no less need to find warrant for what it signified. Wilde became the first writer in English since Christopher Marlowe to make a case for it in public. One of his ways of doing so is to attack homosexuality's enemies the puritans. He does so in his plays in the Nineties as he demonstrates, in one play after another, that moral questions are too complex to be solved by puritan mottoes. He never defended homosexuality overtly, except once at his trial, and the present generation, happily uncloseted, are sometimes indignant with him for not having made himself more convincingly and openly the victim of society (the first 'homintern martyr', in Auden's phrase). I think Wilde felt he could be more effective by opening a window here and there than by seeking martyrdom through taking off the roof, and given the age in which he lived, that monstrous age, who can say that he was wrong? He saw himself as a rebel, not as a missionary. Homosexuality was not a cause, it was a way of affronting complacency. In three works, between 1889 and 1892, Wilde therefore outraged heterosexual smugness.

The first was *The Portrait of Mr W. H.*, which played with the idea that Shakespeare was a homosexual, and that he wrote the sonnets to his 'dearmylove', Mr. W. H. He does not actually endorse the view, but he disseminates it. Wilde had begun his perilous campaign to bring this forbidden theme into literature by reconstructing the image of Shakespeare himself. He continued this campaign in *The Picture of Dorian Gray*. Dorian not only espouses decadence, he decays in every way except physically, the physical decay being consigned till the book's end to his portrait. He is driven to ruin men and women alike, as if his love in either mode were genuine only to the extent that it is tainted. As in *A Rebours* or for that matter in *The Waste Land*, a later decadence, both forms of love are introduced as equally corrupt. Wilde did not celebrate homosexuality, but then, neither did Proust. In both writers, this deviation is described in terms of unhappiness. But to mention it at all in a society which pretended it did not exist was courageous, and for Wilde, as events proved, foolhardy. The book is also a criticism of the aesthete type, who samples sins and regrets it. Dorian lacks the motive of art, has only its artificializing mechanism. He enslaves instead of emancipating himself. We almost forgive him because he is so beautiful.

In *Salome* the pageboy loves the Syrian soldier, but this is only one of the erotic relationships suggested. For the Syrian, like Herod, loves

Salome, Salome loves John the Baptist, John the Baptist loves Jesus. All love appears as deviation, and no deviation is superior to any other. All bring their tragic consequences. Wilde improves upon the Bible also by making Iokanaan as hysterical in hatred as Salome is hysterical in love, so that the reader feels about the same concern for his being decapitated as for her being smothered. Originally Wilde intended to have both of them decapitated, as if to confirm their parity. He said elsewhere that renunciation, like excess, brings its own punishment, chastity being just as tendentious as debauchery. Mario Praz finds that *Salome* exhibits the *femme fatale* in all her cruelty, but it seems to exhibit rather the uncontrollability of passion. Though Praz claims the play is all plagiarized, and is baffled by its surviving better than other versions, the reason is simple – only Wilde's *Salome* reconstitutes the entire legend, St. John as well as Salome, and in terms of a strong and original attitude.

With these writings Wilde stretched the domain of literature: he suggested that art might deal critically with moral taboos as part of an effort to remake the world. As Herbert Marcuse says, art shatters everyday experiences and anticipates a different reality principle. Wilde did for English literature almost single-handedly what a score of writers in France had been attempting for a dozen years. The result was soon apparent. A. E. Housman was empowered to write, in the year of Wilde's trial, *A Shropshire Lad,* with its thinly veiled interest in boys; he sent it to Wilde as he was being released from prison. The next year Rhoda Broughton, who did not like Wilde but was quick to sense the way the wind was blowing, wrote her novel *Faustina* which is the first lesbian novel in English. Even Henry James wrote a series of works which took advantage of the freedom that Wilde had won for art even while losing his own freedom. Among them perhaps the most important for my purpose is *The Turn of the Screw* (1897), in which James indicates that boy and valet, and girl and governess, pair off for long hours together, and that the boy is expelled from school for some unnameable act of corruption of his schoolmates, which is described as being 'against nature'. Of course his offense is never specified. By presenting, even if with deliberate vagueness, homosexuality in terms of the corruption of children by adults, James follows Wilde's lead in broaching the subject, and he too associates it with bad conduct, though he himself had the same inclinations. It is in large part thanks to Wilde, then, both to his books and to his trial testimony, that the taboo against writing about homosexual behavior or other forms of sexuality began to be lifted in England. Opening our eyes has been the principal labor of modern literature.

In only one of his works did Wilde attempt to say what the renaissance would be like. That is *The Soul of Man under Socialism*. It would be a time when art would be triumphant, when people would develop freely, when there would be a new Hellenism devoid of the slavery that marked the old Hellenism, when nobody would have to be concerned about the poor, because there would be no poor, nobody would fight for property, because there would be none, nobody would marry because marriage, being merely an extension of property, would also be abolished. In his letter to Douglas, *De Profundis*, Wilde imagined in muted terms that Christ, whom he now accepted at last, but as the supreme aesthete, would bring about a renaissance by being recognized as a model – for Christ created himself, out of his own imagination, and asserted the imagination as the basis of all spiritual and material life. There are no laws, only exceptions. Sin and suffering were for him modes of perfection. So Wilde found a place for suffering, at last, as leading to reconstitution of the terms of existence.

Yeats was in many ways a disciple of Wilde. When he was eighteen he heard Wilde give a lecture in Dublin, and when he was twenty-two he met Wilde at the home of William Ernest Henley. This was the famous occasion when Wilde praised Pater's book on the Renaissance – 'It is my golden book. I never travel anywhere without it, but it is the very flower of decadence; the last trumpet should have sounded the moment it was written.' 'But,' someone interjected, 'would you not have given us time to read it?' 'Oh, no,' said Wilde, 'there would have been plenty of time afterwards, in either world.' Wilde was praising Pater for his decadence, and also suggesting that Pater's readers might as likely go to hell as to heaven. He recognized the ambiguity of Pater's morality.

But the decisive moment in the early relationship of Wilde and Yeats came after the Christmas dinner at Wilde's to which Yeats was invited in 1888, when he was twenty-three. At 16 Tite Street he saw the extraordinary décor – drawing room and dining room done in white, not only walls but furniture and rugs too, the only exception being the red lampshade suspended from the ceiling. This cowled a terra cotta statue which stood on a diamond-shaped cloth in the middle of a white table. After dinner Wilde brought out the proofs of his essay, 'The Decay of Lying', and read it to Yeats. It had a profound effect. Yeats was quite prepared to believe that lies were better than truth, for he had already written in 'The Song of the Happy Shepherd',

> The woods of Arcady are dead
> And over is their antique joy
> Of old the world on dreaming fed
> Grey Truth is now her painted toy.

He would say this more vigorously in his verse dialogue, 'Ego Dominus Tuus', where the first of the two speakers, Hic, pleads for sincerity and veracity so that one can be what one really is, and the second, Ille, pleads for masks and images to enable one to be more than one really is. Ille of course wins. In his edition of Blake Yeats redefined truth in the light of aestheticism: it is 'the dramatic expression of the most complete man'. Pater and Wilde would have approved.

Much of 'The Decay of Lying' deals with the value of images in shaping our awareness of the world. Wilde insists, for example, that 'the whole of Japan is a pure invention. There is no such country, there are no such people.' It is a concoction of the artists, to which they have given the name 'Japan'. Yeats would do something similar with Byzantium, which in his poems must be taken as a pure invention also. It bears no resemblance to the historical Constantinople, but is a city of imagination made by its artists, a magnificent 'instead' conjured up by an aging Irishman seeking an antidote for his own time. In his first poem on the subject, Yeats made the city somewhat static, and he wrote a second poem to give it the dynamism that he like Wilde regarded as essential to avoid art's repeating itself.

Although Yeats in the Nineties scouted the idea of literary decadence, he wrote many poems about the decadence of the modern world. When he says in 'The Second Coming', 'Things fall apart, the centre cannot hold, / Mere anarchy is loosed upon the world', he has at least the satisfaction of finding in the rough beast that 'slouches towards Bethlehem to be born' an image of the mock-renaissance that decadence will bring. His poetry is full of anguish over the world's decadence in poem after poem:

> Though the great song return no more
> There's keen delight in what we have:
> The rattle of pebbles on the shore
> Under the receding wave.

When Edward VII is crowned he writes

> I have forgot awhile
> Tara uprooted, and new commonness
> Upon the throne and crying about the streets
> And hanging its paper flowers from post to post ...

But it was not only English decadence he resented, it was Irish

12

decadence too, as in 'Romantic Ireland's dead and gone, / It's with O'Leary in the grave', or, more largely, 'Many ingenious lovely things are gone.' Yet he never loses hope, and a renaissance is almost always in the offing. 'Easter 1916', which declares that 'A terrible beauty is born', makes the claim that in tragic failure Ireland has achieved heroic rebirth. The great sacrifice is a true Easter, as the poet is the first to recognize.

Yeats identified decadence much as Wilde did, as all the things that the Victorians celebrated as evidence of health. He spoke derisively of 'that decadence we call progress'. The Victorian poets had allowed morality and religion to fill their art with impurities, such as the 'doctrine of sincerity'. Victorian morality was particularly blame-worthy. So he says in *A Vision* (1925), 'A decadence will descend, by perpetual moral improvement, upon a community which may seem like some woman of New York or Paris who has renounced her rouge pot to lose her figure.' He insisted even in his early work that fantasy and caprice would lose their necessary freedom if united either with good or with evil. Wilde sometimes referred distantly to a 'higher ethics', which would completely revise moral standards, and Yeats was prompted to try to redefine good and evil, in terms of an aesthetic point of view. In *A Vision* he said that for men of the coming age, good would be that 'which a man can contemplate himself as doing always and no other doing at all'. This definition underlies poems such as the ones in which Yeats sanctions 'the wild old wicked man', or praises Crazy Jane against the Bishop, or pleads for vital personality instead of dead character, for laughter instead of solemnity. For he too like Wilde knew the terrible unimportance – or even danger – of being earnest. Artists are in league with lovers because they too are in search of an amplified consciousness. Appropriately, however, when Yeats in 'Under Ben Bulben' denounces the present,

> Scorn the sort now growing up
> All out of shape from toe to top,
> Their unremembering hearts and heads
> Base-born products of base beds,

as if all beds could not be called base – or no beds at all, he asks the Irish *poets* to overcome this decadence. It is they who must engender renaissance of the imagination, to rescue 'this foul world in its decline and fall',

> ... gangling stocks grown great, great stocks run dry,
> Ancestral pearls all pitched into a sty,
> Heroic reverie mocked by clown and knave.

> ('A Bronze Head')

Like Wilde, Yeats insists on the ulterior motive of art to reshape the world in which we live. This renaissance is always in the making. Sometimes it is present in the deeds of great men, in intense love, in images of poets or in the way the language, often clogged and impeded, suddenly begins to dance.

And here we come to recognize that each Yeats poem is likely to begin in decadence, and to end in renaissance. The decay may be physical, as in 'The Tower', or 'Sailing to Byzantium', or cultural, as in 'Nineteen Hundred and Nineteen'. There are of course many variations – sometimes the point is to show that apparent decadence is not true decadence, as in 'No Second Troy', and sometimes, as in 'The Cold Heaven', the decadence continues into the afterworld, where heaven proves to be hell. But in general the poems present decadence in order to overcome it. The mind contends with some decadent fact or thought or image, then puts it aside in favor of some radiant recovery, a renaissance in little. Yeats does the same thing when he takes up whole civilizations, as if they too at recurrent intervals were artistically rescued from decadence. He expresses this idea most powerfully in 'The Gyres':

> Conduct and work grow coarse, and coarse the soul,
> What matter? Those that Rocky Face holds dear,
> Lovers of horses and of women, shall,
> From marble of a broken sepulchre,
> Or dark betwixt the polecat and the owl,
> Or any rich, dark nothing disinter
> The workman, noble and saint, and all things run
> On that unfashionable gyre again.

Lovers of horses and of women – Yeats would have said artists directly but he avoids the term, not wishing to be totally aesthetic. The term 'artist' had become much less honorific than it was in Wilde's time, yet the artist's role in conjuring up the best of life out of marble or air is implicit.

In Wilde and Yeats 'decadence' becomes the term to turn upon their antagonists. The decadents are those who accept the acquisitive, insensitive, unimaginative world, with all its morality, sincerity and seriousness. This world exists only as a distortion of reality, as Blake would also have said. Wilde could celebrate art more directly in his time than was possible in Yeats's more ironical age, and while Yeats believed as fully as Wilde did that the mind of man can be rescued by art, he had to be wary in praising a faculty that others were quick to belittle. If Yeats is occasionally circumspect, Joyce is even more so. By his time silence, exile, and cunning are required. Yet, though he would not have said so, Joyce was in the same tradition.

He rarely discusses decadence or renaissance in general terms as Wilde and Yeats had. The word 'aesthetic' was used by him to describe a philosophical theory, not adjectivally to pat art on the back. He even called Yeats an aesthete in a derogatory way, meaning that Yeats had been too ethereal and so had drifted about. Joyce wanted his renaissance closer to earth. He began by particularizing the waste-land qualities of life in Ireland. He has Mr. Dedalus say at the Christmas dinner in *A Portrait*, 'A priestridden godforsaken race.' In 'The Day of the Rabblement', Joyce's first published work, he called the Irish the 'most belated race in Europe'. Later Stephen Dedalus in *A Portrait* says that Ireland is 'the old sow that eats her farrow'. Joyce, as a writer of fiction based on close observation, makes a more detailed attack upon hypocrisy than either Wilde or Yeats – he shows his countrymen pretending to piety and goodness but actually using religion and morality to curb individual lives with cruelty and repressiveness. In *Dubliners* he presented his initial indictment of Ireland, in terms of its inertness, repression and corruption.

Yet *Dubliners* does not rest in the portrayal of decadence. It establishes by tacit antithesis what it is the country lacks. Even while he portrays the fallen state of his countrymen, Joyce introduces three elements of possible relief. The first is a sympathy, usually latent and unstated, for thwarted lives. The second is the evident pleasure taken by the author in Dublin humor. If Joyce were merely excoriating, the humor would be a continual irrelevance. But it is not irrelevant, it keeps suggesting that even squalor can be funny, as if to enable us to withdraw a little from mere disgust or horror, and yet by prodding the muscles with which we laugh to keep us from detachment. Through humor we tumble to our likeness with others. The third is the reserved, fastidious diction and occasional bursts of lyricism. It is as if Joyce were proclaiming that all is chaos, but doing so in heroic couplets. When even the most mentally impoverished situations are described so deftly, so reservedly, so lyrically, the style itself offers the lost rhythms, the missing emotional possibilities, the absent structure. The age weeps, the rhythm smiles. So as hopes are dashed, enterprises doomed, love unrequited or warped, sympathy, humor and lyricism keep reminding us that life need not necessarily be so incomplete. Joyce is not being inconsistent then, in the last story of *Dubliners*, 'The Dead', where his hero is forced to acknowledge that there can be passion in parochialism and primitivism. The country may be decadent, yet still worth saving.

If the description of decadence is by example rather than generalization, so is the description of renaissance. Yet that Joyce hoped for a renaissance was something he did say explicitly, though in less grandiloquent language, on a few rare occasions. The first was in his semi-autobiographical narrative essay entitled 'A Portrait of the Artist', not the book that came later. He ends that essay with a promise of what, thanks to the artist, is to come:

> To those multitudes, not as yet in the wombs of humanity but surely engenderable there, he would give the word: Man and woman, out of you comes the nation that is to come, the lightening of your masses in travail; the competitive order is employed against itself, the aristocracies are supplanted, and amid the general paralysis of an insane society, the confederate will issues in action.

The later novel, *A Portrait of the Artist as a Young Man,* uses a different method from *Dubliners,* in that decadence is described not from various points of view but entirely through the growing consciousness of it in the mind of the inchoate artist. The criticism of decadence is much the same but looks different because of this focus. Stephen's future depends upon his becoming an artist, but the future of Ireland depends upon it too. So he asks himself, as he thinks of his decadent countrymen, 'How could he hit their conscience or how cast his shadow over the imaginations of their daughters, before their squires begat upon them, that they might breed a race less ignoble than their own.' At the book's end, Stephen announces that he is going forth for the millionth time to 'encounter the reality of experience and to forge in the smithy of my soul the uncreated conscience of my race'. Joyce has stolen conscience away from the Church and given it to art. He wishes to emphasize that his art will work with reality, not Zolaesque reality, which is distortion in the name of the body, and not mystical distortion, which is in the name of the soul – but it is through art that he hopes to bring about this great change. As he wrote in a letter to his wife on 22 August 1912, 'I am one of the writers of the generation who are perhaps creating at last a conscience in the soul of this wretched race.'

Joyce had read Wilde, regarded him as a hero of literature, a victim of society; he had Buck Mulligan mock Wilde's idea of a new Hellenism, but what Mulligan mocks is what Joyce doesn't mock. Even if Joyce would not have used that slogan, *Ulysses* with its Greek title was intended to bring something like a new Hellenism about. Because *Ulysses* does so many things – Joyce worried at one point whether he was trying to do too much – this basic impulse has been lost. Yet Joyce like Stephen in *Stephen Hero* considered art to be the vital center of life. When he speaks of a conscience he means something different from the conscience then prevalent – something in tune with Wilde's higher ethics, more Hellenic than Christian. It is a conscience which is always in search of more freedom for itself, and hence for both artist and his audience.

Readers of *Ulysses* have pondered endlessly whether the principal characters are reborn. They do not need to be. Their consciences have gradually defined themselves as exemplary in action and thought against the powers of the world. In *Circe* they resist final attempts to subdue them. They are the race less ignoble than their fellows for which the artist has forged a conscience. Stephen poses the negative aspect of the new era and the new conscience when he points to his head and quotes Blake against subjugation of his spirit or body, 'But in here it is I must kill the priest and the king.' Bloom poses the affirmative aspect when he advocates 'the opposite of force, hatred, history, all that', as truly life – and when pressed says, 'Love, I mean the opposite of hatred.' Molly Bloom is needed to complete the picture to raise their fragmentariness to lyricism, and to show by her general approval of Bloom and Stephen that nature, to which she may be a little closer than they, responds to the values of art – sensitivity, discrimination, sympathy, understanding, and intensity of feeling. Although she is described as fleshly, she is no fleshlier than Hamlet. For her too the mind affects everything. The tenor of her thoughts is to acknowledge grudgingly that her husband, who recognizes her wit and musical talent and inner nature, is a better man than Blazes Boylan. 'I saw he understood or felt what a woman is,' she says. Penelope recognizes Ulysses not by his scar but by his imagination. All three characters achieve a freedom from hypocritical spirituality or empty materiality. In reading about them, the reader takes on the new conscience too. Joyce like Wilde and Yeats had a fifth gospel, a vision, a new Bible. So reading *Ulysses,* if that book is properly understood, is a means of emancipation. One is freed by it to read about freedom.

Decadence then had its uses for Wilde, Yeats and Joyce, as a pivot around which they could organize their work. Each in his different way summons up an opposite to decadence, the promise of an 'unfashionable' age for which as artists they constitute themselves heralds. They are not decadents but counter-decadents. Or we could say that they went through decadence to come out on the other side.

1983

Yeats Without Analogue

WHEN we think of Yeats's mind in concentration, brooding upon silence, as he said, 'like a long-legged fly upon a stream', we may well hesitate to clatter in armed with our new-fangled muskets – our readers' guides and commentaries, our iconographies and identities – and to aim them at that noble quarry. The danger was brought home to me when the editor of a continental encyclopedia invited me to write an article about Yeats. Being understandably fearful of American caprices, he supplied me with detailed instructions on how to proceed. I should be sure to show Yeats as a late Pre-Raphaelite, as a member of the Rhymers' Club and of the *Savoy* group, as a symbolist in the school of Mallarmé, as a leader in the revival of William Blake, as a participant in the Celtic Renaissance. I should make clear that he was a friend of Oscar Wilde, of Madame Blavatsky, of Lady Gregory, of the magician MacGregor Mathers, of Ezra Pound. I should demonstrate the effect upon Yeats of other arts. The prescription was intimidating, and as I tried to follow it my misgivings increased. Was Yeats really a jack-of-all-movements? Did he potter about in the past? Was he an other-people's-friend? And while the encyclopedist was German, I have an uneasy feeling that I have not been blameless in helping to establish the kind of criticism of Yeats which made this detailed assignment a logical outcome. But I will not incriminate only myself. Yeats is in some present peril everywhere of being swallowed up by the great whale of literary history. We must do what we can to help him out of that indiscriminate belly.

To be told that what looks new is really old, that every step forward is a step backward, is hard on trail-blazers, and Yeats was impatient enough with those of us who edit and annotate lines young men tossing on their beds rhymed out in love's despair. We need not, however, repudiate editing or annotating; Yeats comforts us elsewhere when he says that 'truth flourishes where the student's lamp has shone.' But to read the literature on Yeats is to come to feel that the search for his sources and analogues has become disproportionate, and that a tendency is growing to turn all that

marvellously innovative poetry into a résumé of what other people
have written. An inspired résumé, of course, but still a résumé.
Sometimes the résumé includes what other people have painted or
carved, too. Some years ago, for example, G. D. P. Allt and T. R.
Henn suggested that Yeats's poem, 'Leda and the Swan', grew out
of a painting of this subject by Michelangelo and possibly also out
of a drawing of Jupiter and Ganymede by the same artist. Later
Giorgio Melchiori, developing these hints in an important book,
reproduced three copies of Michelangelo's lost picture, the drawing
too, a picture of Leda and the swan by a follower of Leonardo and
one by Gustave Moreau, and then a Hellenistic statue of the same
subject. Seven in all. But the conclusion to which a study of these
works of art brings one is that Yeats has done something different
from any; not only are his graphic details at variance (none of the
works shows the bird's beak holding the nape of Leda's neck), but
the whole intellectual weight is distinct.

In Michelangelo what is expressed is the suave perfection of the
union of human and divine. Under the pressure of Christian doctrine,
there is no irony recognized in this union. Yeats has a different
object, as he makes clear at once:

> A sudden blow, the great wings beating still
> Above the staggering girl . . .

For Yeats the significance of this mating is that it is not tender
or easy; the bird, filled with divine power and knowledge, is still
the brute blood of the air. The incongruities are glossed over by
Michelangelo, in Yeats they are heightened. The sense of dispro-
portion, of shock, of rape, is captured in those phrases which describe
the blow, the flapping of huge wings, the strange dark webs, the
catching of the helpless Leda. She is dazed and overcome, not cajoled,
and the god, once the sexual crisis is past, lets her drop from his
indifferent beak. I do not mean that Yeats is a naturalist as Michelangelo is an idealist; both of these positions are too easy. Rather
what Yeats does is to let both views of the subject coalesce, to see
them with double sight, and this is why his poem is modern as
Michelangelo's painting is not. Melchiori shows intelligently how
fond Yeats was of the personality of Michelangelo, but whether fond
or not, Yeats belongs to a different persuasion from the Renaissance.

The issue of a pictorial source for 'Leda and the Swan' was drawn
more sharply when Charles Madge published in the *Times Literary
Supplement* a reproduction of a Greek bas-relief which Yeats probably
saw in the British Museum. This carving is much more convincing
than Henn's or Melchiori's examples; in it the details are in fact the

same as in the first part of the poem. The resemblance is too close for coincidence. The only question is, what does it prove? Melchiori wrote a letter to the editor conceding that this illustration was more apt than his own, but declaring that it confirmed his theory that visual imagery had priority for Yeats. But does it? 'Priority' has become an offensive word, and it is not an easy thing to determine. Presumably Yeats knew from his reading who Leda was before he saw the bas-relief at the British Museum. Is it not hopeless to attempt to determine through which sense a poet is most deeply affected? For example, if we were to grant that the bas-relief helped Yeats to frame the octave of the sonnet, what inspired the next three lines?

> A shudder in the loins engenders there
> The broken wall, the burning roof and tower,
> And Agamemnon dead.

There is nothing in the bas-relief to suggest these after-effects of the coupling. Is it useful to speculate on how Yeats conceived of the image of burning? Did he see a fire, hear the crackling of flames, smell burn, scorch his hand, taste something that was too hot? Or did he remember Marlowe's description of 'flaming Jupiter' when he appeared not to Leda but to 'hapless Semele'? Or Rossetti's refrain of 'Tall Troy's on fire'? Even if we determined beyond doubt that Yeats had seen a picture of a fire, or a bas-relief of it, or read a poem, we could still not explain the telescoping of historical events in those lines. Or the stages of the sexual violation which are probably implied in the series of images – the broken wall, the burning roof and tower, and Agamemnon dead. It is conceivable that he found these out by personal experience, and that the suggested relation of sexual stages to historical events came as an ironic echo of the octave from his own mind, not someone else's. And if we admit this possibility, we can ask more peremptorily what is the use of trying to isolate creative motivation. The only effect is to minimize the role of the poet in shaping his impressions.

We can go further and say that, given this bas-relief, Yeats's poem does not necessarily emerge from it. He uses its details in so far as they are convenient, but his emphasis is not the Greek artist's either. For the Greek the rape of Leda by the swan was apparently a magnificent variety of sexual assault; he was interested in its minute physical oddities; the god and the woman receive his equal attention. In Yeats, however, the interest is centered on the mortal woman, on the psychological implications for her and, by extension, for us. We watch Leda's reactions, not the god's. And Yeats goes beyond the strangely assorted pair to meditate on the destructiveness of sexual passion, on its power to upheave the world. At the end of the poem, he exclaims in bewilderment at the disparity between gods and men, between the minds as well as the bodies of Zeus and Leda. The generating theme of the poem is a feeling he had from childhood, of the tantalizing imperfection of human life; his own experience told him that power and knowledge could never exist together, that to acquire one was to lose the other. All Yeats's poetry embodies this theme. Leda and the swan are only one of many embodiments of it in his verse. When we study that verse we put source after source behind us until we are in the poet's mind, not in the British Museum.

If painters and sculptors have not provided us with enough analogues, we have all been unable to resist comparing Yeats with William Blake. Certainly Yeats had a passion for Blake and certainly he spent three years from 1889 to 1892 strenuously editing and commenting on the Prophetic Books. It is tempting to relate Blake's Four Zoas to Yeats's Four Faculties, but even if such connections can be made, is it not time to emphasize the disconnections instead? When we think of Blake, we think of a mind of almost unprecedented assertiveness. When we think of Yeats, we think of a force of almost unprecedented modulation. Blake, as Yeats himself tells us, 'beat upon the wall / Till truth obeyed his call'. Yeats in his dealings with truth is rather a great cat than a beater upon walls. Blake condemns the world of the five senses, Yeats gives it substantial acceptance. Blake is determined that England should become heaven, Yeats is not sure that even Ireland will achieve this goal. Blake impresses us by his initial and unswerving conviction, Yeats by his serpentine struggle towards bold declaration. Blake commits himself to his own system and spends most of his creative years elaborating it in special terms. Yeats remains ambiguous about his symbology, lodges it in prose, and never uses its special terms in his verse unless they have accepted as well as eccentrically personal meanings. Finally, Yeats wrote an explanation of Blake, a favor that Blake, who hated explanations, would never have done for Yeats.

Since Yeats is not Blake, perhaps he is Mallarmé. Graham Hough contends that the early Yeats at least belongs to the French symbolists. 'Symbolism', Hough points out, 'moves in the direction of an impassable gulf.... For the symbolist poet there is no question of describing an experience; the moment of illumination only occurs in its embodiment in some particular artistic form. There is no question of relating it to the experience of a lifetime, for it is unique, it exists in the poem alone.' And he finds in the early Yeats the symbolist doctrine full-blown, though contaminated a little by a non-literary occultism. The fact that it is contaminated at all should warn us. I cannot concede to Hough that even in the early Yeats there is any desire for an autonomous art, separated from life and experience by an impassable gulf. We have been taught so often that we live in a degenerate age, that the audience has become obtuse and sterile, that writers have detached themselves from it perforce, that we are almost embarrassed when we bethink ourselves of the sizeable number of our best writers who are not alienated, not isolated, not even inaccessible. Yeats's early dream was not to live in an ivory tower, but on an Irish island, not in unnature, but in nature, not in a place he had never seen, but in a place he had grown up. If there was anything that he shied away from it was the separation of his art from his life, of his work from his audience. Consider all those interrelations he set up between himself and his public by founding Irish literary societies in London and Dublin, by attaching his affections to a woman who was an Irish nationalist, by writing poems which should be Irish, local, amorous. All these poems confirm an intention to stay on earth, however much he may hint at the existence of another world.

When Yeats seriously contemplates leaving the observable world, he customarily points out what a mistake it would be. For example, in one of his earliest poems, 'The Seeker', the hero is so enraptured by the pursuit of an other-worldly ideal that he cannot fight in battle, and men say his heart has been stolen by the spirits. At last, after a lifetime of unheroic behavior and tenacious searching, he reaches the visionary figure he has sought. But she is no image of transcendent beauty, instead she is a 'bearded witch', and when asked her name replies, 'Men call me infamy.' Yeats suppressed this object-lesson for symbolists about the danger of isolating experience from an ideal, but its theme is common to many poems he retained.

In 'Fergus and the Druid' Fergus begs the gift of other-worldly wisdom; receiving it, he is appalled and laments,

> But now I have grown nothing, knowing all.
> Ah! Druid, Druid, how great webs of sorrow
> Lay hidden in the small slate-coloured thing!

So far from yielding to another world of the spirit, Yeats in his verse is always demonstrating that we had better cling to this one. In the poem which he put at the beginning of his second volume of verse, 'To the Rose upon the Rood of Time', he acknowledges his fear that he may do what Mallarmé perhaps wished to, and 'learn to chaunt a tongue men do not know'. Yeats testifies to his determination to keep in touch with common things, with the weak worm, the field mouse, with 'heavy mortal hopes that toil and pass'. He acknowledges the call of isolation, but affirms that he will resist it. His next volume, *The Wind Among the Reeds*, also begins with an appeal from the other world, this time from the Sidhe who call, 'Away, come away.' We listen to their musical voices without obeying. Occasionally someone is taken away, like the child the fairies steal in *The Land of Heart's Desire*, but the fairies are baleful and predatory here. In Yeats's later poetry the same struggle is portrayed: it becomes the theme of such poems as 'Vacillation' and 'A Dialogue of Self and Soul', but while the poet tries to play fair, the dialogue, and his vacillation, have always the same resolution. To follow the soul into another world is to give up one's heart and self, and worst of all for a poet, to give up one's tongue, for in the presence of that unblemished world our tongue's a stone, in the simplicity of fire we are struck dumb. The poet is committed to this world by his profession as well as by his temperament.

How different all this sounds from Mallarmé, for whom the artist treats experience as gingerly and probingly as a detective looking for the incomprehensible crime which appearances cover up. Mallarmé constitutes the poet a specialist in reality, a detective writing for detectives. What can be said in the open is not worth saying. Mallarmé's acknowledged image of the poet is the awesome magus who evokes by words an intangible reality. But this is a French magus more than an Irish one. Yeats, who knew magic at first hand as Mallarmé did not, took a homelier view of it. One thinks of his experiments in putting certain substances under his pillow to see what effect his dreams might have upon them, or they upon his dreams. And for Yeats the incantatory word is not something achieved by exclusion of much of the mind; it is achieved by a spiritual struggle of the whole being, of which the poetic imagination forms a part, and it is inside, not outside, the stress of experience. Unassumingly, too, Yeats does not talk of the magician as a manufacturer but an importer; his images are not created new but come from the Great Memory, a kind of collective imagination. In Mallarmé the attempt is to separate the poem from all that is not poem, to abolish the poet, to free an object originally palpable so that it becomes impalpable. All real bouquets render up their fragrance to form an essence they do not themselves possess.

In Yeats, the emphasis is on the tangibility of the images which the artist cleans and perfects, and on the struggle to clean and perfect them. The poet is not ostracized from his poem, he is its all-important inhabitant. The act of creation itself is curiously democratic for Yeats, comparable to other forms of intense endeavor, so that the poet can represent his work as human too. He must write with such airs that one believes he has a sword upstairs. The desire to see Mallarmé in Yeats has encouraged a misconception of some of his best poems. His pursuit of images is held to be an escape from experience, when the images are rather focuses of experience. In 'The Circus Animals' Desertion', Yeats at first seems to take another view, as when he says,

> Players and painted stage took all my love,
> And not those things that they were emblems of,

but even here the word 'emblems' recalls to us the dependent character of the images. And his conclusion recognizes firmly the dependence of art upon life:

> Those masterful images because complete
> Grew in pure mind, but out of what began?
> A mound of refuse or the sweepings of a street,
> Old kettles, old bottles, and a broken can,
> Old iron, old bones, old rags, that raving slut
> Who keeps the till. Now that my ladder's gone,
> I must lie down where all the ladders start
> In the foul rag- and bone-shop of the heart.

An excellent critic interprets these lines to mean that Yeats is in despair at the idea of lying down in his heart, at being 'left to live merely, when living is most difficult, life having been used up in another cause'. But this is reading Yeats's words without considering their intonation. While the poet is disgusted for the moment with his own heart, he is well aware that this heart has engendered all his images. He pleads necessity for what he does by desire; he *wants*, in short, to lie down in the foul rag- and bone-shop of the heart. For, as he says in 'Two Songs from a Play',

> Whatever flames upon the night
> Man's own resinous heart has fed,

and in 'Vacillation',

> From man's blood-sodden heart are sprung
> Those branches of the night and day
> Where the gaudy moon is hung.

At the end of the poem 'Byzantium', Yeats, having described the miraculous creations which are produced in art, suddenly recalls the flood of time from which they come, and sees the time-world as made up of passionate images too:

> Those images that yet
> Fresh images beget,
> That dolphin-torn, that gong-tormented sea.

We have been asked to believe that these lines express Yeats's revulsion from the welter of experience, when clearly they imply that even from the vantage point of Byzantium that welter is fascinating.

So I do not think we can describe Yeats as alienated or even as aloof, either from his own experience or from other people's. From childhood on he is delighted with the life of peasants, with Irish life. Mallarmé, always straining to avoid space and time, would find Irish nationalism an absurdity, as perhaps it is, though Yeats did not think so. Yeats even wrote his poem, 'To Ireland in the Coming Times', to establish his rightful place once and for all as Ireland, his claim to be counted one with the Irish poets Davis, Mangan, Ferguson. And at the end of his life he wrote a poem to make sure that his body after death should be Irish too:

> Under bare Ben Bulben's head
> In Drumcliff churchyard Yeats is laid.

Yet I do not find it very helpful either to consider Yeats, as some would do, one of a group of Irish poets who freshened up Celtic legends. Yeats could be and wanted to be provincial, but he could also be cosmopolitan. When he wrote *A Vision*, he forgot he was an Irishman. And while he calls the fairies by their Irish name of the Sidhe, I suspect that they too are internationalists. His later versions of preternatural beings are, except in the play *The Dreaming of the Bones*, indifferent to race although they retain their interest in families and in individuals. Irishness is an essential quality, but a secondary one.

Perhaps then we should pursue another direction by seeing Yeats as a follower of the occult tradition or, as it has been renamed by one critic, the Platonic tradition. But here too his allegiance is doubtful. If we try to think of him as a Platonist we have to remember he wrote a poem to say, 'Those Platonists are a curse, ... God's fire upon the wane', and another in which he said, 'I cry in Plato's teeth.' If we mean by Platonism the later followers of Plato, we have to remember that Yeats also wrote, 'I mock Plotinus' thought', and that he buffeted Plotinus as well as Plato about in several poems. At moments his theories seem to coincide with Plato's, as in that heroic defense of a woman's primping, 'Before the World Was Made'. In a way she agrees that this world is a copy of a more Platonic one, but the real theme is her deliberate energy in attempting to override human imperfection. Plato's philosophy is used only to the extent that it can be made Yeatsian, the extent to which the bodiless can be bodied.

If we ally Yeats with the occultists who followed in secret a metaphysical tradition, we will find him asserting his independence of them too. There is danger in connecting him too closely with either MacGregor Mathers or Madame Blavatsky, for he quarrelled and broke with both of them. In so far as occultism is cloistered and moralistic – and most magicians are tediously moralistic or immoralistic – Yeats stands apart from them. In so far as they hope to alter the phenomenal world, Yeats is very skeptical. The phenomenal world is not so easily dismissed, or at least not for long. In so far as they hold converse with spirits and win from them preternatural powers, Yeats is only sporadically credulous and then for his own reasons. Fundamentally he is like Queen Edain in 'The Two Kings', who rejects the advances of an immortal lover so as to stay with her mortal one. We long for immortal essences but when they accost us we resist. The poet, firm among the five senses, imagines their perfection, not their abandonment. He tolerates the ideal only when it is covered with what Yeats calls 'casual flesh'.

In seeking to emphasize the degree to which Yeats is unlike Michelangelo or Plato or Blavatsky or Mallarmé or Blake, I have the ulterior motive of offering another view. What is the mental atmosphere that makes Yeats's poems so individualistic? We might try to establish first the outer borders of his mind, with the initial admission that, as Yeats said, these are constantly shifting; and then its inner qualities. The intimation that seems to have been with him from his earliest days is that life as we generally experience it is incomplete, but that at moments it appears to transcend itself and yield moments of completeness or near-completeness, moments when, as he says half-humorously in the poem 'There', 'all the barrel-hoops are knit, ... all the serpent-tails are bit.' In his early work Yeats conceives of the boundary line between the worlds of completeness and incompleteness as twilit, in his later work it is lit by lightning. Whether the light is blurred or stark there are strange crossings-over.

The trespassers come from both directions, from this world to that, from that world to this. The fairies or Sidhe would like to translate us, to possess us, to catch us in nets of dreams, to tempt us, to remind us of what we lack and they have, and sometimes they succeed. More often they only manage to make us miserable. Something about the world of generation saddens them, as if the separation of worlds were difficult for them, too, to bear and caused them suffering. In middle life Yeats discards the fairies (as he already had given up the Rose), and begins to call the denizens of the other world antiselves or simply ghosts; in his later work they are usually spirits in his verse, daimons in his prose. Under their changed names, they continue to busy themselves about us.

Some readers of Yeats are put off by this metaphysical population, and by his related interest in all sorts of extrasensory perception. Could Yeats really have believed in these things? they ask. But to ask this question is to show that one is several generations in time behind Yeats, who asked with more point whether the word 'belief' belonged to our age at all. Yeats used many locutions to avoid the term 'believe', and it can be said that nothing is further from his mind than simple credence. The word 'God' he generally skirted with the same dexterity. In the poem, 'Mohini Chatterjee', there is the line, 'I asked if I should pray.' A critic interpreting this poem says, Yeats asks if he should pray to God; but Yeats doesn't mention God, and it is not at all certain that he is addressing himself to that early authority. He may be invoking his deeper self, or some daimon or group of daimons, or some indeterminate object or he may be meditating with an even vaguer audience, praying to no one and to nothing, just praying. Occasionally Yeats does make use in his verse of supernatural machinery or of preternatural machinery, but always without precise or credal commitment.

He needs this machinery because of his conviction, as I have indicated, that there is a conceivable life which is better than human life in that it is complete, undiminished, unimpairable. Let us call this the daimonic world. In relation to the daimons we are mere abstracts. Yeats astonishes us by the bluntness with which he makes clear the defects of our own world. But having made clear its limitations, he suddenly enters upon its defense. It has pain, it has struggle, it has tragedy, elements denied to the daimons. Seen from their point of view, life always fails. Yet it does not fail utterly, for man can imagine their state even if he cannot participate in it. And the capacity to imagine is redemptive; man, in a frenzy at being limited, overthrows much of that limitation. He defiantly asserts his imaged self against futility, and to imagine heroism is to become a hero.

And now we are led from a comparison of worlds to one of people. Man, according to Yeats's view, is a being who is always endeavoring to construct by fiction what he lacks in fact. Born incomplete, he conceives of completeness and to that extent attains it. We outfling ourselves upon the universe, people the desert with our fertile images.

The hero does this unconsciously, the artist consciously, but all men do it in their degree. The dead bone upon the shore in 'Three Things' sings still of human love. Space and time are unreal, Yeats sometimes concedes to the philosophers, but he says they are marvellously unreal; they, and life and death, heaven and hell, day and night, are human images imposed like form upon the void. Yeats looks at two withered old women, Eva Gore-Booth and Constance Markiewicz, and writes of them,

> The light of evening, Lissadell,
> Great windows open to the south,
> Two girls in silk kimonos, both
> Beautiful, one a gazelle.

The girls in the gazebo of the country house are summoned up by the poet as more real than the decrepit women; if the great gazebo of the world is false, it must be true as well. It is true when it conforms, as at moments it does, to our image of perfection.

But the mind has another glory besides its power to create: it can also destroy. Man lowers his plumb-line into the darkness and establishes measurement, form, number, intellect. But he has hardly established all these before he casts the line away, as if every imaginative construct could only momentarily satisfy his creative need and must then be demolished. 'What's the meaning of all song?' Yeats asks in 'Vacillation', and replies, 'Let all things pass away.' His most powerful statement of this kind is in the poem called 'Meru', where the hermits on the Indian mountain sum up in themselves this dissatisfaction with every human fabrication. They are Asiatic hermits, but Yeats recognizes that every mind has an Asiatic aspect which would destroy the shows of this world – shows which he associates with Europe. We live in 'manifold illusion'; and, as Yeats puts it in another poem, 'mirror on mirror mirrored is all the show.' Having put on our finery we take it off again. We strip the masks we have created for ourselves. We descend into our own abyss; if we cannot burn up the gazebo, we scornfully aspire to do so. The urge to destruction, like the urge to creation, is a defiance of limits; we transcend ourselves by refusing to accept completely anything that is human, and then indomitably we begin fabricating again. As Yeats says in 'Lapis Lazuli',

> All things fall and are built again,
> And those that build them again are gay.

If we try to relate Yeats's poems more narrowly to the contrast between daimons and men on the one hand, and between man and his limitations on the other, I think we will see that each such contrast gains its force from a confrontation of passive acceptance with energetic defiance. It would be so easy to grant, as any objective witness would, that the poet's daughter should not associate with a man who has the worst of all bad names. When he admonishes her, however, she replies unanswerably: 'But his hair is beautiful, / Cold as the March wind his eyes.' In a greater poem, it would be so easy to concede that Maud Gonne had behaved badly towards Yeats; but the sense of 'No Second Troy' is that this aspect of her life is of no consequence, and the important thing is that she has tried to live by the high laws of imagination. The poet is always faced with a common-sense solution, as by a sort of minimum wage, and always chooses to take nothing rather than take that. If Maud Gonne's energies were destructive, that was because she lived in a world of outworn images and had to destroy them. The pacific soul, which Yeats contrasts in his later verse with the military self, always offers a conventional way to heaven, and the self always rejects it, preferring the turmoil of this world, with its desperate search for words and images, to an easy and dumb-striking heaven. Every poem establishes alternatives to indicate only one choice is worth making, and that the agonized, unremunerative, heroic one.

These are not Yeats's ideas or beliefs; they are the mental atmosphere in which he lived, or if that term sounds too climatic, they are the seethings, the agitations of his mind which he learned to control and direct. His symbolism has to be understood not as a borrowing from Mallarmé, but as the only way in which he could express himself. 'I have no speech but symbol,' he wrote. His symbols are condensations of his theme that all struggle is futile except the struggle with futility, his recognition of the problem of the empty cornucopia, the crowded void. Each symbol is a kind of revolving disc, like Yeats's wheel or the moon with its dark and light phases in *A Vision*. We can compare the tower in the poem of that name with the one in 'The Black Tower'; in the first it is intellectual aspiration, in the second it is the insubstantiality of that aspiration. The image of the tree also has its two sides, not only in the poem, 'The Two Trees', but when it emerges as an epitome of unity in 'Among School Children' and then as an image of decay in 'the old thorn tree' of 'A Man Young and Old'. The dance is frantic, purposeless destruction in 'Nineteen Hundred and Nineteen', while in 'Among School Children' it is composed perfection. 'The Peacock' is a symbol of the lavishing imagination, while in another poem, 'Nineteen Hundred and Nineteen', when the blind Robert Artisson brings the mad Lady Kyteller peacock feathers, it seems some image of beauty gone hollow.

Not only are the symbols double-natured in different poems; they usually take on shifting implications within the same poem, as if they were being slowly revolved. The ancestral houses described in 'Meditations in Time of Civil War' summon up glory only to remind us of its transience. In 'Two Songs from a Play', the staring virgin brings her divine child to begin a new cycle of time, as if it were the only cycle, yet the muses know that there are many cycles, that this has all been done before and will be done again. The pomp of the new god is contrasted with images of darkness and nullity; as Yeats says in one of his finest images of the doubling involved in all identity, 'The painter's brush consumes his dreams.' 'Only an aching heart', he declares ('Meditations in Time of Civil War'), 'conceives a changeless work of art.' 'The Tower' that dominates the countryside has ruin in its history; on the other hand, 'The Black Tower', so ruined as to be indefensible, finds defenders. The great-rooted blossomer is the tree in its springtime only, the perfection of dancing is achieved only momentarily before the turmoil of the greenroom begins again. Yeats is fond of showing how ambiguous the word 'dream' itself is, since it is at once something brilliantly imagined, and something delusive, real and unreal, 'flowers' ('I pray that I ever be weaving') and 'cold snows' ('Meditations'). But all his key words share in this property; youth is strength and folly, old age is wisdom and debility. Images of substance are always on the verge of nothingness, narrowly balanced: 'The boughs have withered because I have told them my dreams.' 'Through all the lying days of my youth / I swayed my leaves and flowers in the sun; / Now I may wither into the truth.' Even art participates in this double nature. For though all-powerful in its own realm, that realm is balanced uneasily between this world and the daimonic one. If it became daimonic it would be ethereal, insubstantial; if it became human, it would be helpless. Yeats summarizes this condition of art in 'Byzantium' where he writes of those artistic fires of Byzantine forges that they are

> Dying into a dance,
> An agony of trance,
> An agony of flame that cannot singe a sleeve.

In art the fires are all-powerful, but in life they have no effect at all. The same mediation is evident in 'Sailing to Byzantium', where the bird is at once more than human in its golden perfection, and less than human in its toylike character; out of generation, it yet must sing of generation, of what is past, passing, or to come, irrevocably dependent upon the nature which it affects to spurn.

Not only do the symbols turn like wheels, but the intellectual or thematic content of each poem balances two meanings contingent upon each other. The poem 'Friends', for example, begins with two orthodox examples of friendship, Lady Gregory and Mrs. Shakespear, and then takes up Maud Gonne who is totally unfriendly. The secret of the poem is that she has unconsciously given him more than the others gave consciously, that she did so because she represented a more fundamental energy. In 'The Magi' Yeats plays upon the standard picture of the magi dazzled by Christ's miraculous birth, and perplexes them with his human death. In 'The Second Coming' he accepts the title from Christianity but represents the new god as destructive rather than benign, a monster rather than a lamb. In 'The Cold Heaven' a hideous afterlife, where injustice prevails, confronts the naked soul in search of paradise. Or, to take a lighter example, there is his short poem with the long title, 'On Hearing That the Students of Our New University Have Joined the Agitation against Immoral Literature',

> Where, where but here have Pride and Truth
> That long to give themselves for wage,
> To shake their wicked sides at youth
> Restraining reckless middle-age?

The poem's subtlety derives from its conceiving of Pride and Truth not as draped Grecian caryatids but as middle-aged prostitutes. Yet the denigration is mocking, as if he would remind us how lofty a wage pride and truth really demand.

I sometimes think that we could try to codify the laws that govern the complexities of Yeats's poetry. Every poem offers alternative positions. While the choice between them may surprise us, we can be sure it will be based upon a preference for what is imprudent, reckless, contrary to fact, but that in so choosing the poet does not act out of folly but out of understandable passion. The alternative is never completely overwhelmed, but remains like the other side of the moon, or, to use another of Yeats's images, like some imprisoned animal, ready to burst out again with its message of common sense or of renunciation of the world. The basic choice of the poem is reflected in the symbols, which either contain the same alternative or at any rate imply them, as day implies night. The poem ends not in a considered conclusion, but in a kind of breathlessness, a breakthrough from the domain of caution and calculation to that of imprudence and imagination; the poem gathers its strength from putting down one view with another, from saying, against the utmost opposition, what must be said.

Usually the poems take one of two directions: either they are visionary, concerned with matters of prophecy, of the relations of the time-world and daimonic timelessness, or they are concerned with human enterprise, the relations of people with each other or with their own secret hopes and ambitions. In the visionary poems such as 'Leda and the Swan' or 'The Second Coming', Yeats is concerned to intermesh the divine world with the animal, to show the world of time as centaurlike, beautiful and monstrous, aspiring and deformed. In the poems which deal with artists or with heroes or with other men, he wishes also to show how brute fact may be transmogrified, how we can sacrifice ourselves, in the only form of religious practice he sanctions, to our imagined selves which offer far higher standards than anything offered by social convention. If we must suffer, it is better to create the world in which we suffer, and this is what heroes do spontaneously, artists do consciously, and all men do in their degree.

To represent his themes Yeats originally tried to dislodge conventional attitudes by a slow rhythm which would attenuate sense and draw it onwards, as it were, into new possibilities. Sense would make way like some equerry before the sovereign spirit. Gradually he substituted for this rhythm of longing and fascination a rhythm of conquest. Like Jupiter, the daimons penetrate our world by shock, and we in turn surprise them by sudden incursions, as when, in an ordinary shop, our bodies of a sudden blaze. We do not hope to intermingle but to encroach upon each other. The language of this struggle needs to be vigorous, for it must bring us beyond statement, to the central agitation of the mind, where mission and futility brother each other, where as in the sun destruction and creation go on at once. The mind is a rage, not a warehouse. And while Michelangelo and Blake and Mallarmé and the rest may be tutelary spirits on the perimeter of this consciousness, at its center we see only and supremely Yeats.

1964

Becoming Exiles

IN ACCORDING the title *Exiles* to his only play, Joyce recognized the density of this word. The twentieth century has been thronged with exiles and expatriates. They can easily be distinguished: expatriates are blithe, exiles dour; expatriates live somewhere nice, exiles somewhere dingy. The exile feels separated from his country as a sinner feels separated from his god; but unlike the sinner, the exile feels that he has been true and his country false. James Joyce had been on the Continent only a few weeks when he announced to his brother that he considered himself to be a voluntary exile. Although he returned to his country three times, he made even less effort than Richard Rowan does in the play to settle back there, and after each of his three visits Joyce left with his old rancor renewed.

So in writing *Exiles* he was animated by much the same mixture of rancor and nostalgia that animates Richard Rowan. Joyce was inclined to see life as a series of betrayals – his father took much the same view – and he experienced enough of them to feel that his expectations had been justified. Richard says, 'There is a faith still stranger than the faith of the disciple in his master', and when Robert Hand asks what it is, replies, 'The faith of a master in the disciple who will betray him.' Such a view of his own experience was not inevitable; in some ways Joyce might have regarded himself, as Yeats regarded himself, as lucky.

It was true that when Joyce eloped with Nora Barnacle to Zurich in October 1904, the job that was supposed to await him at the Berlitz School in Zurich did not exist: an English employment agency had betrayed him. Still, within a week he found another Berlitz job, in Pola. To be transferred from that at the end of six months may momentarily have seemed a misfortune, but his transfer to Trieste enabled him to shift from Berlitz School teaching to more lucrative private tuition, and among his pupils was the writer Italo Svevo who furnished him with a good deal of the character of Leopold Bloom. Luck again. When the First World War broke out, Joyce's brother was interned by Austria; Joyce however had the good fortune to be allowed to go to Zurich. If he seemed for a while adrift there, it was not long before he obtained first one wealthy patron and then another, in days when patrons were in short supply. Although he had great difficulties during eight years in finding a publisher, at the end of that time he quickly became known in England and America, and by the age of forty he was famous around the western world. His really bad luck came later, when his eye troubles became acute and his daughter dangerously ill. But long before these Joyce had molded himself as misfit, outcast, *poète maudit*, exile. He always regarded himself as poor, too, even when he was dining in Fouquet's almost every night. (A room in the restaurant has been christened the Salle James Joyce, in recognition of this inveterate customer.) In other words, exile was a state for which Joyce was peculiarly suited, quite apart from the events which brought it about. In *Ulysses* Stephen Dedalus suggests that we go forth into the world expecting to encounter external phenomena but always meet ourselves.

So it's not surprising that Joyce's first autobiographical fiction, begun in 1904 and finished in 1914, should have ended with Stephen Dedalus going off into exile. Once this was decided upon – and it seems to have been decided subsequent to his own departure in 1904, since the very earliest version of 'A Portrait of the Artist' concludes in a kind of socialist revolutionary manifesto rather than in exile – Joyce needed a theme of comparable power to culminate his subsequent books. In *Giacomo Joyce*, which he decided not to publish, the ending is simply one of frustration and separation of Giacomo from his handsome pupil. She does not want his advances to become serious, and the last words are 'Love me, love my umbrella'. What it lacked was a contest, a conflict. Instead of looking for a completely new theme for *Exiles* and *Ulysses*, something post-exilic, Joyce decided that exile could include a much larger idea than mere physical separation, voluntary or involuntary, from one's native land. It could include disaffection of a political and social kind, and Joyce wanted his works to have a political and social context. Expressed another way, it could be alienation in general, an alienation based upon betrayal.

For this Joyce had many examples. At the age of nine he had composed a poem about the betrayal of Parnell in Committee Room 15, where his followers voted him out of the leadership of the Irish party. Joyce, fourteen years later, wrote another poem on the same subject for his character Joe Hynes to recite in 'Ivy Day in the Committee Room'. Hynes's poem is doggerel but moving; it compares what happened to Parnell with what happened to Christ. Grandiloquent as the comparison is, Joyce was not beyond making it with his own life. He needed something more intense than voluntary exile to sharpen the similarity.

The necessary incident occurred in 1909, when he was twenty-seven. It was during a time of great tension, his first return to Ireland after five years away. The outlines of the incident are known, but are so mightily entrenched in the outlines of *Exiles* that we may remind ourselves of them.

Joyce's ship docked at the Kingstown pier in July 1909. Almost the first thing he saw was a rear view of his friend Oliver Gogarty, whom he avoided meeting. In a letter he mentioned seeing Gogarty's 'fat back' on the pier. In *Exiles* Bertha Rowan tells Robert Hand that she had seen Hand on the pier when she arrived, and noticed that he had got fat. Momentarily, at least, Robert Hand is Gogarty. Whenever Joyce conceived of an adversary, in his later works, he levied upon his experience with Gogarty. Blake had his Hayley, Joyce had his Gogarty. Their last meeting had been in the Martello tower on the morning of 19 September 1904, when Gogarty jestingly shot some pots and pans down on the recumbent Joyce's head. The joke, if that was what was intended, was lost upon Joyce. He took it as his expulsion, and, being in the mood to find larger symptoms in small details, he decided to leave Ireland. The letter he wrote a few hours later, asking Nora Barnacle to leave the country with him, has survived. Gogarty made several attempts by correspondence to heal the breach. He did not like implacable animosities, though his malicious and witty tongue often created them. Now in 1909 he learned that Joyce had come back to Dublin. Radiating affluence and good will – both sourly taken notice of by Joyce – Gogarty breezily drove him down in a new motor car to his house in the country. Gogarty was already becoming famous as a surgeon and a poet – that is, he was famous as a surgeon to his readers and as a poet to his patients. He took the occasion to implore Joyce not to put him into his books, but Joyce refused to promise anything except that he would use him artistically if he used him at all. With this Gogarty had to be content.

The meeting with Gogarty was criss-crossed enough with difficulties, but an even more upsetting meeting occurred with Vincent Cosgrave. Cosgrave had been a crony of Joyce for years; cynical and indolent, he furnished most of the character of Lynch, Stephen's walking companion in both *A Portrait* and *Ulysses*. It was while walking with Cosgrave that Joyce had first met and spoken to Nora Barnacle in Leinster Street. After Joyce's departure from Dublin he and Cosgrave had exchanged a letter or two, and Joyce thought of Cosgrave as loyal when Gogarty was not. We can therefore imagine how jolted he was when Cosgrave announced that, on the nights when Nora in 1904 had told Joyce she was having to work and could not meet him, she was actually out with Cosgrave. Joyce felt consternation.

He wrote to Nora to ask if it were true, because if so they must part forever. The unlikelihood of Cosgrave's story did not dawn on him until he consulted still another old friend. J. F. Byrne, the main model for his character Cranly. Byrne had a taste for conspiracy as vivid as Joyce's, and at once proposed to him that Cosgrave was in league with Gogarty to break Joyce's spirit. Meanwhile Joyce learned from his brother that Cosgrave, far from being a successful suitor for Nora, had been an unsuccessful one. As Joyce recognized the degree of animosity which must have underlain Cosgrave's concocted story, his jealousy and rage subsided, without disappearing. The situation was artistically determining: it established a relation between the betrayal of his country, which he felt he had suffered in voluntary exile, and the betrayal by his friend with his wife. It was appropriate that he should have returned from exile to absorb this enlargement of his theme.

Yet the play *Exiles* is not confined to the false claims of Cosgrave or the false friendship of Cosgrave and Gogarty. A third and more complex element came from still another of Joyce's friends, a man whom even Joyce acknowledged to be 'a decent kind of a fellow'. This was Thomas Kettle, a classmate of Joyce at University College, and like Joyce a regular visitor to the hospitable at-homes of David Sheehy, M.P., and his good-looking daughters. When Joyce made his decisive departure from Dublin in 1904 he paid Kettle the compliment of leaving with him his only manuscript of *Stephen Hero*. But he quickly became uneasy, perhaps because he remembered how in *Hedda Gabler*, by his favorite dramatist, Hedda had destroyed a manuscript left with her husband. He therefore wrote to his brother Stanislaus to take back the manuscript from Kettle, not because Kettle would do anything so nefarious as Hedda, but because he was too polite to suspect treachery, and some 'impostor', as Joyce described his enemies, might wheedle it away from him.

Kettle of course gave up the manuscript, without resentment. His career, which took a public direction, was one that Joyce followed from abroad with interest. For a short period in 1906 Kettle edited a newspaper called the *Nationist*. He had a special point of view towards Irish problems. As he would write in the preface to his book, *The Day's Burden* (1910) – a book Joyce obtained – 'My only counsel to Ireland is, that in order to become deeply Irish, she must become European.' In *Exiles*, when Robert Hand borrows a cigar from

36

Richard, he says, 'These cigars Europeanize me. If Ireland is to become a new Ireland she must first become European.'

Stanislaus Joyce proposed submitting some of Joyce's poems to Kettle for his paper, and Joyce was willing; but Kettle, before anything could be done, gave up editing the paper after only three months. He went into politics instead, and was elected M.P. for North Tyrone in 1906. The following year his connection with Joyce became less tenuous. In that year *Chamber Music* was published, and Kettle wrote one of the two Irish reviews of the book. He praised it, but could not forbear to note how remote from all the problems facing Ireland and the modern world Joyce's verses were. When in *Exiles* Robert Hand composes a leader for a newspaper about Richard Rowan's return, he falls into much the same language as Kettle. Kettle had begun his review with the sentence, 'Those who remember University College life of five years back will have many memories of Mr. Joyce.' Robert Hand rephrases it, 'Those who recall the intellectual life of Dublin of a decade since will have many memories of Mr. Rowan.' Kettle had suggested that *Chamber Music* was kindred with Paul Verlaine; Robert Hand allies Richard Rowan rather with the fierce indignation of Swift – a writer more appropriate to Joyce's prose than to his verse.

Kettle's obvious liking for Joyce prompted Stanislaus Joyce to propose to his brother that their friendship might be cultivated. But his brother replied, 'my influence on male friends is provocative. They find it hard to understand me, and difficult to get on with me even when they seem well equipped for those tasks.' He regretted also that Kettle was bent on securing Irish independence by parliamentary means, which he was sure would never work. Still, he bore the complimentary review of *Chamber Music* in mind. Just after he had come to Dublin in 1909, Joyce heard that a position might be available in modern languages in the Intermediate Examinations. He asked Kettle to recommend him for it. Kettle cordially agreed, and, having himself just become a professor at the National University, he suggested that Joyce stand for a chair in Italian there. Joyce was willing enough, but discovered that Kettle was misinformed about the nature of the appointment, which was only a minor lectureship instead of a professorship. He could get it, he wrote his brother, evidently on the basis of Kettle's sponsorship, but it would not be worth having. This is obviously the genesis of the attempt by Robert Hand in *Exiles* to secure a chair in modern languages for Richard Rowan.

So far the relationship with Kettle was too tenuous to offer Joyce much more than incidental ideas for his play. But, at least in Joyce's imagination, it became more intimate. Kettle asked to see the new version of Joyce's novel, and Joyce was grateful enough to arrange for Stanislaus to send it on from Trieste by registered mail. But about the time it arrived, he learned that Kettle was going to be married, and concluded that his sardonic book would ill consort with nuptial pleasures. Though he did not tender the manuscript, he took a great interest in the marriage. Kettle's bride-to-be was the prettiest daughter of the Sheehy family, Mary Sheehy. Joyce had often seen her at her family's house; he had once gone on a walk into the Dublin mountains with a group that included her. This occasion had been a romantic one, at least in his mind, for he wrote two poems of *Chamber Music*, 'What counsel has the hooded moon' (xii) and 'Lightly come or lightly go' (xxv), to Mary Sheehy as a result. He never allowed her to know how taken he was with her, and when I met Mary Sheehy Kettle in 1953 and told her of Joyce's secret passion for her, she said she had never suspected anything of the kind.

Three days before Kettle and Mary Sheehy were to be married, Joyce attended a reception at the Gresham Hotel. He was presented to about twenty people, perhaps by Kettle, as a man who was 'going to be the greatest writer of my country'. This praise of him as a writer was associated with the rather wincing experience of seeing his old beloved marry his friend. The marriage took place on the 8th of September. Joyceans will recognize this as one of those dates which bear a talismanic significance to Joyce, for he gave it to Molly Bloom as her birthday. Dates in Joyce's writings are rarely chosen at random. The choice encourages me to propose something much more extravagant, that Mary Sheehy was a kind of model for Richard Rowan's other attachment, Beatrice Justice, in *Exiles*. You will recall that Richard has been corresponding with her since he left Ireland, and that Bertha is jealous of Beatrice because she knows that Beatrice can understand the books which are beyond her own capacity. A partial confirmation is that Richard Rowan has written sketches – we are not told whether in prose or verse – to Beatrice Justice, but has never shown them to her. Joyce had done the same for Mary Sheehy.

Think how extraordinary it must have seemed to Joyce that Kettle should review so favorably a book of poems that included two addressed to his future wife. It was the kind of irony Joyce enjoyed. As if to compound it, he resolved that his wedding present to the new couple should be a copy of *Chamber Music*, especially bound for them in Trieste. For a man with little money to spend, and not prone to giving wedding presents freely, a gift for a bridal pair that contained rival attentions to the bride had a symbolic weight. Was it a kind of fingertip adultery? Did Joyce hope that the poems he had written Mary Sheehy would at last meet her gaze, that her eyes would be penetrated by the emotions he had felt and shaped long ago? That these questions appear to be posed by Joyce's gift leads us to recognize a point that might otherwise escape notice, that Joyce put not only Kettle, Cosgrave and Gogarty into Robert Hand, but also something of himself. This is borne out by the theory of Shakespeare that Stephen concocts in *Ulysses*, where he agrees that Shakespeare is to be identified with villains in the plays as well as heroes. 'His unremitting intellect', Stephen declares, 'is the hornmad Iago willing that the Moor in him shall suffer.' It is also the Moor, willing that the hornmad Iago in him should make him suffer.

The Kettles were to honeymoon in Austria, and Joyce invited them to visit him and Nora there. They promised to do so, but perhaps thought better of it. At any rate, the next time Joyce mentions Kettle in his letters it is to indicate that he doesn't feel free now to ask help for another brother, Charles Joyce. There is no reference to Kettle after this until 1912 when Joyce made his last visit to Dublin. On this occasion he was trying to persuade or compel an Irish publisher to fulfill his contract to publish *Dubliners*. The publisher was balking, and Joyce went to Kettle for help. Help was not forthcoming. Kettle took against the stories, and complained that the second story, 'An Encounter', about a pervert, was 'beyond anything in its outspokenness' he had ever read. When Joyce defended it by saying that he had actually met the man in the story, Kettle replied, 'We have all met him.' 'I'll slate that book,' he told Joyce, a serious threat from one of Joyce's two Irish reviewers. It was clear that Joyce, in Kettle's eyes, was now not ignoring the nationalist movement, as in *Chamber Music*, but actively flouting it. Joyce had here a basis for the equivocal attitude of Robert Hand, when he remarks in his newspaper article about Richard, 'Not the least vital of the problems which confront our country is the problem of her attitude towards those of her children who, having left her in her hour of need, have been called back to her now on the eve of her longawaited victory, to her whom in loneliness and exile they have at last learned to love.' Baldly stated, Thomas Kettle having married Joyce's sometime sweetheart, was prepared to attack his work. Much of the plot of *Exiles* could now take shape in Joyce's mind.

For the rivalry of Robert and Richard is directed towards Beatrice Justice as well as towards Bertha Rowan. Robert has been secretly engaged to Beatrice, while Richard has carried on a kind of epistolary courtship. As for their rivalry over Bertha, Joyce could remember what Cosgrave had falsely claimed about his association with Nora. Kettle was in no sense a model for Robert's adulterous leanings. But back in Trieste, Joyce found a further example, and one closer to his play. For some years he had been friendly with his pupil Roberto Prezioso, editor of *Il Piccolo della Sera*, the Triestine newspaper. Prezioso commissioned Joyce to write nine articles about Ireland for the newspaper, and it was probably he who wrote the several flattering comments in the *Piccolo* about Joyce's lectures on *Hamlet* in 1912 and 1913. Prezioso was accustomed to dropping in on the Joyces, and when Joyce was away, being something of a ladies' man, would stay conversing with Nora. Joyce seems to have encouraged these visits. Nora boasted to a woman friend that Prezioso had said to her, 'The sun rises for you.' The remark was evidently also reported to Joyce, because he has Bloom in *Ulysses* say, 'The sun shines for you,' and in *Exiles* has the Rowans' maid say to Bertha about her husband, 'Sure he thinks the sun shines out of your face, ma'am.' At some point Prezioso made a direct overture to Nora. Joyce, informed of it, was not the complaisant husband one might have expected. He was jealous and went to see Prezioso and upbraided him, presumably for violating friendship and trust. Prezioso burst into tears. As late as 1916 Nora Joyce was still dreaming about Prezioso weeping, and her husband was still interpreting. No wonder, then, that Richard's rival should be named, like Prezioso, Robert.

But with Joyce's interest in anatomizing his own soul – 'what can a man know but what passes inside his own head?', he asked his brother – he did not leave the matter there. He was the first to recognize that his own motives were more divided than he allowed Prezioso to know, for in 1918 or 1919 Nora Joyce said to their friend Frank Budgen, 'Jim wants me to go with other men so he will have something to write about.' Although she failed him in this wifely duty, she did go so far in indulgence as to address a letter to him, 'Dear Cuckold'. It was not only a fantasy to spice up the marriage. Joyce relished the bitter savor of Nora's possible but never realized infidelities. I have suggested that he was present in Robert as well as Richard, and this conclusion is borne out by the fact that when Robert Hand calls Bertha 'a wild flower blowing in a hedge', he is quoting a letter of Joyce to Nora of 2 December 1909, 'you are always my beautiful wild flower of the hedges.' And when Hand tells her, 'There is one word I have never dared to say to you,' he is echoing Joyce who – to Nora's distress in their days of courtship – could never bring himself to say that he loved her. Richard Rowan admits his collusion in his own cuckoldry when he says to Robert, 'in the very core of my ignoble heart I longed to be betrayed by you and by her – in the dark, in the night – secretly, meanly, craftily. By you, my best friend, and by her. I longed for that passionately and ignobly, to be dishonoured for ever in love and in lust, to be ... To be for ever a shameful creature and to build up my soul again out of the ruins of its shame.' Robert has reason to say that Bertha and he have only obeyed Richard's will, that even his proposal of a duet between their two souls for Bertha has been roused in his brain by Richard.

This notion of willing one's own destruction is deeply imbedded in Joyce. In *Ulysses* Stephen sings to Bloom the ballad of the Jew's daughter, in which a Christian child is killed; the commentary Stephen offers is to the effect that the child is immolated, 'consenting'. That one somehow contrives one's own destiny as well as suffers it is also indicated in *A Portrait of the Artist*. There Stephen notes that Cranly appears to have designs upon his girl. He comments, 'Is he the shining light now? Well, I discovered him. I protest I did. Shining quietly behind a bushel of Wicklow bran.' Jealous, he yet consoles himself by the thought that he has brought Cranly out of obscurity to his girl's attention. The relation of Stephen and Cranly also foreshadows that of Richard and Robert, for Cranly asks Stephen if he can bear being alone, 'not to have any one person ... who would be more than a friend, more even than the noblest and truest friend a man ever had.' 'Of whom are you speaking?' Stephen asks. 'Cranly did not answer.' I met Byrne twice, and the first thing he said to me was that homosexuality was not even known in his day in Dublin. Joyce says in his notes to *Exiles* that the relation between Richard and Robert is a mixture of jealousy with love: 'The bodily possession of Bertha by Robert, repeated often, would certainly bring into almost carnal contact the two men. Do they desire this? To be united, that is carnally through the person and body of Bertha as they cannot, without dissatisfaction and degradation – be united carnally man to man as man to woman?' In the play Richard says he longs to put his arm around Robert's neck, and feels at moments a special 'brotherhood' with him. Joyce is trying to anatomize not only love but also friendship, including its homosexual component. From this point of view the woman is a vehicle through which the two men possess each other as well as her. In *Giacomo Joyce* the most cryptic scene is one which appears to be a dream, though it is not so denominated, in which Giacomo is making love to a hairdresser while Gogarty has come to be introduced to Nora. Something of the situation of *Exiles*, in which love is an *égoisme à quatre*, is implicit here.

*

But Joyce saved for *Ulysses* an even more thorough examination of the theme of betrayal, as applied to adultery. Bloom, like Joyce, like Richard Rowan, loves keyholes; Joyce makes clear the voyeuristic aspect which is undoubtedly an ingredient in jealousy, so that he has Bloom witness Molly's infidelity and be goaded by her into noting all its details. It cannot be said that he has encouraged this affair, but he does propose an exchange of Italian and music lessons between his wife and Stephen Dedalus, and though the proposal is tentative and unlikely to be carried out, it seems to connect with Prezioso's visits to Nora, and with Robert's visits to Bertha. Though Richard has helped to set off the forces which then obsess him, he is tortured by doubt – he cannot know what Bertha and Robert have done together. Joyce used to say that the world is based upon doubt as the world hangs in the void. The question that Bloom explores is different but related: he does not doubt, he knows that his wife has committed adultery. His response is to reconcile himself, because we are sexual from our mother's wombs, and everyone must participate in fidelity and infidelity; whether or not there is copulation, there is ocular penetration or reception, and fantasy. Even if the body is loyal, the mind may be truant. So in *Giacomo Joyce* Giacomo brags at one point, about his pupil, 'Her eyes have drunk my thoughts: and into the moist warm yielding welcoming darkness of her womanhood my soul, itself dissolving, has streamed and poured and flooded a liquid and abundant seed. Take her now who will.' Before this is dismissed as nonsense, remember that it is Christian nonsense: 'Whosoever looketh on a woman to lust after her hath committed adultery with her already in his heart.' If we are all lusting after each other, with varying degrees of intensity, Bloom must have the right of it when he insists that adultery is a much more venial offense than

theft, highway robbery, cruelty to children and animals, obtaining money under false pretenses, forgery, embezzlement, misappropriation of public money, betrayal of public trust, malingering, mayhem, corruption of minors, criminal libel, blackmail, contempt of court, arson, treason, felony, mutiny on the high seas, trespass, burglary, jailbreaking, practice of unnatural vice, desertion from armed forces in the field, perjury, poaching, usury, intelligence with the king's enemies, impersonation, criminal assault, manslaughter, wilful and premeditated murder.

Yet this is not the attitude taken in *Exiles*, and evidently Joyce wished to cast betrayal in different roles and to measure different reactions to it. To regard infidelity as corporeal is in *Exiles* to fall into materialism and into what Blake called Single Vision. In his notes for his play, Joyce insists that 'The soul like the body may have a virginity. For the woman to yield it or for the man to take it is the act of love.' It is really Bertha's soul that Richard is trying to woo. But Robert's point of view, a different one, is also given some credibility. 'The blinding instant of passion' – meaning physical passion – is what he longs for. His is the voice of corporeal love, of what he calls the eternal law of nature. 'Call it brutal, bestial, what you will,' he says, confident that it has its own claim. A woman, he says, is like a stone, a flower, or a bird. Richard timidly objects that 'the longing to possess a woman is not love', and when challenged by Robert for a definition of love, he says it is 'to wish her well'. (This is the Italian way of saying 'I love you': '*Ti voglio bene*.') Robert wishes to deal with love as completely physical, an exaltation of the body. Richard insists that it must be considered metaphysical, an act of union: 'Have you', he asks Robert – and we realize that he is now defining love more precisely – 'the luminous certitude that yours is the brain in contact with which she must think and understand and that yours is the body in contact with which her body must feel?' Robert replies cautiously, 'Have you?' and Richard says, 'Once I had it.'

At the end of *Exiles*, as at the end of *Ulysses*, the physical world seems on the verge of becoming metaphysical. So when Molly Bloom says of her husband, 'I knew he understood or felt what a woman is', she is praising Bloom for a quality that the exclusively physical Boylan lacks, imagination. In the final scene of *Exiles* Richard speaks of a wound to his soul – 'a deep wound of doubt which can never be healed'. This doubt is like that in a play of Strindberg that Joyce knew, *The Father*, in which the Captain thinks that his son may not be his son, and in spite of his wife's protestations (like Bertha's) remains unconvinced. Richard has longed 'to be united' with Bertha 'in body and soul in utter nakedness', but the nakedness is primarily the soul's nakedness. Robert, beaten in this battle which is one of wits rather than of bodies, decides to go into the exile from which Richard has come, as if exile were the state of rejection rather than any geographical position.

We do not know what happened that night at the end of the second act, and Joyce is at pains to keep us from knowing. Richard must be entitled to his wound of doubt. Adultery is not a casual matter. On the other hand, he cannot really be unsure that Bertha is and will continue to be devoted to him. He even says that he wants to be in a state of 'restless living wounding doubt'. Yet there is a way in which people who live in such doubt must be to some extent in perpetual exile from each other.

In rehearsing the backgrounds of *Exiles*, I have tried to suggest that this a better play than it may first appear. It has of course many weak spots: Beatrice remains a shadowy figure, and Robert does not have a high degree of reality. But Richard and Bertha come through quite well, strange as their conduct may appear. Joyce wanted the play to be, like his other works, an 'extravagant excursion into forbidden territory', in this case particularly the investigation of the cuckold. In his notes for *Exiles* he speaks of newly discovered drafts of *Madame Bovary* in which the focus of attention shifts away from the lovers and on to the cuckolded husband. He suggests also that 'As a contribution to the study of jealousy Shakespeare's *Othello* is incomplete.' In these notes – which Joyce wrote with such formality as to suggest that he imagined their eventual publication – he does not mention another play of Shakespeare, *Cymbeline*. Yet *Cymbeline* is much closer, for in it as in *Exiles* there is a fidelity test. Iachimo falsely claims to have seduced Posthumus's wife Imogen. But in the end Posthumus is disabused. What Joyce found in the play is a reflection of Shakespeare's personality: as Stephen Dedalus says in *Ulysses*, 'In *Cymbeline*, in *Othello* he is bawd and cuckold.' Joyce does try to complete the diagnosis of jealousy, to anatomize it further, and the depiction of it that he gives is exceedingly complex. The jealous person at once relishes the attention paid to the loved one and hates it. He longs to arouse the envy of others by the possession of a beautiful object. Yet to delight in possession is to allow the conceivability of dispossession, to rely on constancy is impossible because it can only exist as a relation to inconstancy; what is absent calls attention to what is present. He may feel, as Richard does, that the very idea of faithfulness belongs to an era of private property that should be superseded. One cannot steal what one has given, no one can break into an open door. Richard, indignant at the idea of owning a wife, still longs for her total commitment to him. To achieve it, however, he must subject it to a test, and in so doing he shoulders the burden of uncertainty: she may be physically unfaithful, she may be spiritually unfaithful. Her assurance that she is not the first does not preclude her having been the second. And on the second point her own witness, however sincere, can never evoke certainty.

For Bertha the problem does not center in jealousy, though she expresses some jealousy of Beatrice, knowing that Beatrice's mind and Richard's mind have a mutual attraction. For her the problem centers mostly in freedom. How can she be free when she feels bound, when she wants to be bound? On the other hand, how can her husband claim that she is free when he makes her freedom his gift, and when he watches her like a hawk, or only averts his eyes to see better what she is thinking? We can never achieve Richard's ideal of two people possessing each other in utter nakedness.

In the sentiments evoked by sexual betrayal and jealousy Joyce found a parable of the dilemma of all creators, whether of books or of worlds. Joyce's notes speak of the play as 'a rough and tumble between the Marquis de Sade and Freiherr v. Sacher Masoch'. But in the artist creator these sentiments converge, as if all creation were sado-masochistic. Shakespeare is all in all of us, ostler and butcher, bawd and cuckold; God cannot help resembling him. So Stephen Dedalus tells us. But I think Joyce would have said that the same could be said of everyone, to the extent that we all create, at least in part, the situations we suffer from, and the minds that render us prone to suffering. Exiles all of us from the promised land, we return to it in vain.

Ez and Old Billyum

AT THE time of their first meeting in London, in 1908, Ezra Pound was twenty-three to W. B. Yeats's forty-three. Pound did not, like Joyce six years earlier, find Yeats too old to be helped. Instead, he declared, with humility and yet some arrogance of his own, that Yeats was the only poet worthy of serious study, and in later years he recalled without chagrin having spent the years from 1908 to 1914 in 'learning how Yeats did it'. What he learned was the 'inner form of the lyric or short poem containing an image', as in 'The Fish' ('Although you hide in the ebb and flow / Of the pale tide when the moon is set'), and 'the inner form of the line' (probably its rhythmical merger of 'dull, numb words' with unexpected ones). Yeats offered further an example of 'syntactical simplicity'; he had, for example, cut out inversions and written with what Pound as late as 1914 considered 'prose directness', in 'The Old Men Admiring Themselves in the Water': 'I heard the old, old men say, /"Everything alters." '

That Pound had already studied Yeats intently before coming to London is disclosed by the volume *A Lume Spento*, which he published in Venice on his roundabout way to England from Wabash College, and republished in 1965 with a new preface describing the poems as 'stale cream-puffs'. They are so, but show something anyway about the confectioner. The second poem, 'La Fraisne' (Old Provençal for ash tree), has a long 'note precedent' in Latin and Old Ezraic. Before explaining that the speaker in the poem is Miraut de Gazelas when driven mad by his love for Riels of Calidorn, Pound indicates that he wrote the poem in a mood like that of Yeats's *The Celtic Twilight*, a title which was intended to suggest a vague borderline between the physical and metaphysical worlds. He felt himself 'divided between a self corporal and a self ætherial', or, as he defines it further, 'trans-sentient as a wood pool'. Such states, in which time is contained and transcended, possess Pound again, most notably in the descriptions of paradisal moods in the *Cantos*, but 'La Fraisne' itself does not offer this pitch of feeling. In the course of his self-exegesis, Miraut identifies himself with the ash tree; at one time he was a wise councillor, but now he has left 'the old ways of men' to lose himself in sylvan metamorphosis. He seems to follow the lead of two characters in Yeats's early poetry: Fergus, who abdicated to drive his brazen cars in the forest, and another royal abdicator, Goll, who belongs to the same dynasty as Arnold's 'Mycerinus'. Pound's line, 'Naught but the wind that flutters in the leaves', echoes 'The Madness of King Goll', where the refrain is: 'They will not hush, the leaves that round me flutter – the beech leaves old.' Miraut's thought that he is merging into the boles of ash wood owes something, like Pound's other early poem, 'The Tree', to Yeats's poem, 'He Thinks of His Past Greatness When a Part of the Constellations of Heaven': 'I have been a hazel-tree and they hung / The Pilot Star and the Crooked Plough / Among my leaves in times out of mind....'

Other lines in 'La Fraisne', where Miraut has 'put aside this folly and the cold / That old age weareth for a cloak', and where he announces, 'For I know that the wailing and bitterness are a folly', echo words like 'wail' and 'folly' from the diction of Yeats, and derive more particularly from his poem, 'In the Seven Woods', where the speaker has 'put away the unavailing outcries and the old bitterness / That empty the heart'. Blistered in Provence, Miraut has been patched and peeled in Yeats's first, third, and fourth volumes of verse, as well as in *The Celtic Twilight*.

Yet the proximity to Yeats does not prevent 'La Fraisne' from being identifiably Pound's configuration. Yeats portrays the madness of King Goll as a heroic state of mind superior to sanity, while Councillor Miraut's mental condition is more equivocal, even pathetic. Pound diverges also, after three stanzas, from the formal regularity on which Yeats always insisted, so that he can attempt to capture his hero's incoherence. In a passage, bold in 1908, he makes use of a series of broken sentences:

> Once when I was among the young men...
> And they said I was quite strong, among the young men,
> Once there was woman...
> ...but I forgot...she was..
> ...And I hope she will not come again.
>
> I do not remember.....
>
> I think she hurt me once, but..
> That was very long ago.

These are perhaps the most important dots in English poetry. They show Pound already essaying what in *Mauberley* he calls a 'consciousness disjunct'. In the later poem the pauses represent hesitations instead of panicky repressions:

> Drifted ... drifted precipitate,
> Asking time to be rid of ...
> Of his bewilderment; to designate
> His new found orchid. ...

In the *Cantos*, like Eliot in *The Waste Land*, he usually leaves out dots, as if no one expected any longer the considerate guidance that prevailed in earlier poetry. But this mode begins in 'La Fraisne'.

If Pound translated Yeats, then, like one of his troubadours, sometimes literally and sometimes freely, Yeats responded to the change in atmosphere with which Pound surrounded his borrowings, and he did not dismiss him as an imitator. When he read *A Lume Spento*, with which Pound must have introduced himself, he called it 'charming', an adjective Pound knew to be reserved. Still, Yeats could hardly have read the poem entitled 'Plotinus' without being tempted to rewrite it, syntactically and otherwise:

> As one that would draw thru the node of things
> Back sweeping to the vortex of the cone. ...
>
> And then for utter loneliness, made I
> New thoughts as crescent images of *me*.

The vortexes are premonitory of Pound's later Vorticist movement, but they also, with cones and crescents, anticipate metaphors of *A Vision*. Pound cannot be said to have put them into Yeats's head, for Yeats knew Plotinus well already, but he must have given them a new spin.

Yeats liked better Pound's book *Personae*, which appeared in April of the following year, 1909. The title proudly drew attention to the very point that had vexed William Carlos Williams in the first book, the assumption of a series of exotic roles. For Pound, it was an attempt, by encompassing more situations and moods, to follow Walter Pater's advice and extend the self horizontally. Yeats's purpose in the seemingly similar doctrine of the mask, which he was then cultivating in early drafts of *The Player Queen*, and must have discussed with Pound, was a vertical deepening of the self by fusion with its opposite. For Yeats, Pound's theory, like Arthur Symons's version of Pater's impressionism, was too volatile and rootless, and suspiciously international. But, beyond the theory, he detected the young man's extraordinary talent; and Pound wrote elatedly to Williams, just after *Personae* was published, 'I have been praised by the greatest living poet.' This snub almost silenced Williams.

Yeats was in fact as pleased with his new friendship as Pound was. In December 1909, he wrote Lady Gregory that 'this queer creature

Ezra Pound ... has become really a great authority on the troubadours.' So much erudition of course amused him a little, too, and now or later he humorously accused Pound of trying to provide a portable substitute for the British Museum. He liked the way Pound devised to recite verse so that it sounded like music, with strongly marked time, yet remained intelligible, and he credited it with being a better method than that of Florence Farr, which a decade earlier he had so highly praised. But he noted also that Pound's voice was poor, sounding 'like something on a bad phonograph'. It may have been just the American accent emigrating to an Irish ear. Pound, for his part, thought Yeats's method of 'keening and chaunting with a *u*' absurd, and while he could effect no improvement, he obliged Yeats to admit, after half an hour's struggle, that poems such as those of Burns could not be wailed to the tune of *The Wind among the Reeds*. Each poet enjoyed condescending to the other.

Pound, as he began to flabbergast London with his passionate selections and rejections, found that his allegiance to Yeats was not shared by other writers whom he respected. The movement away from nineteenth-century poetry had begun. As John Butler Yeats wrote to his son, 'The poets loved by Ezra Pound are tired of Beauty, since they have met it so often....I am tired of Beauty my wife, says the poet, but here is that enchanting mistress Ugliness. With her I will live, and what a riot we shall have. Not a day shall pass without a fresh horror. Prometheus leaves his rock to cohabit with the Furies.' The vogue of ugliness was sometimes companioned by an insistence on man's limited and finite condition. T. E. Hulme was already in 1908, when he and Pound met, denouncing the romantic bog and leading the way to the classical uplands; by his rule. Yeats was wet and dim when he should have been dry and clear. On still other grounds T. S. Eliot, who battled Yeats for Pound's soul a few years later, declared Yeats an irrelevance in the modern world. By 1912 D. H. Lawrence, originally an admirer of Yeats, could say, 'He seems awfully queer stuff to me now – as if he wouldn't bear touching,' and he objected to Yeats's method of dealing with old symbols as 'sickly'. Another friend of Pound's, Ford Madox Ford, though not unreceptive to other monstrosities, informed Pound that Yeats was a 'gargoyle, a great poet but a gargoyle'.

Pound's determination to make it new combined with this voluble pressure to stint a little his admiration of Yeats as a model. Writing in *Poetry*, the then new Chicago review, in January 1913, he explained that Ford and Yeats were diametrically opposed because one was objective, the other subjective. While he grandly pronounced Yeats to be 'the only poet worthy of serious study', he felt compelled to warn that the method of Yeats 'is, to my way of thinking, very dangerous'. The magistrate was severe: 'His art has not broadened much during the past decade. His gifts to English art are mostly negative; i.e., he has stripped English poetry of many of its faults.' Yeats continued to fall short. In 1913 Pound wrote Harriet Monroe that Ford and Yeats were the two men in London, 'And Yeats is already a sort of great dim figure with its associations set in the past.' In the *Pisan Cantos* (LXXXII), the two men are weighed again,

> and for all that old Ford's conversation was better,
> consisting in *res non verba*,
>> despite William's anecdotes, in that Fordie
>> never dented an idea for a phrase's sake
>
> and had more humanitas

Such reservations did not prevent Pound from regarding Yeats as a splendid bridge from Mallarmé and the symbolists, which he could afford to cross on his way to founding Imagism and then Vorticism. These movements, full of don'ts, extolled light, clarity, and in general a Polaroid view of the verse line. Pound knew, however, as Hulme, Lawrence and Ford did not know, that Yeats was still adaptable, and as eager to leave the '90s behind as they were. The books of verse he published in 1904 and 1910 reacted against his early manner, but he was still dissatisfied, and kept looking about for incitements for further change. Pound was a perpetual incitement, mixing admiration with remonstrance.

Another spur, now improbable, was Rabindranath Tagore, whom Yeats met in June 1912. Tagore's poetry brought together, Yeats felt, the metaphors and emotions of unlearned people with those of the learned, coupling the fastidious with the popular in the way that he had commended to Joyce ten years before. Yeats remarked to Pound, unhinged by the same enthusiasm, that Tagore was 'someone greater than any of us – I read these things and wonder why one should go on trying to write.' Pointing to a description in Tagore's poem, 'The Banyan Tree', 'Two ducks swam by the weedy margin above their shadows, and the child ... longed ... to float like those ducks among the weeds and shadows,' Yeats proclaimed, 'Those ducks are the ducks of real life and not out of literature.' His friend Sturge Moore was helping Tagore with the translation, and Yeats joined in the task, arguing with Moore about words. (He allowed Tagore to use the word 'maiden', though in a later stage of dictional disinfection, when he was translating the *Upanishads* with another Indian, he insisted upon the word 'girl'.) Soon he recognized that

Tagore was 'unequal' and sometimes dull, but he saw mainly 'great beauty', and wrote a fulsome introduction to *Gitanjali*.

Pound's own role in the modernization of Yeats began at first, like that of most mentors, uninvited. In October 1912 he persuaded Yeats to give *Poetry* a start with some new poems. Yeats sent them to Pound for transmittal, appending a note to ask that the punctuation be checked. The note was bound, as Pound said ruefully later, 'to create a certain atmosphere of drama'. He could not resist exceeding mere compliance by making three changes in Yeats's wording. In 'Fallen Majesty', he impudently if reasonably deleted 'as it were' from the final line: 'Once walked a thing that seemed as it were a burning cloud.' In 'The Mountain Tomb', he worried over the lines, 'Let there be no foot silent in the room, / Nor mouth with kissing or the wine unwet', and altered 'or the' to 'nor with'. Then, with 'To a Child Dancing Upon the Shore',

> Being young you have not known
> The fool's triumph, nor yet
> Love lost as soon as won,
> Nor he, the best labourer, dead,
> And all the sheaves to bind ...

Pound thought long and deep and then changed 'he' to 'him'.

At peace, he sent the poems on 26 October to Harriet Monroe with the comment: 'I don't think this is precisely W. B. Y. at his best ... but it shows a little of the new Yeats – as in the "Child Dancing". "Fallen Majesty" is just where he was two years ago. "The Realists" is also tending toward the new phase.' Pound, though he had liked the hardness of 'No Second Troy', was weary of prolonging the celebrations of Maud Gonne as she had been twenty years before. On the other hand, he welcomed the increasing directness that Yeats now usually aimed at. He conveyed something of these opinons to Yeats, and at the same time duly informed him of the small changes he had made.

To his surprise, Yeats was indignant at this American brashness, and Pound had to carry out mollification proceedings as recorded in his letters to Miss Monroe. For rhythm's sake Yeats insisted upon restoring the spiritless 'as it were' to 'Fallen Majesty', though a year later he rewrote the line to get rid of it. But Pound's other two revisions shook him. At first he modified the second passage to read, 'Nor mouth with kissing nor *the* wine unwet', but by the proof stage he recognized that unwet wine would not do, and Pound's version, 'nor with wine unwet', appears in *Poetry*. In the third instance, the battle of the pronouns, he insisted upon 'he' rather than 'him', but, made aware of the grammatical sin, put a period after the third line to replace the comma. On 2 November, Pound transmitted these partial restorations to Miss Monroe with the remark, 'Oh *la la*, ce que le roi désire!' Later the same day, he reported a last change, eliminating 'Nor' before 'he':

Final clinic in the groves of philosophy.

Love lost as soon as won. (full stop)
And he, the best labourer, dead

peace reigns on parnassus.

Still enthralled by Tagore's verse, and still stung by Pound's criticism, Yeats felt the challenge to his powers. It was probably now that he confided to Pound, 'I have spent the whole of my life trying to get rid of rhetoric. I have got rid of one kind of rhetoric and have merely set up another.' For the first time in years he asked for help, as his letters to Lady Gregory of 1 and 3 January 1913 make clear. In the former he writes: 'I have had a fortnight of gloom over my work – I felt something wrong with it. However on Monday night I got Sturge Moore in and last night Ezra Pound and we went at it line by line and now I know what is wrong and am in good spirits again. I am starting the poem about the King of Tara and his wife ['The Two Kings'] again, to get rid of Miltonic generalizations.' (Pound had made 'Miltonic' a derogatory epithet.) Yeats was later to redefine what he and Pound had crossed out as 'conventional metaphors', presumably those turned abstract by overuse. In his second letter to Lady Gregory he indicates that the whole experience has given him diarrhea:

My digestion has got rather queer again – a result I think of sitting up late with Ezra and Sturge Moore and some light wine while the talk ran. However the criticism I have got from them has given me new life and I have made that Tara poem a new thing and am writing with a new confidence having got Milton off my back. Ezra is the best critic of the two. He is full of the middle ages and helps me to get back to the definite and the concrete away from modern abstractions. To talk over a poem with him is like getting you to put a sentence into dialect. All becomes clear and natural. Yet in his own work he is very uncertain, often very bad though very interesting sometimes. He spoils himself by too many experiments and has more sound principles than taste.

A letter which Pound sent Harriet Monroe summarizes the sound principles if not the questionable taste he must have communicated to Yeats. In terms ostentatiously graceless he called for 'Objectivity and again objectivity, and expression; no hind-side-beforeness, no straddled adjectives (as "addled mosses dank'), no Tennysonianness of speech: *nothing* that you couldn't in some circumstance, in the stress of some emotion, *actually say*. Every *literaryism*, every book word, fritters away a scrap of the reader's patience, a scrap of his sense of your sincerity.' Though Yeats had been able to reconstruct much of his diction, he needed a jolt to complete the process. This Pound, by virtue of his downrightness, his good will, his unintimidatable character, his sense of himself as shocker, was peculiarly fitted to administer. For him, as for Auden later, poems were contraptions, and most of them were inefficient and needed overhaul. He had trained himself, like no one else, for the very task Yeats demanded of him. That Pound was able to give advice, and Yeats, notwithstanding age and fame, to take it and to admit having taken it, made their friendship, unlike many relations of literary men, felicitous.

The experience was, like most medicine, more than a little painful for Yeats; having requested Pound's help once, he had to submit to occasional further reproofs. He showed Pound 'The Two Kings' when it was finished, and Pound informed him (and said later in a review of *Responsibilities*) that it was like those *Idylls* written by a poet more monstrous even than Milton. Yeats wrote his father of this harsh verdict, and his father reassured him by saying that the poem had supremely what Tennyson never achieved – namely, concentration. Yeats took heart and believed that Pound this time was wrong. But he was none the less gratified when Pound, on reading the untitled last poem in *Responsibilities*, and especially the last lines – 'till all my priceless things / Are but a post the passing dogs defile' – remarked that Yeats had at last become a modern poet. An image of urination had finally brought Pound to his knees.

Yeats, while acknowledging Pound's critical penetration and quite liking him as a person, was perplexed about his poetry. He quarreled with the rhythms of its free verse as 'devil's metres'. Many of the poems did not seem to Yeats fully achieved. When in 1913 Harriet Monroe offered him a prize for 'The Grey Rock', Yeats urged her in December to give it to Pound instead; he said candidly, 'I suggest him to you because, although I do not really like with my whole soul the metrical experiments he has made for you. I think those experiments show a vigorous creative mind. He is certainly a creative personality of some sort, though it is too soon yet to say of what sort. His experiments are perhaps errors, I am not certain; but I would always sooner give the laurel to vigorous errors than to any orthodoxy not inspired.' Although Pound's work was not to Yeats's taste any more than Joyce's, he could not fail to sense that here, too, was a kind of alien talent. The following year he spoke at a *Poetry* dinner in Chicago, and said again of Pound, 'Much of his work is experimental; his work will come slowly; he will make many an experiment before he comes into his own.' But he read two poems which he judged of 'permanent value', 'The Ballad of the Goodly Fere' and 'The Return'. The latter he complimented, in that slightly histrionic rhythm for which Joyce mocked him in *Ulysses*, as 'the most beautiful poem that has been written in the free form, one of the few in which I find real organic rhythm'. He quoted it again later in *A Vision*, where it jibed with his theory of cyclical repetition. He was consciously, doggedly allowing virtue in Pound's work, though he had no wish to enroll in the new school which his former pupil had opened. On many matters they continued to dispute, and Pound summarized almost with satisfaction the quarrelsomeness of a meeting the next year: 'The antipodes of our two characters and beliefs being in more vigorous saliency.'

During the winter of 1913–14, and the two following winters, Yeats wished to be away from London with a secretary who could do some typing and also read to him Doughty's poems and (anticipating Auden) Icelandic sagas. He had formed the plan with Pound as companion in mind, and Pound with misgivings agreed to put himself out for the sake of English letters. He expected that Yeats would sometimes amuse him but often, because the occult was so irresistible a subject, bore him. To his partial surprise, life with Yeats in a four-room Sussex cottage proved contented and placid. He wrote Williams that Yeats was 'much finer *intime* than seen spasmodically in the midst of the whirl'. With more polish he described life at Stone Cottage nostalgically in Canto LXXXIII:

> There is fatigue deep as the grave.
> The Kakemono grows in flat land out of mist
>   sun rises lop-sided over the mountain
>   so that I recalled the noise in the chimney
> as it were the wind in the chimney
>   but was in reality Uncle William
> downstairs composing
> that had made a great Peeeeacock
>   in the proide ov his oiye
>   had made a great peeeeeeecock in the...

54

> made a great peacock
> in the proide of his oyyee
>
> proide ov his oy-ee
> as indeed he had, and perdurable
>
> a great peacock aere perennius...

While Yeats's aristocratic pride and his 'hearing nearly all Words-worth / for the sake of his conscience but / preferring Ennemosor on Witches' amused Pound still, he recognized that these two foibles received a kind of immortal warranty by their reflection in 'The Peacock' and 'The Witch'.

At Stone Cottage, Pound taught Yeats after a fashion to fence, while Yeats offered reciprocal lessons, as dreaded, in spiritualism and related subjects. These proved, however, more apposite to his own interests than Pound had anticipated. For when Yeats was writing essays for Lady Gregory's *Visions and Beliefs in the West of Ireland*, setting them in the context of the *tradition à rebours*, Pound was devoting himself to editing Ernest Fenollosa's translations of the Noh plays of Japan. These were just as crowded with ghosts and other extraterrestrial creatures. East and West met in the astral envelope as well as in Connemara. In the edition he now made of the plays, *'Noh' or Accomplishment* (1916), Pound refers frequently to parallels furnished him by Yeats, and speaks with unwonted respect of such matters as 'the "new" doctrine of the suggestibility or hyp-notizeability of ghosts', though he preserves his dignity by an alibi: only the merit of the Japanese poetry has brought him to this pass. Pound's versions of Noh convene a kind of grand international festival with entries from India, Japan, England, the United States, and Ireland. The Samurai are particularly at home in Kiltartan or Aran:

> I've a sad heart to see you looking up to Buddha, you who left me alone, I diving in the black rivers of hell. Will soft prayers be a comfort to you in your quiet heaven, you who knew that I'm alone in that wild, desolate place?
>
> Times out of mind am I here setting up this bright branch, this silky wood with the charms painted on it as fine as the web you'd get in the grass-cloth of Shinobu, that they'd be still selling you in this mountain.
>
> I had my own rain of tears; that was the dark night, surely.

The Noh plays were more to Yeats's taste than to Pound's: by

1918 Pound was prematurely dismissing them as a failure. He linked them in this disgrace with Yeats's long essay, *Per Amica Silentia Lunae*, which with its hypothesis of antiselves and daimons must still have seemed too occult for the mint assayer's son. Whether he also dismissed the prefatory poem to this work, 'Ego Dominus Tuus', is not clear, though his allusion to it as a dialogue of 'Hic' and 'Willie' (for 'Ille') perhaps implies some dissatisfaction, beyond his unwillingness to resist polylingual jokes. He was prepared to believe again, as he said in 1920, that Yeats was 'faded'.

Yeats had entered a period of much greater assurance. The Noh plays, so fortuitously put in his hands, had won without his being aware of it the battle with naturalistic drama which he had himself been fighting in beleaguered fashion. Here was the authorization he needed for leaving probability in the lurch, by abolishing scenery so the imagination would be untrammeled, by covering faces with masks, by portraying character in broad strokes – emptied of Ibsen's convincing details – through isolating the moment in which some irrevocable deed separates a man from his fellows as well as from his own idiosyncrasies. He was also prompted to new and more reckless devices, the symbolic dance as a climax to suggest the impingement of the timeless upon the actual, the preternatural shudder from the sudden lighting-up of a ruined place, the assumption of someone else's human form by a spirit or god. Yeats saw how he might focus an entire play, as he had entire poems, on a single metaphor. That the Noh plays were often blurred in effect did not ruffle him; the form, he saw, could be improved. He kept the strangeness and increased the dramatic tension, splicing natural with preternatural in order, unpredictably, to heighten the human dilemma. The Yeatsian paradox was to explode verisimilitude by miracle for the purposes of a more ultimate realism.

The result was the first of his plays for dancers, *At the Hawk's Well*, and to some degree almost all his subsequent plays. Happily, Ezra Pound proved to have an aptitude for the criticism of drama as well. He offered many suggestions about scenery and timing; he found the indispensable Japanese dancer Michio Itō; and he helped Yeats to clarify the play. For a time, it seemed that his dramatic ability might receive professional sanction. He wrote a skit which Yeats encouraged him to enlarge, thinking it might be suitable for presentation at the Abbey Theatre, but it was adjudged, by the then manager, too full of indecencies. Then Yeats recommended to Lady Gregory that Pound fill in as manager of the Abbey for a four-month period, but this plan also was vetoed. Surviving these rebuffs, Pound remained indispensable; he observed Yeats locked in struggle with a long-unfinished tragedy, and irreverently proposed it be made a comedy instead. The firecracker went off, Yeats was exhilarated, and *The Player Queen* reached completion. Both Pound's moral impudence about experience and Yeats's theme in the play – the necessity of lying – would have pleased Wilde.

In the midst of Vorticism and daimonism both poets were distracted toward marriage. Yeats had trouble unmaking the fealty to Maud Gonne as symbol, if not as woman, which he had so often declared. He wrote a poem, 'His Phoenix' (which Pound dismissed as 'a little bad Yeats'), to contrast her more gaily than usual with the current lot of women, 'There's Margaret and Marjorie and Dorothy and Nan, / A Daphne and a Mary who live in privacy', with the defiant conclusion, 'I knew a Phoenix in my youth, so let them have their day.' He was indulging here a private joke by making a list of Pound's girl friends. Among them Dorothy was pre-eminent. This was Dorothy Shakespear, with whose mother, Olivia, Yeats had been in love during the Nineties. Pound married Dorothy in April 1914. Then Yeats, after the Easter Rebellion had widowed Maud Gonne, felt duty bound to offer her marriage, though he hesitated to bed an obsessive conviction. (Pound saw her in the same way: when he wished to characterize Yeats's occult interests, just as when Yeats wished to characterize Pound's political ideas, each compared the other to Maud Gonne.) Her refusal was a relief. The next year Yeats married Georgie Hyde-Lees, a cousin and close friend of Pound's wife, and Pound served as best man. The two poets met often after their marriages. After Pound went to the Continent in 1920, they met in Paris in 1922, in Sicily in 1925, in Rapallo in 1928, 1929–30, 1934, and in London in 1938. Yet, as so often, separate households made for a subtle disconnection of friendship.

Pound's work had become more ambitious. After *Lustra*, he wrote *Propertius*, *Mauberley* and the first *Cantos*. Yeats disconcerted him in 1916 by saying that Pound's new work gave him 'no asylum for his affections'. Pound wrote the criticism to Kate Buss, but cautioned her about repeating it. Perhaps in part because he recognized some justice in it, Pound moved away from purely satirical poems like many in *Lustra*, and in the *Cantos* (LXXXI) he subscribes fully to Yeats's principle:

> What thou lovest well remains,
> > the rest is dross
> What thou lov'st well shall not be reft from thee
> What thou lov'st well is thy true heritage

It is hard to discover Yeats's views of Pound's new works. He told Pound in 1920 that he liked *Mauberley*, and he tried to suspend judgment about the *Cantos*.

His attitude toward Pound between 1915 and 1925 can however be elicited from *A Vision*, the book he began in October 1917 just after his marriage. In the characterology which formed a large part of this book, Yeats classified contemporaries and men of the past in terms of phases of the moon. Pound was slowly becoming an abstraction, something analyzed at a distance. The early drafts, written between 1918 and 1922, placed Pound with Nietzsche as denizen of the twelfth lunar phase, called the phase of the Forerunner. He is Forerunner to men of fuller consciousness including, with chronological indifference, Yeats himself. But when the book was published in 1926, Pound's name was omitted; Yeats probably feared to give pain. Though Phase 12 was not a bad perch, Pound occupied it in a disharmonious way. The Phase 12 man who is 'in phase' follows Zarathustra's exhortation by heroically overcoming himself. (Yeats speaks elsewhere of Pound's effort at total self-possession, but does not seem to have regarded it as successful.) He is thereby enabled to assume his true mask which is lonely, cold, and proud, and to formulate a subjective philosophy that exalts the self in the presence of its object of desire. While Yeats may have thought of Imagism as offering an aesthetic philosophy of this kind, he had primarily in mind Nietzsche's projection of a superior world. In phase, the Phase 12 mind is a jetting fountain of personal life, of noble extravagance. It loathes abstraction as much as Pound did, and everything it considers comes clothed in sound and metaphor.

But if the man of this phase is 'out of phase', the result is much less satisfactory. Unable to discover his true mask, he assumes almost in frenzy a series of self-conscious poses. Here Yeats must have thought of Pound's *Personae*, and perhaps of Pound's own Bergsonian statement in *Gaudier-Brzeska*: 'One says "I am" this, that, or the other, and with the words scarcely uttered one ceases to be that thing. I began this search for the real in a book called *Personae*, casting off, as it were, complete masks of the self in each poem. I continued in long series of translations, which were but more elaborate masks.' Always in reaction, yet according to Yeats always hesitant, the out-of-phase man becomes a prey to facts, which drug or intoxicate him. More by chance than choice, he turns to a false mask, which offers instead of splendid loneliness the isolation of some small protesting sect; and he defends this role by 'some kind of superficial intellectual action, the pamphlet, the violent speech, the sword of the swashbuckler'. He oscillates between asserting some pose or, if preoccupied with outward things, asserting a dogmatism about events which depends too much upon the circumstances that produced it to have lasting value. Yeats is thinking here of Pound's adherence to Major Douglas's theories of social credit.

Even if Yeats penciled Pound into Phase 12, he could not fail to think of him also for Phase 23, which is the phase of our age and of its dominant art. Ultimately, he decided to transfer Pound completely to this later and less desirable phase; he saw him as neither arch-individualist nor forerunner but as a dissolving mind, subject to losses of self-control. What immediately impelled this unhappy demotion was the sight of Pound feeding all the stray cats in Rapallo in 1928. This undifferentiated pity, pity 'like that of a drunken man', was quickly connected by Yeats to the hysterical pity for general humanity left over from the Romantic movement. He had observed and blamed it in other writers, notably Sean O'Casey and Wilfred Owen. All three now seemed to belong to Phase 23, the theme of which is Creation through Pity.

The man of Phase 23 studies the external world for its own sake, and denies every thought that would make order of it. Instead of allowing the fountain of the mind to overflow, as in Phase 12, he lets the cauldron of the world boil over. Not only is causation denied, as Pound once remarked to Yeats, only sequence being knowable, but even sequence is destroyed. Yeats returned to this idea of A Vision in other essays; in the Oxford Book of Modern Verse he complained of the Cantos specifically: 'There is no transmission through time, we pass without comment from ancient Greece to modern England, from modern England to medieval China; the symphony, the pattern, is timeless, flux eternal and without movement.' In subsequent art, violations like Pound's have ceased to appear violative, but Yeats was not yet accustomed to them. He found an Eastern parallel for such work not in Pound's favorite Easterner, Confucius (who to Yeats seemed an eighteenth-century moralist, pulpited and bewigged), but in Sankara, the ninth-century founder of a school of Vedantism which conceives of mental and physical objects as 'alike material, a deluge of experience breaking over us and within us, melting limits whether of line or tint; man no hard bright mirror dawdling by the dry sticks of a hedge, but a swimmer, or rather the waves themselves' The new literature of the Cantos, of Virginia Woolf's novels, melted limits of plot, of logic, of character, of nationality, of authorship. In a letter, Yeats complained that Pound and his school prided them-selves on what their poems did not contain, all that might stop the flood, the conscious mind's capacity for intelligibleness and form.

Remembering his old view that Pound was too preoccupied with experiment, Yeats in *A Vision* asserts that in Phase 23 everything is seen from the point of view of technique and is investigated technically rather than imaginatively. Technical mastery offers the man of his phase his only refuge from masterless anarchy. Denying its subjective life, the mind delights only in the varied scene outside the window, and asks to construct a whole which is all event, all picture. Because of this submission to outwardness, the man of Phase 23 wishes to live in his exact moment of time as a matter of conscience, and, says Yeats, defends that moment like a theologian. He has in mind here Pound's Imagist predilection, as well as his forever and dogmatically 'making it new'.

Yeats noticed also that men of this phase, not only Pound but Joyce and Eliot, were apt to contrast some present scene with a mythical one. By holding apart what should be joined, the Phase 23 mind heralds further loss and eventual extinction of personality, and a world in which rights are swallowed up in duties and force is adored so that society turns into a mechanism. At variance with some of his later prose, Yeats explicitly deplores here an inevitable alliance of this phase and its succeeding phases with a regimented state.

After the first edition of *A Vision* was published early in 1926, Yeats grew dissatisfied with some of it, included the pretense that it was translated from an Arabic manuscript. In 1928 he came to Rapallo intending to work on it some more. He showed Pound a chorus he had translated 'From the *Antigone*' ('Overcome – O bitter sweetness ...') and was again convinced of his neighbor's critical acumen. After looking over what 'the Yeats' (as Pound jocularly called him) had written, Pound saw that the eighth line of the poem must become the second; he made changes in the ninth and tenth lines also. Yeats accepted the corrections. They may have given him an idea, which was half a jest, of complimenting Pound by prefacing *A Vision* with a series of papers under the common title, 'A Packet for Ezra Pound'. The irony of this tribute was that of all Yeats's books *A Vision*, with its detailed scheme of life and the afterlife, was most antipathetic to Pound's conception of art as liberated from deliberate rule or abstract theory. So 'A Packet' would pit Yeats against his surest castigator.

Acting on this impulse, Yeats began the 'Packet' with a description of Rapallo and then a discussion of the poet 'whose art is the opposite of mine'. He summarized a conversation he had had with Pound about the *Cantos*, and explained the poem enough (as he wrote a friend) to keep Pound neighborly. He did his best, in fact, to present sympathetically Pound's mode of marshaling in spurts certain increasingly enforced themes, though he admitted being unable to overcome his feeling that the *Cantos* were fragmentary that in them conventions of the intellect were abolished to satisfy an illusion that what is primal is formless, and that discontinuity had become a shibboleth.

Yeats also included in 'A Packet' a letter to Pound warning the expatriate against accepting public office: 'Do not be elected to the Senate of your country. I think myself, after six years, well out of mine. Neither you nor I, nor any other of our excitable profession, can match those old lawyers, old bankers, old business men, who, because all habit and memory, have begun to govern the world. They lean over the chair in front and talk as if to half a dozen of their kind at some board-meeting, and, whether they carry their point or not, retain moral ascendancy.' Pound, deep in correspondence with several Senators, was not at all convinced. In Canto LXXX he responded, 'If a man don't occasionally sit in a senate / how can he pierce the darrk mind of a / senator?' As for the bankers, Pound's special detestation, he devoted his pasquinade, 'Alf's Eighth Bit', in the *New English Weekly* (1934) to reforming Yeats's view of them:

> Vex not thou the banker's mind
>   (His *what?*) with a show of sense,
> Vex it not, Willie, his mind,
>   Or pierce its pretence
> On the supposition that it ever
> Was other, or that this cheerful giver
> Will give, save to the blind.

The only other part of *A Vision* on which Pound commented directly was not from 'A Packet' but from the ending. Yeats wrote there: 'Day after day I have sat in my chair turning a symbol over in my mind, exploring all its details, defining and again defining its elements, testing my convictions and those of others by its unity, attempting to substitute particulars for an abstraction like that of algebra ... Then I draw myself up into the symbol and it seems as if I should know all if I could but banish such memories and find everything in the symbol.' From Pound's point of view, symbols interfered with experience instead of letting experience coalesce into its natural pattern. In Canto LXXXIII he alluded to Yeats's perorative remarks, and connected them with 'Sailing to Byzantium' (a poem Pound had published in *The Exile* in 1928), where Yeats had asked to be gathered into 'the artifice of eternity'. Contrary to Yeats, Pound insisted,

> Le Paradis n'est pas artificiel
> And Uncle William dawdling around Notre Dame
> in search of whatever
>   paused to admire the symbol
> with Notre Dame standing inside it
> Whereas in St Etienne
>   or why not Dei Miracoli:
> mermaids, that carving,

Pound differs with Yeats on architecture as on paradise; he ironically suggests that Mary's presence is diminished rather than enhanced by the symbolic portentousness of her cathedral. He subtly compares her to Yeats ingested into his own cathedral-like *Vision*. As churches, Pound prefers less solipsistic structures like St. Etienne in Périgueux or Pietro Lombardo's Santa Maria dei Miracoli in Venice, and he repeats his earlier praise of Tullio Lombardo's carvings of sirens or mermaids on the latter church. As literature, Pound prefers to *A Vision* those poems of Yeats where there is less sense of the writer's being cocooned. His mild example is 'Down by the Salley Gardens', from which he slightly misquotes a few lines later:

>   the sage
>   delighteth in water
>   the humane man has amity with the hills
>
>   as the grass grows by the weirs
>   thought Uncle William. . . .

Yeats did not live to read the mixed blame and praise meted out to him in the *Pisan Cantos*, but he had another occasion to sample Pound's opinion of him. At the age of sixty-nine he wondered if he might not be too old for poetry. Fearing to outwrite his talent, he went to Rapallo in June 1934 primarily to show Pound a new play, *The King of the Great Clock Tower*. Pound was hard to divert from politics; he took the play, however, and next day rendered his verdict, 'Putrid!' In recounting this experience, Yeats allowed it to be thought that this was all Pound said, and that it was a sign, like his violent political *parti pris*, of a mind too exacerbated to be reliable. But in a journal begun at Rapallo that June he does Pound more justice. What Pound told him was that the lyrics of the play were written in 'Nobody language' and would not do for drama. Far from defying this judgment, Yeats was humbled by Pound's criticism of his diction, willing as always to undergo any indignity for the work's sake. In his notebook he wrote, 'At first I took his condemnation as the confirmation of my fear that I am now too old. I have written little verse for three years. But "nobody language" is something I can remedy. I must write in verse, but first in prose to get structure.' He liked the new songs well enough to publish the play with a preface which, without mentioning Pound by name, wryly repeated his verdict. At the same time, as if to guard against any possibility that Pound's criticism might still apply even after revision, Yeats wrote another play on the same theme, *A Full Moon in March*, where the songs of the head (which is lopped off in both plays) are more concrete. He also let Pound know, through Olivia Shakespear, that *The King of the Great Clock Tower* had been his most successful play at the Abbey.

Pound was not abashed; he had reverted to the pejorative view of Yeats's work as 'dim' or 'faded' that he had taken from time to time in the past, and he wrote Basil Bunting in 1936 that Yeats was 'dead', 'clinging to the habit of being a writer', that the recent poetry was 'slop'. In another letter to Bunting he found 'increasing difficulty' in 'reading the buzzard'. For Pound, Yeats, in spite of devoted ministrations, had come alive only for brief intervals. But at the last meeting of the two poets, which took place late in 1938 in London, Pound said he liked very much some of Yeats's recent poems, and Yeats, accustomed to Pound's impertinent rebuff, was proportionately disarmed by his praise. A late testimonial of Pound's quizzical admiration for Yeats is a parodic version of 'Under Ben Bulben' written in a Wabash version of Irish dialect, which he published in 1958:

> Neath Ben Bulben's buttocks lies
> Bill Yeats, a poet twoice the soize
> Of William Shakespear, as they say
>
> Down Ballykillywuchlin way.
>
> Let Saxon roiders break their bones
> Huntin' the fox
>   thru dese gravestones.

Yeats in his last years made a fresh effort to formulate his view of Pound without recourse, this time, to the symbology of *A Vision*. He was compiling his *Oxford Book of Modern Verse*, and the preface provided a good occasion to fence with his old fencing-master. As he thought about Pound and selected three of his poems ('The River-Merchant's Wife: A Letter', a passage from *Propertius*, and Canto XVII), Yeats remarked to Dorothy Wellesley that Pound's work conveyed 'a single strained attitude', that Pound was 'the sexless

American professor for all his violence'. In the preface he said more discreetly: 'When I consider his work as a whole I find more style than form; at moments more style, more deliberate nobility and the means to convey it than in any contemporary poet known to me, but it is constantly interrupted, broken, twisted into nothing by its direct opposite, nervous obsession, nightmare, stammering confusion.' The trait of nobility mentioned by Yeats was one that Pound had lauded in reviewing *Responsibilities* in 1916; returning the compliment, Yeats prefixed the word 'deliberate' to indicate how a consciously assumed role might flag at moments into total disorder. Not having achieved personal unity, Pound, in Yeats's view, had failed in his effort to get all the wine into the bowl. Pound did not respond directly, though in the *Cantos* he remarks briefly, but twice, that Yeats, like Possum (Eliot) and Lewis, and unlike Orage, 'had no ground to stand on'. Orage stood on the firm ground of Major Douglas's economics.

While not retreating from his innovations, Pound often owned the tentativeness of the method he adopted for the *Cantos*. When in 1917 he published in *Poetry* the first versions of Cantos I, II, and III, he was almost apologetic in contrasting their broken form with Browning's: 'You had one whole man? / And I have many fragments.' At the same time, 'the modern world / Needs such a rag-bag to stuff all its thoughts in.' This humility prompted him until 1937 to treat the published *Cantos* as only 'drafts', and they became final just by passage of time, not change of heart. In his late writings, he returns, as in Canto CXVI, to his old sense of brave yet possibly unrealized effort:

> but the beauty is not in the madness
> Tho my errors and wrecks lie about me.
> and I cannot make it cohere.

Pound, in fact, always recognized some force in Yeats's objections.

For his part, Yeats did not summarily dismiss what Pound was attempting. The Japanese professor Shotaro Oshima went to visit him in the summer of 1938, and expressed dissatisfaction with the poems collected in Pound's *Active Anthology*. Yeats replied, 'Even those pieces composed by ellipsis have a triumphant combination of the visual and the imaginative.' He had come to identify Pound with ellipsis. In some of his later poems he endeavors to make room for a comparable if not identical agitation, by incorporating in them a direct challenge to the symmetry of the universe. He produces disruption by a refrain that embodies most of the hesitations, denials, and unspoken thoughts which Pound conveyed by ellipsis or discontinuity. So in 'What Then?' the ghost of Plato is summoned to question in the refrain everything that has been affirmed in the body of the stanza:

> 'The work is done,' grown old he thought.
> 'According to my boyish plan;
> Let the fools rage, I swerved in naught,
> Something to perfection brought';
> *But louder sang that ghost, 'What then?'*

With such devices Yeats, who had generally conceived of reality under the figure of a sphere, acknowledges another force, which might be called the *anti-sphere* – a contemptuous, unassimilable force which mocks our enterprise. Plato's ghost is a more reputable symbol for anarchy than Pound would have used, but in its lofty way it counters any hope of accommodation, any contentment with established forms. Perhaps Pound's liking for Yeats's last poems came from understanding that they were not unconcessive, that they too acknowledged the domain of incoherence.

The relationship of the two men had long ceased to be that of master and disciple. Though Pound referred to Yeats as 'Uncle William' or 'Old Billyum', it was he who after 1912 often assumed the avuncular role. As a matter of fact, they be-uncled each other. The sense that Yeats could profit from his corrections must have reinforced Pound's sense of his own independent talent. To have kept Yeats up to the mark was a heady accomplishment. But Pound went his own way and, notwithstanding his penchant for quoting, and lecturing, Yeats in the *Cantos*, their later work is quite dissimilar. The principal and determining divergence between them remains their conceptions of form, which for Yeats is usually an hourglass, mined until it turns over, while for the later Pound, in so far as it can be characterized at all (and both he and his critics have had difficulty), it is an impromptu breakthrough, not to be prepared in advance or enshrined in retrospect. Yeats was eager to offset Pound's world, one of seeming flow but actually, as he insisted to Stephen Spender, static and tapestry-like, with his own, which brought solids to the melting-point.

The two poets were equally engrossed in what Pound calls 'top flights of the mind', moments often signaled in him by a pool of water, in Yeats by a sense of being blessèd or birdlike or of shaking all over. Their metaphysics are not the same, however, for Pound at least on some occasions insists upon the power of the objective, external image to compel or lure the mind to recognize it, as if he found Yeats too arbitrary in his constructions, while at other times he declares, 'UBI AMOR IBI OCULUS EST', or as he says elsewhere,

> nothing matters but the quality
> of the affection –
> in the end – that has carved the trace in the mind
> dove sta memoria. . . .

The two positions were dovetailed by Pound's insistence that the writer needs above all 'continuous curiosity', to insure that enough life will be 'vouchsafed' for him to work with; but curiosity and observation are, as he reiterates in the *Cantos*, only a start, the vital ingredient being love. While Yeats also asserted the importance of love, he meant by it something more ardent, sexual, and individualized, less humanitarian, less cultural than Pound meant. He thought, moreover, that curiosity was too unimpassioned a quality, and that affections which were too eclectic and international could only diminish imaginative intensity.

The two writers agreed that they lived in an age of decline, 'beastly and cantankerous' for Pound, 'half dead at the top' for Yeats. ('My dear William B.Y. your 1/2 was too moderate,' the *Pisan Cantos* admonished.) For Yeats the cure was to condense and arrange experience. Pound thought this procedure could only lead to premature synthesis, born from an insufficient 'phalanx of particulars'. For Pound, the cure was to probe, experiment, accumulate until things – some things at any rate – shone with their intrinsic light: Yeats thought such experimentation might reach no end. Pound's view of experience is as 'improvisatory', as informalist, as Yeats's is formalist. The city of the imagination for Yeats is Byzantium, taken by assault; for Pound it is Fasa, the African city described by Frobenius, built and patiently built three times again until it becomes 'in the mind indestructible', an image of perfection so remote as to carry that special arcane inflection which is Pound's. But while Fasa is, like Ithaca, essential as journey's end, the incidents on the way to it beset Pound's mind with cryptic relevance or with unresolved irrelevance. Helter-skelter may or may not lead to epiphany; it sometimes exists only because Fasa must confront an opposite, and many varieties of helter-skelter will serve. The lack of inevitability is a guarantee of authenticity, of an honesty not to be gulled by aesthetics. Pound's art in the *Cantos* is coagulative, Yeats's in his poems is exploitative; the poets face each other in an unended debate.

1966

'He Do the Police in Different Voices'

LLOYDS' most famous bank clerk revalued the poetic currency half a century ago. As Joyce said, *The Waste Land* ended the idea of poetry for ladies. Whether admired or detested, it became, like *Lyrical Ballads* in 1798, a traffic signal. Hart Crane's letters, for instance, testify to his prompt recognition that from that time forward his work must be to outflank Eliot's poem. Today footnotes do their worst to transform innovations into inevitabilities. After a thousand explanations, *The Waste Land* is no longer a puzzle poem, except for the puzzle of choosing among the various solutions. To be penetrable is not, however, to be predictable. The sweep and strangeness with which Eliot delineated despair resist temptations to patronize Old Possum as old hat. Particular discontinuities continue to surprise even if the idea of discontinuous form – to which Eliot never quite subscribed and which he was to forsake – is now almost as familiar as its sober counterpart. The compound of regular verse and *vers libre* still wears some of the effrontery with which in 1922 it flouted both schools. The poem retains the air of a splendid feat.

Eliot himself was inclined to pooh-pooh its grandeur. His chiseled comment, which F. O. Matthiessen quoted in *The Achievement of T. S. Eliot* (1935), disclaimed any intention of expressing 'the disillusionment of a generation', and said that he did not like the word 'generation' or have a plan to endorse anyone's 'illusion of disillusion'. To Theodore Spencer he remarked in humbler mood, 'Various critics have done me the honour to interpret the poem in terms of criticism of the contemporary world, have considered it, indeed, as an important bit of social criticism. To me it was only the relief of a personal and wholly insignificant grouse against life. It is just a piece of rhythmical grumbling.'

This statement is prominently displayed by Mrs. Valerie Eliot in her excellent decipherment and elucidation of *The Waste Land* manuscript (1971). If it is more than an expression of her husband's genuine modesty, it appears to imply that he considered his own poem, as he considered *Hamlet*, an inadequate projection of its author's tangled emotions, a Potemkin village rather than a proper

67

objective correlative. Yet no one will wish away the entire civilizations and cities, wars, hordes of people, religions of East and West, and exhibits from many literatures in many languages that lined the Thames in Eliot's ode to dejection. And even if London was only his state of mind at the time, the picture he paints of it is convincing. His remark to Spencer, made after a lapse of years, perhaps catches up another regret, that the poem emphasized his *Groll* at the expense of much else in his nature. It identified him with a sustained severity of tone, with pulpited (though brief) citations of biblical and Sophoclean anguish, so that he became an Ezekiel or at least a Tiresias. (In the original version of the poem John the Divine made a Christian third among the prophets.) While Eliot did not wish to be considered merely a satirist in his earlier verse, he did not welcome either the public assumption that his poetic mantle had become a hair shirt.

In its early version *The Waste Land* was woven out of more kinds of material, and was therefore less grave and less organized. The first two sections had an over-all title (each had its own title as well), 'He Do the Police in Different Voices', a quotation from *Our Mutual Friend*. Dickens has the widow Higden say to her adopted child, 'Sloppy is a beautiful reader of a newspaper. He do the Police in different voices.' Among the many voices in the first version, Eliot placed at the very beginning a long conversational passage describing an evening on the town, starting at 'Tom's place' (a rather arch use of his own name), moving on to a brothel, and concluding with a bathetic sunrise:

> First we had a couple of feelers down at Tom's place,
> There was old Tom, boiled to the eyes, blind ...
> – ("I turned up an hour later down at Myrtle's place.
> What d'y' mean, she says, at two o'clock in the morning,
> I'm not in business here for guys like you;
> We've only had a raid last week, I've been warned twice....
> So I got out to see the sunrise, and walked home.

This vapid prologue Eliot decided, apparently on his own, to expunge, and went straight into the now familiar beginning of the poem.

Other voices were expunged by Ezra Pound, who called himself the '*sage homme*' (male midwife) of the poem. In Pound's own elegy on a shipwrecked man, *Hugh Selwyn Mauberley* (1920), the hero is unnamed, except in the title, and like Eliot's protagonist, he is more an observing consciousness than a person, as he moves through salons, aesthetic movements, dark thoughts of wartime deaths. But

Mauberley's was an aesthetic quest, and Eliot deliberately omitted this from his poem in favor of a spiritual one. (He would combine the two later in *Four Quartets*.) When Eliot was shown *Mauberley* in manuscript, he had remarked to his friend that the meaning of a section in Part II was not so clear as it might be, and Pound revised it accordingly. Now he reciprocated.

Pound's criticism of *The Waste Land* was not of its meaning; he liked its despair and was indulgent of its neo-Christian hope. He dealt instead with its stylistic adequacy and freshness. For example, there was an extended, unsuccessful imitation of *The Rape of the Lock* at the beginning of 'The Fire Sermon'. It described the lady Fresca (imported to the waste land from 'Gerontion' and one day to be exported to the States for the soft-drink trade). Instead of making her toilet like Pope's Belinda, Fresca is going to it, like Joyce's Bloom. Pound warned Eliot that since Pope had done the couplets better, and Joyce the defecation, there was no point in another round. To this shrewd advice we are indebted for the disappearance of such lines as:

> The white-armed Fresca blinks, and yawns, and gapes,
> Aroused from dreams of love and pleasant rapes.
> Electric summons of the busy bell
> Brings brisk Amanda to destroy the spell . . .
> Leaving the bubbling beverage to cool,
> Fresca slips softly to the needful stool,
> Where the pathetic tale of Richardson
> Eases her labour till the deed is done. . . .
> This ended, to the steaming bath she moves,
> Her tresses fanned by little flutt'ring Loves;
> Odours, confected by the cunning French,
> Disguise the good old hearty female stench.

The episode of the typist was originally much longer and more laborious:

> A bright kimono wraps her as she sprawls
> In nerveless torpor on the window seat;
> A touch of art is given by the false
> Japanese print, purchased in Oxford Street.

Pound found the décor difficult to believe: 'Not in that lodging house?' The stanza was removed. When he read the later stanza

> – Bestows one final patronising kiss,
> And gropes his way, finding the stairs unlit;

> And at the corner where the stable is,
> Delays only to urinate, and spit

he warned that the last two lines were 'probably over the mark', and Eliot acquiesced by canceling them.

Pound persuaded Eliot also to omit a number of shorter poems that were for a time intended to be placed between the long poem's sections, then at the end of it. One was a renewed thrust at poor Bleistein, drowned now but still haplessly Jewish and luxurious under water:

> Full fathom five your Bleistein lies
> Under the flatfish and the squids.
>
> Graves' Disease in a dead jew's/man's eyes!
> Where the crabs have eat the lids ...
>
> That is lace that was his nose ...
>
> Roll him gently side to side
> See the lips unfold unfold
>
> From the teeth, gold in gold. ...

Pound urged that this, and several other mortuary poems, did not add anything, either to *The Waste Land* or to Eliot's previous work. He had already written 'the longest poem in the English langwidge. Don't try to bust all records by prolonging it three pages further'. As a result of this resmithying by *il miglior fabbro*, the poem gained immensely in concentration. Yet Eliot, feeling too solemnized by it, thought of prefixing some humorous doggerel by Pound about its composition. Later, in a more resolute effort to escape the limits set by *The Waste Land*, he wrote *Fragment of an Agon*, and eventually, 'somewhere the other side of despair', turned to drama.

Eliot's remark to Spencer calls *The Waste Land* a personal poem. His critical theory was that the artist should seek impersonality, but this was probably intended not so much as a nostrum as an antidote, a means to direct emotion rather than let it spill. His letters indicate that he regarded his poems as consequent upon his experiences. When a woman in Dublin remarked that Yeats had never really felt anything, Eliot asked in consternation, 'How can you say that?' *The Waste Land* compiled many of the nightmarish feelings he had suffered during the seven years from 1914 to 1921, that is, from his coming to England until his temporary collapse.

Thanks to the letters quoted in Mrs. Eliot's introduction, and to various biographical leaks, the incidents of these years begin to take shape. In 1914 Eliot, then on a traveling fellowship from Harvard, went to study for the summer at Marburg. The outbreak of war obliged him to make his way, in a less leisurely fashion than he had intended, to Oxford. There he worked at his doctoral dissertation on F. H. Bradley's *Appearance and Reality*. The year 1914–15 proved to be pivotal. He came to three interrelated decisions. The first was to give up the appearance of the philosopher for the reality of the poet, though he equivocated about this by continuing to write reviews for philosophical journals for some time thereafter. The second was to marry, and the third to remain in England. He was helped to all three decisions by Ezra Pound, whom he met in September 1914. Pound had come to England in 1908 and was convinced (though he changed his mind later) that this was the country most congenial to the literary life. He encouraged Eliot to marry and settle, and he read the poems that no one had been willing to publish and pronounced his verdict, that Eliot 'has actually trained himself *and* modernized himself *on his own*'. Harriet Monroe, the editor of *Poetry*, must publish them, beginning with 'The Love Song of J. Alfred Prufrock'. It took Pound some time to bring her to the same view, and it was not until June 1915 that Eliot's first publication took place. This was also the month of his first marriage, on 26 June. His wife was Vivien Haigh-Wood, and Eliot remained, like Merlin with another Vivian, under her spell, beset and possessed by her intricacies for fifteen years and more.

What the newlyweds were like is recorded by Bertrand Russell, whom Eliot had known at Harvard. In a letter of July 1915 reproduced in his *Autobiography*, Russell wrote of dining with them:

> I expected her to be terrible, from his mysteriousness; but she was not so bad. She is light, a little vulgar, adventurous, full of life – an artist I think he said, but I should have thought her an actress. He is exquisite and listless: she says she married him to stimulate him, but finds she can't do it. Obviously he married in order to be stimulated. I think she will soon be tired of him. He is ashamed of his marriage, and very grateful if one is kind to her.

Vivien was to dabble in painting, fiction, and verse, her mobile aspirations an aspect of her increasing instability. Ten years later her husband was to describe her to Russell as 'still perpetually baffling and deceptive. She seems to me like a child of 6 with an immensely clever and precocious mind. She writes *extremely* well (stories, etc.) and great originality. And I can never escape from the spell of her persuasive (even coercive) gift of argument.'

Eliot's parents did not take well to their son's doings, though they did not, as has been said, cut him off. His father, president of the Hydraulic Press Brick Company of St. Louis, had expected his son to remain a philosopher, and his mother, though a poet herself, did not like the *vers libre* of 'Prufrock' any better than the free and easy marriage. To both parents it seemed that bright hopes were being put aside for a vague profession in the company of a vague woman in a country only too distinctly at war. They asked to see the young couple, but Vivien Eliot was frightened by the perils of the crossing, perhaps also by those of the arrival. So Eliot, already feeling 'a broken Coriolanus', as Prufrock felt a Hamlet *manqué*, took ship alone in August for the momentous interview.

His parents urged him to return with his wife to a university career in the States. He refused: he would be a poet, and England provided a better atmosphere in which to write. They urged him not to give up his dissertation when it was so near completion, and to this he consented. He parted on good enough terms to request their financial help when he got back to London, and they sent money to him handsomely, as he acknowledged – not handsomely enough, however, to release him from the necessity of very hard work. He taught for a term at the High Wycombe Grammar School, between Oxford and London, and then for two terms at Highgate Junior School. He completed his dissertation and was booked to sail for America on 1 April 1916 to take his oral examination at Harvard; when the crossing was canceled, his academic gestures came to an end. In March 1917 he took the job in London with Lloyds Bank, in the Colonial and Foreign Department, at which he stuck for eight years.

During the early months of their marriage the Eliots were helped also by Russell, who gave them a room in his flat, an act of benevolence not without complications for all parties. Concerned for his wife's health, and fearful – it may be – that their sexual difficulties (perhaps involving psychic impotence on his part) might be a contributing factor, Eliot sent her off for a two-week holiday with Russell. The philosopher found the couple none the less devoted to each other, but noted in Mrs. Eliot a sporadic impulse to be cruel towards her husband, not with simple but with Dostoevskyan cruelty. 'I am every day getting things more right between them,' Russell boasted, 'but I can't let them alone at present, and of course I myself get very much interested.' The Dostoevskyan quality affected his imagery: 'She is a person who lives on a knife-edge, and will end as a criminal or a saint – I don't know which yet. She has a perfect capacity for both.'

The personal life out of which came Eliot's personal poem now began to be lived in earnest. Vivien Eliot suffered obscurely from nerves, her health was subject to frequent collapses, she complained of neuralgia, of insomnia. Her journal for 1 January 1919 records waking up with migraine, 'the worst yet', and staying in bed all day without moving; on 7 September 1919, she records 'bad pain in right side, very very nervous'. Ezra Pound, who knew her well, was worried that the passage in *The Waste Land*,

> "My nerves are bad to-night. Yes, bad. Stay with me.
> "Speak to me. Why do you never speak? Speak.
> "What are you thinking of? What thinking? What?
> "I never know what you are thinking. Think.'

might be too photographic. But Vivien Eliot, who offered her own comments on her husband's verse (and volunteered two excellent lines for the low-life dialogue in 'A Game of Chess': "If you don't like it you can get on with it / What you get married for if you don't want to have children") marked the same passage as 'Wonderful'. She relished the presentation of her symptoms in broken metre. She was less keen, however, on another line from this section, 'The ivory men make company between us,' and got her husband to remove it. Presumably its implications were too close to the quick of their marital difficulties. The reference may have been to Russell, whose attentions to Vivien were intended to keep the two together. Years afterwards Eliot made a fair copy of *The Waste Land* in his own handwriting, and reinserted the line from memory. (It should now be added to the final text.) But he had implied his feelings six months after his marriage when he wrote in a letter to Conrad Aiken, 'I have lived through material for a score of long poems in the last six months.'

Russell commented less sympathetically about the Eliots later, 'I was fond of them both, and endeavoured to help them in their troubles until I discovered that their troubles were what they enjoyed.' Eliot was capable of estimating the situation shrewdly himself. In his poem, 'The Death of Saint Narcissus', which *Poetry* was to publish in 1917 (but then he withdrew it probably as too close to the knuckle) and which he thought for a time of including in *The Waste Land*, Eliot wrote of his introspective saint, 'his flesh was in love with the burning arrows.... As he embraced them his white skin surrendered itself to the redness of blood, and satisfied him.' For Eliot, however, the search for suffering was not contemptible. He was remorseful about his own real or imagined feelings, he was self-sacrificing about hers, he thought that remorse and sacrifice, not to mention affection, had value. In the Grail legends which underlie *The Waste Land*, the Fisher King suffers a Dolorous Stroke that maims him sexually. In Eliot's case the Dolorous Stroke had been marriage. He was helped thereby to the poem's initial clash of images, 'April is the cruellest month,' as well as to hollow echoes of Spencer's *Prothalamion* ('Sweet Thames, run softly till I end my song'). From the barren winter of his academic labors Eliot had been roused to the barren springtime of his nerve-wracked marriage. His life spread into paradox.

Other events of these years seem reflected in the poem. The war, though scarcely mentioned, exerts pressure. In places the poem may be a covert memorial to Henry Ware Eliot, the unforgiving father of the ill-adventured son. Vivien Eliot's journal records on 8 January 1919, 'Cable came saying Tom's father is dead. Had to wait all day till Tom came home and then to tell him. *Most terrible.*' Eliot's first explicit statement of his intention to write a long poem comes in letters written later in this year. The references to 'the king my father's death' probably derive as much from this actual death as from *The Tempest*, to which Eliot's notes evasively refer. As for the drowning of the young sailor, whether he is Ferdinand or a Phoenician, the war furnished Eliot with many examples, such as Jean Verdenal, a friend from his Sorbonne days, who was killed in the Dardanelles. (Verdenal has received the posthumous distinction of being called Eliot's lover, but in fact the rumors of homosexuality remain unwitnessed.) But the drowning may be as well an extrapolation of Eliot's feeling that he was now fatherless as well as rudderless. The fact that the principal speaker appears in a new guise in the last section, with its imagery of possible resurrection, suggests that the drowning is to be taken symbolically rather than literally, as the end of youth. Eliot was addicted to the portrayal of characters who had missed their chances, become old before they had really been young. So the drowned sailor, like the buried corpse, may be construed as the young Eliot, himself an experienced sailor, shipwrecked in or about *l'an trentième de son eage*, like the young Pound in the first part of *Hugh Selwyn Mauberley* or Mauberley himself later in that poem, memorialized only by an oar.

It has been thought that Eliot wrote *The Waste Land* in Switzerland while recovering from a breakdown. But much of it was written earlier, some in 1914 and some, if Conrad Aiken is to be believed, even before. A letter to John Quinn indicates that much of it was on paper in May 1921. The breakdown, or rather, the rest cure, did give Eliot enough time to fit the pieces together and add what was necessary. At the beginning of October 1921 he consulted a prominent neurologist, who advised three months away from remembering 'the profit and loss' in Lloyds Bank. When the bank had agreed, Eliot went first to Margate and stayed for a month from 11 October. There he reported with relief to Richard Aldington that his 'nerves' came not from overwork but from an 'aboulie' (Hamlet's and Prufrock's disease) 'and emotional derangement which has been a lifelong affliction.' But, whatever reassurance this diagnosis afforded, he resolved to consult Dr. Roger Vittoz, a psychiatrist in Lausanne. He rejoined Vivien and on 18 November went with her to Paris. It seems fairly certain that he discussed the poem at that time with Ezra Pound. In Lausanne, where he went by himself, Eliot worked on it and sent revisions to Pound and to Vivien. Some of the letters exchanged between him and Pound survive. By early January 1922 he was back in London, making final corrections. The poem was published in October.

The manuscript had its own history. In gratitude to John Quinn, the New York lawyer and patron of the arts, Eliot presented it to him. Quinn died in 1924, and most of his possessions were sold at auction; some, however, including the manuscript, were inherited by his sister. When the sister died, her daughter put many of Quinn's papers in storage. But in the early 1950s she searched among them and found the manuscript, which she then sold to the Berg Collection of the New York Public Library. The then curator enjoyed exercising seignorial rights over the collection, and kept secret the whereabouts of the manuscript. After his death its existence was divulged, and Valerie Eliot was persuaded to do her knowledgeable edition.

She did so the more readily, perhaps, because her husband had always hoped that the manuscript would turn up as evidence of Pound's critical genius. It is a classic document. No one will deny that it is weaker throughout than the final version. Pound comes off very well indeed; his importance is comparable to that of Louis Bouilhet in the history of composition of *Madame Bovary*. Pound could not be intimidated by pomposity, even Baudelairean pomposity.

> London, the swarming life you kill and breed,
> Huddled between the concrete and the sky;
> Responsive to the momentary need,
> Vibrates unconscious to its formal destiny.

Next to this he wrote 'B-ll-S'. Pound was equally peremptory about a passage that Eliot seems to have cherished, perhaps because of childhood experiences in sailing. It was the depiction at the beginning of 'Death by Water' of a long voyage, a modernizing and Americanizing of Ulysses' final voyage as given by Dante, but joined with sailing experiences of Eliot's youth:

> Kingfisher weather, with a light fair breeze,
> Full canvas, and the eight sails drawing well.
> We beat around the cape and laid our course
> From the Dry Salvages to the eastern banks.
> A porpoise snored upon the phosphorescent swell,
> A triton rang the final warning bell
> Astern, and the sea rolled, asleep.

From these lines Pound was willing to spare only

> with a light fair breeze
> We beat around the cape from the Dry Salvages.
> A porpoise snored on the swell.

All the rest was – seamanship and literature. It became clear that the whole passage might as well go, and Eliot asked humbly if he should delete Phlebas as well. But Pound was as eager to preserve the good as to expunge the bad: he insisted that Phlebas stay because of the earlier references to the drowned Phoenician sailor. With equal taste, he made almost no change in the last section of the poem, which Eliot always considered to be the best, perhaps because it led into his subsequent verse. It marked the resumption of almost continuous form.

Eliot did not bow to all his friend's revisions. Pound feared the references to London might sound like Blake, and objected specifically to the lines

> To where Saint Mary Woolnoth kept the time,
> With a dead sound on the final stroke of nine.

Eliot wisely retained them, only changing 'time' to 'hours'. Next to the passage

> "You gave me hyacinths first a year ago;
> "They called me the hyacinth girl"

Pound marked 'Marianne', and evidently feared – though Mrs. Eliot's note indicates that in his last years, when asked, he denied it – that the use of quotation marks would look like an imitation of Marianne Moore. (He had warned Miss Moore of the equivalent danger of sounding like Eliot in a letter of 16 December 1918.) But Eliot, for whom the moment in the hyacinth garden had obsessional force – it was based on feelings, though not on a specific incident in his own life – made no change.

Essentially Pound could do for Eliot what Eliot could not do for himself. There was some reciprocity, not only in *Mauberley* but in the *Cantos*. When the first three of these appeared in *Poetry* in 1917, Eliot offered criticism which was followed by their being completely altered. It appears, from the revised versions, that he objected to the elaborate wind-up, and urged a more direct confrontation of the reader and the material. A similar theory is at work in Pound's changes in *The Waste Land*. Chiefly by excision, he enabled Eliot to tighten his form and get 'an outline', as he wrote in a complimentary letter of 24 January 1922. The same letter berated himself for 'always exuding my deformative secretions in my own stuff . . .' and for going 'into nacre and objets d'art'. Yet if this was necessity for Pound, he soon resolved to make a virtue of it, and perhaps partially in reaction in Eliot's form, he studied out means of loosening his own in the *Cantos*. There was to be no outline. The fragments which Eliot wished to shore and reconstitute Pound was willing to keep unchanged, and instead of mending consciousness, he allowed it to remain 'disjunct' and its experiences to remain 'intermittent'. Fits and starts, 'spots and dots', seemed to Pound to render reality much more closely than the outline to which he had helped his friend. He was later to feel that he had gone wrong, and made a botch instead of a work of art. Notwithstanding his doubts, the *Cantos*, with their violent upheaval of sequence and location, stand as a rival eminence to *The Waste Land* in modern verse.

1972

Gazebos and Gashouses

THE PUBLIC demeanor of poets toward each other is usually courteous, though it verges on punctilio. But when their private letters are published, posthumously of course, we learn how furious they were with the Nobel Prize committee for overlooking them to favor some inadequate other. The impingement of someone else's poetic world upon theirs also makes them restless, as if their centripetal energy might not suffice to keep them in orbit. Yet as years pass they become accustomed to their rivals, until one of them dies. Then they feel an unexpected regret, for the consequence must be that some unfamiliar competitor, laden with unfamiliar hostility, is likely to replace the late lamented; so they are always eloquent in regretting other poets' deaths. The living poet remains a source of vexation for another reason, that it is never certain which of two poets will *write* the elegy, and which be its *subject*. The feeling that one poet may some day be fertilizing the other's mournful rhyme clouds the relationship of the living.

These sombre reflections may help to prepare for the relationship between W. B. Yeats and W. H. Auden. They met only a few times, often enough to recognize that in poetry and thought they were eminent adversaries. More than one generation separated them, for Auden was born forty-two years after Yeats. Auden's mind was forming when Yeats was in his fifties. Looking back, they find the modern period beginning at different times. For Yeats the death of Victoria marks the change, for Auden the First World War.

In the literary rivalries of the 1920s and 1930s, Yeats was a peculiar encumbrance for young poets. Those who went up to Oxford in the late 1920s – Auden, MacNeice and Spender – were puzzled whether to regard him as a monument or a folly. His intellectual vagaries embarrassed them as primitive, and if that was not, since the Dadaists, an adequate slur, primitive in the wrong way. And yet the verse of Yeats was cultivated and subtle, not to be scouted or easily matched. Even as an older man he persisted in exploring themes such as personal love and general ruin, themes the young poets would have liked to reserve for themselves. His behavior was much less congenial to them than T. S. Eliot's. Eliot was proceeding with stately anguish into middle age and spirituality, while Yeats advanced precipitously, without this American decorum, upon old age and corporeality.

Eliot, as their leader, and their publisher, had the right to exist, or least to co-exist. Bridges and Hardy were uncompetitive codgers from whom technical graces or ineptnesses might usefully be borrowed. Hopkins, while highly influential, was safely dead; one might even feel original in discovering him. Yeats, however, remained intrusive. As Auden observes, not altogether without respect, Yeats refused to play the Twenties game of understatement, or the Thirties game of Social Concern, games for which Auden himself helped to lay down the rules. He had the effrontery to ignore the modern imagery that others considered *de rigueur*. We can detect three ages of poetry: Eliot looked at the gasworks and – despaired; Auden pushed past to go inside and admire the machinery, asking, 'How many horsepower is the large turbine?' much as Hart Crane, at about the same time, looked at his father's cannery works and exulted; as for Yeats, he had long since passed by, thinking of Trojan towers or of Lissadell gazebos. Or we might compare the poets' behavior in houses – Eliot appalled by human habitations and by those who do not own but rent them and crumble with their plaster, Yeats looking for one grand or noble enough to endorse, Auden praising the benefits of the American kitchen or the good toilet in his Austrian house as he probes the significance, immediate and ulterior, of the common actions we spend our lives in performing. Still, Yeats claimed to have a modern consciousness too, even if Auden declined to concede the point. Just as in 1900, before Auden was born, Yeats had denounced Bernard Shaw as a reactionary, because Shaw was caught up in the outmoded scientific epoch, so he was capable of suggesting that the modern poets were not so progressive as they supposed, but were cutting back to flat places in human development where control of environment gave way to barren submission to it.

Auden's attitude to Yeats could not be called sympathetic – sympathy would be gratuitous as well as insulting – but he tries to be judicious in an antic way. Since Auden is more outspoken than most poets, his attitudes enable two phases of modern poetry to confront each other. He began to speak his mind about Yeats before Yeats had died. His remarks show impatience of the power play by which Yeats had taken over English poetry; they vary in their point of attack, as if Auden saw many vulnerabilities yet had trouble finding the weakest spot. His first public mention of Yeats appears to be in the verse 'Letter to Lord Byron' which he wrote in Iceland in 1936, by which time he was twenty-nine and Yeats seventy-one. Auden informs Byron that poetry is not dead:

> Cheer up! There're several singing birds that sing,
>   There's six feet six of Spender for a start;
> Eliot has really stretched his eagle's wing,
>   And Yeats has helped himself to Parnell's heart.

The allusion to Eliot's eagle wing bows respectfully to a metaphor of Eliot, while the reference to Yeats's eating habits maliciously tumbles one of Yeats's metaphors about. In a little poem published the previous year Yeats had said that if De Valera had eaten Parnell's heart, Ireland's imagination would have been satisfied. Auden, while listing Yeats among the genuine poets, found this image portentous. He is probably also responsible for the passage about Yeats in the poem signed jointly by him and MacNeice, their 'Last Will and Testament', where they both determine to 'leave the phases of the moon / To Mr. Yeats to rock his bardic sleep'. We can imagine their private jokes about poets who set themselves up as bards and laid claim, as Yeats did, to having a vision. The refusal to be quite serious about Yeats is one of the forms of their rebellion against him.

But mockery is, in an inside-out way, a compliment. Another poem by MacNeice in *Letters from Iceland* (1937) registers Yeats's influence much more politely with such lines as

> There was MacKenna
> Spent twenty years translating Greek philosophy,
> Ill and tormented, unwilling to break contract,
> A brilliant talker who left
> The salon for the solo flight of Mind,

lines which evoke the troubled spirits of Yeats's 'All Souls' Night'. As for Auden, if we compare his first book, *Poems* (1928), with any of Yeats's early books, they prove surprisingly alike in theme. Both poets concentrate their attention upon the antiphony of unsuccess in love and decline in the world. With Yeats the reverberations are felt in the spheres ('dishevelled wandering stars') while with Auden they are likelier to express themselves in the dream of 'a buried engine-room'. Yeats makes unrequited love a symbol of human aspiration and limit, while Auden, disdaining Yeats's early vocabulary, dwells upon transitoriness of feeling (both for the lover and the beloved), and reviles love as a 'dishonest country', 'a delicious lie', 'brief adherence', 'obsolete or extremely rare'. When, in the poem later entitled 'The Letter', that disappointing communication arrives, it is made part of a canvas of general thwart:

> Nor speech is close, nor fingers numb
> If love not seldom has received
> An unjust answer, was deceived;
> I, decent with the seasons, move
> Different or with a different love,
> Nor question overmuch the nod,
> The stone smile of this country god,
> That never was more reticent,
> Always afraid to say more than it meant.

It is the world of Humphrey Bogart. Like his, the brave words about seasonal passion conceal both considerable anguish and an inner capacity for fidelity and intensity which, rather than acknowledge, the poet would pretend does not exist. The necessary obverse of this seeming derogation of love is in Auden's poems soon afterwards, where love becomes the animating principle of the world, 'the interest itself in thoughtless heaven'. Having got love away from Yeats, and from Petrarch, Auden is free to capitalize and mythologize it once again, as flagrantly as they would do. The country god once so reticent re-opens his mouth.

In later years Auden regretted some tendencies of his early work: 'It is not the fault of Yeats or Rilke that I allowed myself to be seduced by them into writing poems which were false to my personal and poetic nature.' He attributed to his middle age an increasing revulsion to the 'element of "theatre", of exaggerated gesture and fuss, of indifference to the naked truth'. This revulsion was present, however, at the time that the Yeats influence was at its strongest. Already as a young man of twenty and twenty-one, when he wished to speak with an authority comparable to Yeats's on kindred subjects, Auden sensed that his own style was powerful enough to filter Yeats's lines and make them his own. For instance, he describes how, in company with his beloved, he watched buzzards as they swept down the sky:

> I, though a watcher too,
> Saw little where they sped.
> Who could have dreamed that you
> Would turn your head?

The stanza probably echoes a couplet from an early poem of Yeats:

> O heart! O heart! if she'd but turn her head,
> You'd know the folly of being comforted.

Auden fastens on the immediate physical gesture, which he leaves a little enigmatic since it may signify either love renewed or carrion love. For Yeats the turning of the head is totally figurative, like the word 'heart'. Auden permits emblematic gestures to retain something undeciphered as if it were a guarantee of actuality.

Another poem of Auden shows, as Stephen Spender has noted, that Auden had been reading Yeats's 'The Tower', which had just then (in 1928) been published. But again the effect is one of filtering. Yeats had written,

> I choose upstanding men
> That climb the streams until
> The fountain leap, and at dawn
> Drop their cast at the side
> Of dripping stone,

and the scene is instantly eternal. Auden begins more matter-of-factly,

> I chose this lean country
> For seven day content,
> To satisfy the want
> Of eye and ear, to see
> The slow fastidious line
> That disciplines the fell ...

Eternity is expressly denied, for this is a place of seven-day content, a holiday not a Great Year. When Auden speaks of 'eye and ear', he is echoing other lines from 'The Tower', 'Nor an ear and eye / That more expected the impossible', but he is beset rather by the possible. 'The slow fastidious line / That disciplines the fell' is a brilliant adaptation of three lines from 'In Memory of Major Robert Gregory',

> ... cold Clare rock and Galway rock and thorn,
> Of that stern colour and that delicate line
> That are our secret discipline.

Auden makes his presence felt by changing 'delicate' to 'fastidious' and limiting that word with 'slow', a combination of adjectives that Yeats might have considered only at the very end of his career. The word 'discipline', in Yeats always a noun, seems as a verb to come from prose rather than from poetry. One of Auden's great achievements is to bring a new tenseness to the relations of these two modes. Again there is a difference in gravity: Auden finds the conjunction of art and nature more accidental and less integral with his own style; it is only one of several equally cogent morals offered by an obliging landscape. He is unwilling to grant so much iconic prestige, or iconic single-mindedness, to what he observes. Yeats is always moving from particulars to the universal; as in these other lines from 'The Tower',

> I pace upon the battlements and stare
> On the foundations of a house, or where
> Tree, like a sooty finger, starts from the earth,

where 'tree' exists as undifferentiated, having neither genus nor even an article to precede it. Auden's symbols are less fixed and inevitability is not claimed for them.

After Yeats's death in 1939 Auden made several efforts to sort out his mixed feelings about the dead poet's mysterious interfusion into the period. He published a review of *Last Poems*, summing them up with some distaste (a distaste shared with Eliot) for their old-goatishness. In a mock-trial entitled 'The Public v. the Late William Butler Yeats' (1939), Auden shared his divided thoughts among prosecution and defense. 'Yeats as an Example' (1948) praises him on technical grounds for releasing the lyric from 'iambic monotony', and on substantive grounds for introducing serious reflections into occasional poems, though it does not endorse any of the serious reflections themselves. When he came in 1955 to write about Yeats's *Letters*, Auden had prepared himself for rodomontade, and was unusually indulgent when he found that Yeats was fully capable of self-mockery. But in reviewing *Mythologies* in 1959, he protested sharply against Yeats's refusal to distinguish between faith and myth, between what was true and what was just traditional.

He also memorialized Yeats in two poems, one an elegy, the other a limerick, as if he could not think of Yeats except in two conflicting ways. The limerick offers advice for students:

> To get the Last Poems of Yeats
> You need not mug up on dates;
> All a reader requires
> Is some knowledge of gyres
> And the sort of people he hates.

The elegy, 'In Memory of W. B. Yeats', must be unique among elegies in English in that it takes its subject to task even while expressing admiration for his example. It has little to say of regret; may there not be in it even a minuscule touch of relief? It is hard to be sure, because Auden's method in elegy as in love lyric is to underline all that we must not say. Yet he does take the occasion of death to put the poet into manageable proportions, and to alert us to the shortcomings as well as the virtues of the deceased.

The first of the poem's three parts begins, 'He disappeared in the dead of winter', and chills the climate to suit his theme, for it is the climate in which Auden heard of the death, not that in which Yeats died at Roquebrune. He soon declares, 'O all the instruments agree / The day of his death was a dark, cold day.' No epic personages show up, only the barometer is invoked as expert witness. In allowing scientific instruments to express themselves, Auden may be unconsciously underscoring his own freedom from what he noted elsewhere to be a flaw, the failure of Yeats to relate his outlook to science. But chiefly Auden is being himself; he prefers to present himself, as if otherwise he might become dishonest, in the guise of a grieving computer. His instruments were at first allowed, nevertheless, a good deal of emotion: Auden prefixed the threnodic word 'O' to their concurring reports, and the sudden strong rhythm implies what is left unsaid, that Yeats's death is a dark cold blow. In a later version of the poem, Auden (like Yeats an inveterate reviser) says, 'What instruments we have agree', as if their testimony might not be totally reliable, and as if the previous version had been too easily ironic, or had anthropomorphized machinery. The new line almost suppresses the machines, though it tilts toward the opposite danger in Auden, of making restraint sound doctrinaire.

As we know from other works of Auden, such as 'Musée des Beaux Arts', he liked to point out to a generation prone to pathetic fallacy how indifferent surrounding objects are to human activities. An emotion is rendered more poignant by observing creatures and things that have ignored it. This studied irrelevancy is a tactic he shares with Robbe-Grillet: the portrayal of truth by evoking and putting aside a false context. But in this elegy Auden has a special reason. The wolves continue – regardless of the poet's death – to run through the evergreen forests; paradise is still unregained, and the peasant river untempted by the fashionable quays, as if to suggest that the class barrier which Yeats thought to surmount, between the peasantry and 'hard-riding country gentlemen', was fixed regardless of the poet's embrace of both groups. So far it seems that Yeats has merely failed, as (Auden thinks) all poets must, but the next conceit is as complimentary as it is accurate: 'By mourning tongues / The death of the poet was kept from his poems.' Nature is still nature, the classes still persist, but the poems, now as inevitable in the landscape as trees or rivers, survive their maker's disappearance. Bent on avoiding insincerity as well as fulsomeness, Auden finds what may be said genuinely about Yeats's death is that the earth's axle did not break, but that a few thousand will think of this day as of a day when one did something slightly unusual. All the panoply of mourning is subdued, and the panoply of a poet's greatness is put into terms that even a generation skeptical of the reach of poetic genius can accept.

The second part of the poem registers certain complaints against Yeats, comradely complaints. In prose Auden had written that Yeats was 'not conspicuously intelligent', and now he softens that blow a little, 'You were silly like us.' In the version of the elegy first published, this line was in the third person, 'He was silly like us; his gift survived it all'; but Auden then decided to speak directly to Yeats, and to itemize some of the sillinesses. He considers Yeats's poetic motivation to have come from Irishism: 'Mad Ireland hurt you into poetry,' and then he points out that Ireland, for all Yeats's efforts, remains as mad as ever. Now he is led to his own conclusion, expressed in a prose article before being inserted in the poem, 'For poetry makes nothing happen; it is instead / A way of happening, a mouth.' This apophthegm is really a rebuke to the dead poet, for Yeats, as Auden knew, could not stomach the view that poetry was ineffectual, even if splendidly so. It is also questionable in itself, since events cannot be separated from the emotions to which they give birth, nor roused human feelings from subsequent events.

The debate with this formidable corpse continues into the third and final section of the poem, where Auden originally said that Yeats, like Claudel and, of all poets, Kipling, would be pardoned at last because he used language so well. In one of his essays Auden suggests that Yeats's diction was the diction of a just man, even if some of his opinions were unjust – and such a defense may yet prove the best against the multiplying accusations that Yeats was a fascist; here, however, Auden is interested in attesting good poetry as if it could be distinct from good character. The comparison of an Irish nationalist with a British imperialist is casual, and shows the dangers of an apophthegmatic style. Auden quickly became aware of these dangers himself, and he dropped these three stanzas from the elegy in later editions, although anthologies often reprint them. Yeats was in fact scarcely in need of such a defense, or of any sort of pardon, even one granted by Time.

Only in the last verses of the elegy does Auden praise without qualification one attribute, that Yeats celebrated life amid public and private ruin, and so to the inhabitants of a fallen world presented reminders of Eden. If poetry really possesses so much power over men's minds as this, it would seem much more instrumental in life than Auden had earlier admitted. Auden's own poetry, which was full of threats of doom and revolution in the 1930s, shifted then to finding things to live for rather than to die for. In endorsing Yeats's celebrative gift, he may have been bespeaking a turn in his own verse as well.

The mixed feelings which underlie his elegy confirm a pattern of divergence between the two poets which is also present in their biographies. They were grandsons of Episcopalian ministers, though Yeats's grandfather was low church and Auden's high church. Auden's family remained devout through the next generation, while Yeats's father was a skeptic. Auden, described by Isherwood as in childhood startlingly high church, lost his religious belief in adolescence, to regain it in his thirties; he later delivered a sermon in Westminster Abbey. Yeats had little interest in Christianity after his early childhood. He was not an iconoclast, however, but worked out his own iconography in which he conferred on Christianity an especially modest role.

For Yeats, who had spent much of his childhood in Sligo, the ideal landscape was always the pastoral one; looking out at a beautiful Italian countryside with Ezra Pound, Yeats remarked that it was 'Sligo in heaven'. Auden aways preferred another setting, that of the industrial Midlands; his favorite scenic route was the one from Birmingham to Wolverhampton. If Yeats liked lakes, Auden was partial to 'tramlines and slagheaps, pieces of machinery'. I'm not sure how to interpret the fact that Yeats liked towers and Auden lead mines, but – Freud apart, and yet not to give up too easily – these propensities may suggest that Yeats was always struggling to be more than his ordinary self, with a consequent imagery of high places, of figures larger than life, while Auden was pitched lower, struggling to comprehend the self's buried workings or, as he said, 'with prolonged drowning to develop gills'. Masking pleased the one as much as unmasking, the other. While Yeats studied mystical ways to expand consciousness and control the mind, Auden pored over his father's anatomy and pathology books.

Their poetic development also sets them at variance. Yeats's first masters were Rossetti and Morris, mellifluous Pre-Raphaelites. Auden's first master was Thomas Hardy, the sore thumb of late-nineteenth-century poets. Auden chose to be influenced by Old English poetry, Yeats by Old Irish sagas; at first Yeats tended to prettify the ancient material, but he gradually grew tougher, while Auden was tough from the start. In later life Yeats, originally so gracious, became vehement, while Auden, so consciously awkward at first, came to write (even when translating the Eddas) with more suavity. Yeats's early verse suffers from an excess of connectives like 'and', while Auden's is characterized by a lack of them, but both poets grew tired of their chosen mannerisms. One poet they share as a common ancestor, William Blake, but they find different things in him to admire: Auden, who called himself a 'lunatic clergyman', liked especially Blake's moral revolution, while Yeats took up also Blake's deliberate symbolism and eccentric metaphysics. Auden refused to follow, for like Eliot he found Blake in these regions as exasperating as Yeats.

What exactly was the core of Auden's exasperation with his older contemporary? There was first, as he says in 'Yeats as an Example', that interest in Celtic mythology and occult symbolism. To relate these two is symptomatic, since they have no necessary connection; Auden finds them both tiresomely provincial. He complains with mock-snobbery that they are not 'the kind of nonsense that can be believed by a gentleman'. He calls Yeats's interest in the occult 'Southern Californian', and elsewhere connects it with the psychology of the *rentier* class, at its most powerful in England during the time that Yeats was being formed artistically. This economic determinism might be more persuasive if occultism had not been equally powerful in other countries where different economic conditions prevailed, most notably France. Auden himself may not totally have escaped this infection, for when Stravinsky was collaborating with him on *The Rake's Progress*, the composer was startled to learn that his librettist believed in graphology, astrology, the telepathic power of cats, black magic as described in Charles Williams's novels, in categories of temperament (Stravinsky, because he happened to work at night, was booked as a Dionysian), in preordination, in Fate. Auden disavowed some of Stravinsky's listings: while be believed in graphology, as he told me in a letter of 1967, he didn't in astrology. He believed in the power of cats, not as telepathy but as an 'understanding of human discourse and gesture.' He thought black magic possible, but something one shouldn't touch, 'either childish and silly or dangerous to sanity and salvation'. Perhaps we are all occultists a little. But in his work, Auden includes the occult only to overcome it. In this he is opposite to Yeats. The medium in Yeats's play *The Words upon the Window-Pane* is suspected of being a fraud but in the end is shown to have incontrovertible clairvoyant power; while in Auden's and Kallman's *Elegy for Young Lovers*, a woman who sees visions, modeled, as Auden has admitted, on Yeats's wife, is successfully cured of seeing them. In a similar way, the mirrorlike crystal in *The Ascent of F6* lays bare not secrets of the preternatural but traumas of childhood. There are ghosts, but they are within us, and we must get them out, Auden seems to say. They are outside us, says Yeats, and we must take them in.

To such complaints as Auden's, Yeats had answers ready. Provincialism, so distasteful to Auden, was something Yeats sought; he wished to bind emotions to what was local, both in landscape and in traditional images. Moreover he wanted to make his province the world, rather than like Auden, a more consistent traveler, to make the world his province. As for occultism, not every quiver or shudder had to be defended as a genuine expression of the timeless. Yeats believed in the imagination, and held that it had links with a collective mind which could not be explained in terms of scientific psychology. Auden is usually chary of using the word 'imagination', and prefers to say that everyone is 'from time to time excited emotionally and intellectually by his social and material environment', and that this excitement 'in certain individuals produces verbal structures which we call poems'. This diction was foreign to Yeats, who preferred to be taken in by imaginative nonsense because he was attracted to it, rather than to reject it because most people were not. He could also have maintained that he was in his supernatural beliefs much less dogmatic than Auden, in his later phase of revived Christian feeling, became. Auden would have sternly replied, I suppose, that there was no virtue in stickling at the wrong dogma.

Auden also finds fault with Yeats's literary theories. He fervently opposes Yeats's claims for the importance of poetry, and maintains that they are extravagant and dated. When Yeats declares, 'The intellect of man is forced to choose / Perfection of the life, or of the work', Auden comments: 'This is untrue; perfection is possible in neither.' This belief did not however prevent his admittedly composing (with Kallman) the *Elegy for Young Lovers* on the theme here unwittingly proffered by Yeats, or, less explicitly, using Yeats as model for the principal character. When Yeats asks, in 'Sailing to Byzantium', to be turned after death into what Auden calls a mechanical bird, Auden, while granting the stanza's 'utmost magnificence', feels that Yeats is telling 'what my nanny would have called "a story"'. When Yeats writes in 'Under Ben Bulben',

> Cast a cold eye
> On life, on death.
> Horseman, pass by,

Auden says the horseman is a stage prop; a motorist would be more likely. When Yeats remarks of 'The Scholars' that

> Bald heads forgetful of their sins,
> Old, learned, respectable bald heads
> Edit and annotate the lines
> That young men, tossing on their beds,
> Rhymed out in love's despair, . . .

Auden rushes to the scholars' defense, 'Thank God they do. If it had not been for scholars working themselves blind copying and collating manuscripts, how many poems would be unavailable . . . and how many others full of lines that made no sense?' Auden obviously regards Yeats as a balloonist and himself as the man with the pins, an Oxford Yankee at King Cuchulain's court. That he is not merely indulging a hostility to Yeats is proven by his pricking balloons of his own, as when he struck from the poem, 'September 1, 1939', the stanza ending, 'We must love one another or die,' and explained as his reason, 'We'll die anyway.' Auden displays always a loyalty to the common elements of living, and is ready to catch himself short when he finds he has played 'Major Prophet'.

His deflations of Yeats depend upon an initial disagreement; he finds Yeats aesthetic when he should be ethical, and objects to the aesthetic life as an immersion in particulars, a failure to choose the Word instead of just words, and in sum, an abandonment to make-believe. He thinks Yeats prefers, as he himself did sometimes in his early work, sound to sense, and is indifferent to truth, being too much the poet, too little the citizen. Nowhere is the difference plainer than in the prose criticism by the two men of Shakespeare, and particularly of Richard II. To Auden, Richard is an example of the unjust ruler. Of the five qualities which Auden, who loved to rig up lists (though he avoided the kind of apotheosis of lists to be found in Yeats's phases of the moon), prescribes for the just ruler, poor Richard is lacking in four. Prince Hal, on the other hand, has all five and therefore becomes Shakespeare's ideal king. Yeats knew this point of view, or one like it, from earlier criticism, and he disputes it on every count. He insists that Shakespeare understood Richard to be ill-fitted for kingship but preferred him to Henry V, as a boy of fine temperament with weak muscles might be preferred to an athletic lunkhead. So Shakespeare endows Richard with lyricism and Henry with the rhetoric of a leading article. Yeats dismisses any idea that Henry was, after all, successful, for he points out that in the cycle of historical plays Henry's son lost everything that had been seemingly won. 'Shakespeare watched Henry V,' says Yeats in his essay, 'At Stratford-on-Avon' (1901), 'not indeed as he watched the greater souls in the visionary procession, but cheerfully, as one watches some handsome spirited horse, and he spoke his tale, as he spoke all tales, with tragic irony.' Yeats's Shakespeare is on the side of sensitive anarchy, while Auden's is boisterously law-abiding.

Auden's conception of poetry parallels Eliot's anti-Wordsworthian definition of it as 'a superior amusement'. 'If you call it anything else you are likely to call it something still more false,' Eliot said. In his essay, 'Squares and Oblongs' (1948), Auden denominated poetry an impersonal game, though he quickly adds that the game is one of knowledge, a game in which the fun consists in naming hidden relationships. In *New Year Letter* he defines a game as 'any action or series of actions that can be done perfectly'. The frivolity of the game is undercut by the demand for skill and the struggle for perfection, which make the game deadly. Auden remains unsettled whether this perfection in poems is possible or not, but he is firm enough in his desire to shun nobler epithets, and the game's stringent requirements raise it to a super-game, 'a timeless world of pure play', and at the same time a liberation 'from self-enchantment and deception'.

At the end of *The Enchafèd Flood* he belittles his art once again, as if he were surrounded by idolaters of it. The artist can neither have such a heroic importance as the Romantics supposed, nor can he believe in the Art God enough to desire it. We must not think too well of art, he says there, as he had said before, and adds that we must not confuse it with religion. But his attitude toward art antedates his religious conversion, and seems in fact to go back to his childhood when, he tells us, he excluded magic from his childhood games. Now he shakes his finger and says we must recognize dogma again as the foundation for reason and emotion, not their contradiction. This is pious and utterly unlike Yeats.

In *The Sea and the Mirror*, his commentary on Shakespeare's *Tempest*, Auden occasionally echoes Yeats, as in his youth, so as to disagree with him. Yeats in 'The Tower' had asked, 'Oh may the moon and sunlight seem/One inextricable beam, / For if I triumph I must make men mad.' Auden characteristically takes up Prospero at the moment when he has given up magic, because now, 'I shall just be getting to know / The difference between moonshine and daylight.' Auden shows Antonio withstanding Prospero as art god by holding on to his own intransigency and privacy, somewhat as Judas in Yeats's *Calvary* turns against God to express not disbelief but his own identity and free will. Auden wishes to demonstrate that art is not omnipotent, while Yeats indicates that God is not omnipotent and that man is splendidly unsubdued.

At other points the two are not so divergent: that beyond art there is something which Caliban can call 'unrectored chaos' seems to jibe with Yeats's evocations of darkness in his last poems, and that art offers 'feebly figurative signs' of a 'Wholly Other Life' would suit Yeats too, though he would reject 'feebly' and say outright that works of art 'all heavenly glory symbolise'. But for Auden the artist's work is essentially a cunning yet relatively helpless effort to cope with nature or experience. For Yeats art and nature have more revelations to offer, and art is essentially a dialectic between nature – whether revelatory or not – and what Kant calls 'second nature', the artist's own creation from elements nature supplies. This dialectic considers many possibilities, that art depends upon nature, that it interpenetrates nature, that it is powerless in nature, that it shapes nature (as Wilde liked to say), that it transcends nature, and it conceives of nature variously as a temple of symbols or as what Stevens calls 'one insoluble lump' without ulterior meaning.

Auden is aware of this dialectic in Yeats, and uses it a little himself, with less freedom because of his walling off art from religion. He excludes certain possibilities, though he allows art, besides its aesthetic attractions, a certain ethical color, achieved by stripping away illusions and by being kind. In this careful reduction of the status of poetry there is perhaps a wilful self-disparagement, a personal humility gratuitously extended to his art. He presents himself as cutting through folderol. In his early poetry he achieved this effect by being abrupt, by snubbing euphony for dissonance, by insisting that the new password for poetry was enigmatic bluntness rather than, as in the early Yeats, enigmatic beauty. He is pleasantly unintimidated by Yeats, though he often seems to be struggling to maintain his own truculent consistency beyond the need for it. Essentially he wishes to characterize two schools of poetry.

We may join in the attempt too. Yeats did belong to a different persuasion from Auden, less offhand, more peremptory. To call poetry a game, even in an understatement which means that it is secretly, or at least occasionally, more than that, would be inconceivable for him. We can imagine his replying to Auden as he liked to remember Berkeley's replying to Hume, 'We Irish do not hold with this.' He did not concede that poetry and religion had portioned up the creation, or that poetry was subordinate to dogma. He said rather that the priest was the poet's shadow, and he meant that the religions of the world expressed in 'gutturals' what the poets had expressed in 'heavenly labials'. And if Auden had reservations about Yeats, Yeats also had reservations about Auden. In fact, as his letters reveal, Yeats thought of the preface to his *Oxford Book of Modern Verse* as an answer to the question, 'How far do I like the Ezra, Eliot,

Auden school and if I do not, why not?' and then, since he evidently knew the answer to that one, he added the further question, 'Why do the younger generation like it so much? What do they see or hope?' Auden, momentarily forgetting that writing poems was all a game, in turn referred to Yeats's anthology as 'the most deplorable volume ever issued' under the fine Clarendon imprint. (Years afterwards he was mollified to discover in Yeats's letters that Yeats spoke there of his poetry with more liking, though with the appalling vagueness of classifying Auden in the 'Cambridge school'.) In his late plays, *The Herne's Egg* and *Purgatory*, Yeats seems to be attempting some Auden-like abruptnesses in the minor characters' speech (he called it fancifully 'sprung verse'), and in his last prose work, *On the Boiler*, he took occasion to agree with *The Ascent of F6* that monastic abnegation and Western energy (Christ and Caesar) are the two alternatives available now to us.

With Auden prominently in mind, he complained, however, in his essay, 'A General Introduction to My Work', that these young English poets

> reject drama and personal emotion; they have thought out opinions that join them to this or that political party; they employ an intricate psychology, action in character, not as in the ballads, character in action, and all consider that they have a right to the same close attention that men pay to the mathematician and the metaphysician. One of the more distinguished has just explained that man has hitherto slept but must now wake. They are determined to express the factory, the metropolis, that they may be modern.

Remembering that Auden had been teaching school for five years, Yeats went on, 'Young men teaching school in some picturesque cathedral town ... defend their type of metaphor by saying that it comes naturally to a man who travels to his work by Tube.' As they express, he said, not 'what the Upanishads call "that ancient Self" but individual intellect, they have the right to choose the man in the Tube because of his objective importance. They attempt to kill the whale, push the Renaissance higher yet, outthink Leonardo; their verse kills the folk ghost and yet would remain verse. I am joined to the "Irishry" and I expect a counter-Renaissance.' Yeats's statement is as always so figurative as to be variously interpretable, but if he means, as he appears to mean, that the new poets are introducing a flat rationality, he is unjust to that strong sense of the uncanny which, while often masked in Auden by Freudian pseudo-explanation, is always prominent in his early work.

What would Yeats have said if he had had to memorialize Auden instead of Auden's memorializing him? No doubt his portrait of Auden would have become ennobled to the point of archetype, almost beyond recognition. But if Yeats had written in prose, he might have wished Auden to be sillier, or as he might have said, to be more that 'wild old wicked man' whom he presented as his own late image. The claim of being reasonable and honest did not impress him, for Yeats felt that 'poets were good liars who never forgot that the Muses were women who liked the embrace of gay warty lads'. Nor would Yeats have endorsed Auden's affection for the middle style, or, as Marianne Moore more aptly renames it, 'the circumspectly audacious'. If Auden was suspicious of Yeats's later flirtations with aristocracy and even fascism, Yeats was suspicious of Auden's early associations with Communism; it was for Auden's school, he said, a *deus ex machina*, a Santa Claus, offering a happy ending. His own preference, he says, was for tragedy rather than tragicomedy. The zeal for social change meant an attenuation of personality (a word of which Yeats could still, before the Second World War, be fond) because poets, instead of flaunting their selves and seeking identification with their opposites, sought identification with mass movements. When Auden uses the word 'we', he means all humanity, while when Yeats uses the same pronoun he means a limited and elect community.

To Auden's criticism of his mythology as *rentier*, Yeats would have responded that Auden's theology was equally middle-class, and had the further taint of being British. I don't know what Yeats would have made of Auden's change of nationality, from English to American, but if he had indicated more than amusement he would perhaps have taken it for another indication of a mind brusque with its own past as with much tradition. He would not have been pleased by Auden's rejection of the theory that imagination plays its role in the history of the world, and that events are in fact best understood as chains of images, often first generated by poets or by men capable of living at a poetic pitch. In *The King's Threshold*, an early play which reads like a dramatic demonstration of Yeats's essays 'The Symbolism of Poetry' and 'Magic', the poet Seanchan declares that because the poets have christened gold, kings have appeared to wear the crown; and in a late poem, 'The Man and the Echo', Yeats remorsefully questions himself about the effect of *Cathleen ni Houlihan*, 'Did that play of mine send out / Certain men the English shot?' And it is apparent that the answer is yes, that the Easter Rebellion stemmed from images which Yeats's patriotic play helped to generate in men's minds. Auden would insist, 'Art is not life, and cannot be / A midwife to society', but Irishmen in the audience, who felt their national feeling suddenly conscripted and marshaled, have testified that Yeats's play did affect them in this way.

Yeats's view of poetry as working like a subterranean force to alter men's lives does not sentimentalize its effects as necessarily virtuous or humanitarian. 'When did the poets promise safety, King?' asks the poet in *The King's Threshold*. Yeats would agree with Stevens that 'poetry is a destructive force.' In temerariously excluding Wilfred Owen from the *Oxford Book of Modern Verse* (he said in a letter that Owen was 'all blood, dirt, and sucked sugar-stick') and Sean O'Casey's *The Silver Tassie* from the Abbey Theatre repertoire (he found it 'anti-war propaganda'), Yeats made clear that for him poetry, or indeed any art, cannot find its end in pity. It expresses a more volcanic energy, and its consciousness of this Blake-like energy enables poetry to cry out in joy when everything about it falls in ruin.

Yet in espousing the cause of art Yeats is aware of the consequences. He characteristically puts his statement of poetry's power in the form of a remorseful question rather than of a flat declaration. Not that less is being claimed – Yeats's conception of poetry is here as radical as Shelley's, though in its dialectical range it also includes the sour and un-Shelleyan recognition (as in 'Byzantium') that poetical flames cannot singe a sleeve – but there is more modulated assertion, as if the poet, despairing of other forms of persuasion, drew us, half-startled and not quite of the same mind, into his own perplexities. Confuting the notion that poetry is ineffectual, he here suggests its insidious, demonic power. Auden argues against Shelley that not the poets, but the secret police, are the unacknowledged legislators of the world; Yeats's contention is rather that poets are the world's unacknowledged agitators, continually troubling the actual with the aspirant. Auden likes to regard the poet as an averter of panic, a member of the fire brigade (praise which he accords to Eliot – who appropriately was a fire warden – in his poem on the latter's sixtieth birthday). But for Yeats the poet does not put out fires, he starts them. He is a conflagrationist. Auden wants to get a grip on things as they are, Yeats to reshape them so they take on new properties. He is interested in flagrancy while Auden is interested in apprehension.

Their treatment of love suggests the difference in attitude. Maud Gonne seems essential to Yeats's view of things; some overwhelming defeated passion is needed to agitate the mind to its extremities. In Auden such fanfare over disappointment would be excessive; he finds it in Yeats a bit 'literary'; his own love poems, we have noted, emphasize that amorous feeling is 'half-humbug and half true', they applaud love but insist upon the painful awareness that time wrings the feelings and diverts them. He speaks more of friendship than love, and, it may be, sets more store by it. Auden moves away from explosion, as since Hiroshima all have moved, while Yeats is always moving towards it. Auden. as if turning Yeats inside out, made himself the spokesman for all the things that are not included in this overmastering passion.

Their views constitute a running dialogue, formulated by them more or less in this way:

YEATS: I believe in the poet's evocation of disembodied powers which, assuming form through the mind, effect changes in the world. The proper metaphor for poetry is magic.

AUDEN: Poetry is not magic. Insofar as it has an ulterior purpose, this is, by telling the truth, to disenchant and disintoxicate.

YEATS: Truth is the dramatic expression of the highest man, of the poet as hero.

AUDEN: The poet no longer fancies himself a hero; he is an explorer of possibility.

YEATS: Say impossibility rather.

AUDEN: All that is passé with the Romantic movement, thank God. Crying has gone out and the cold bath has come in.

YEATS: The whale is extinct and the little fish lie gasping on the strand.

AUDEN: The artist no longer wanders about in exile, he builds irrigation ditches like Faust in his old age, he votes in elections.

YEATS: The artist has much more in common with the flood than with irrigation. He breaks out of every social dam or political enclosure.

AUDEN: You belong to the school of Mallarmé; you think of yourself as a god who creates the subjective universe out of nothing.

YEATS: You belong to the school of Locke; you split the world into fragments and then worship the cutting edge.

AUDEN: Your world is a chimera.

YEATS: Yours is an urban renewal project.

Before the poets become too heated, perhaps we may try to placate them a little. Yeats is apt to say more than he means, Auden to say less. Yeats regarded himself as a romantic – a school which, like Eliot, Auden professed to detest; yet the bold positions which Yeats shares with Romantic poets appear in his verse often with a modern wariness and qualification. They are outposts flung up with a keen sense of imperilment. Auden regarded himself as a classicist, yet that term implies a much more settled manner and matter than his work displays. He may be described more profitably as an anti-romantic within the Romantic tradition. He would have liked to sing, he declares, 'In the old grand manner/Out of a resonant heart', but he has been forced by the debasement of words and values to adopt 'the wry, the sotto-voce, / Ironic and monochrome'. It is not like Auden to blame the age for his style, and in fact from the start he clearly preferred to reject the idealization of art and the manner that accompanies it. Yet at moments he was not adamant. In *The Sea and the Mirror* Prospero asks Ariel to show in his mirror what Nature is for ever, and when he does so, says, 'one peep ... will be quite enough.' But if the mirror of art can show even one peep at nature in its eternal form, then it must be more powerful than he customarily allows. In *The Dyer's Hand*, Auden repeatedly emphasizes that poetry is a rite, surrounded with awe. Instead of limiting it to an engaging but futile game, he has it subtly remaking the relations of the sacred and the profane, perhaps also of the real and the unreal, of the one and the many. This is about as much as Yeats would claim. At another door, Auden's anti-mythological attitude would seem to be a myth of its own, a belittlement of traditional glories only to make a reduced but very solid residual claim, like stripping a Victorian house of its gingerbread in order to display its solidity.

At least once in later poems Yeats and Auden converge on the same subject. This is a moment of lay sanctity experienced in a restaurant. Auden is full of casual and seemingly gratuitous detail:

In Schrafft's

Having finished the Blue-plate Special
And reached the coffee stage,
Stirring her cup she sat,
A somewhat shapeless figure
Of indeterminate age
In an undistinguished hat.

Yeats's poem on a similar theme comes in the series called 'Vacillation':

My fiftieth year had come and gone,
I sat, a solitary man,
In a crowded London shop,
An open book and empty cup
On the marble table-top.

Auden carries the commonplaceness of the shop a little further than Yeats, and he limits the intensity of the experience described.

Characteristically the latter is not his own, but that of someone 'shapeless' he doesn't know, of indeterminate age, who wears an undistinguished hat, as if she were describable only in negative terms. The religious imagery is operated differently in the two poems: it serves Yeats to describe a blasphemous encroachment of the human upon the divine, while in Auden an earthier god makes his positive incursion upon the human, an incursion less weighty, less implicating, more sanguine. Auden's metaphor is genuinely religious and yet ironically reduced: food in the tabernacle of the belly constitutes a certain good.

The movement has been from candid intensity to intense candor. Auden's offhand, unassuming tone, his disinfected vocabulary, take on some of their authority by disavowing what in Yeats is so assuming, so infected. As Proust remarks, 'A powerful idea communicates some of its strength to him who challenges it.' If Yeats, and poets like him, had not already extolled the poem as a terrestrial paradise, a fragment of Eden, a symbol of heaven, Auden might have felt less disposed to belittle it as a 'verbal contraption'. These terms are not mutually exclusive: they represent different kinds of assertion and defiance at different moments. Yeats with overstatement, and Auden with understatement, circle furtively toward each other, caught in the same galactic system.

1967

Crab-Apple Jelly

THE STORIES of Frank O'Connor refresh and delight long after they are first read. They pass into our experience like incidents we have ourselves known or almost known. Generous in spirit, acute in perception, they sum up a provincial culture in terms that are less provincial, but never cosmopolitan. Detachment from his own country was not one of Frank O'Connor's aims. Nobody was more aware than he of the mules, crows, foxes, who with dogs, horses, gazelles, and doves populated in human form his island home, and nobody was more unwilling to give up the local fauna. His stories preserve in ink like amber his perceptive, amused, and sometimes tender observations of the fabric of Irish customs, pieties, superstitions, loves, and hates. He wrote at the moment when that fabric was being slowly torn by modern conditions. 'Crab-apple jelly' was his own description of the sweet and tart mixture thus compounded. His best stories stir those facial muscles which, we are told, are the same for both laughing and weeping.

Frank O'Connor himself was a man of great affections that were just below the surface of expression, ready to emerge in the form of actions or literary insights. Not that the stories were spontaneous bursts; except for a few such as 'My Oedipus Complex' and 'Bridal Night', which almost wrote themselves, he sifted, shaped, revised, revised again. A story might be given fifty forms before he was satisfied with it, and then be given still another before it was republished. The question of form was always dominant, because what he called the 'glowing center of action' depended upon dense, accurate, and yet poetic presentment. It must not, he insisted, be described naturalistically 'as if it were a leg of mutton.'

Avant-garde methods of narration did not interest him either. He saw that his own talent required, like Yeats's poetry, the sense of an actual man, talking. That man, under whatever cover, was his own spirited, flashing self, bountiful and painstaking. However peculiar the things the characters did, they must appear incontestably real. The kernel of a story might be heard in a pub or on the street, but gathering or inventing the necessary detail, infusing the whole with a theme so powerful and simple that it could be written on a postcard, and commanding the reader's assent as all that was fluid became solid, required stamina as well as enthusiasm. It was a stern regimen, Flaubert among the bogs.

Few writers from humble circumstances have begun quite so humbly as Frank O'Connor did. He was born in 1903 in Cork, a city that prided itself on being unlike Dublin. Yeats would one day praise him for his sharp Corkman's eye. O'Connor himself would speak afterward with affection of the city's 'warm dim odorous feckless evasive southern quality', but in his youth he was more conscious of what he called in an early letter its 'barbarous mediocrity'. Neither view was possible for him in childhood, when hunger and squalor were what he could see of the city. His real name, Michael O'Donovan, he shared with his father, a soldier who had played the big drum in the band and after discharge from the British army worked sometimes as a navvy. Tall and handsome, the father looked to his bookish son like the young Maxim Gorky. Unfortunately he drank heavily in a more indigenous tradition.

The only child in this household regarded himself as a mother's boy, and it was Minnie O'Donovan who rendered conceivable his escape from his surroundings in all but memory. She was pretty and unusually polite, a grace as unexpected as it was pleasant. Perhaps it was the latter quality that made her, as he recorded, suspicious of emotional demonstrativeness; and it may have encouraged him to scrutinize such outbursts for their real worth. Mrs. O'Donovan went out each day to do housework, and brought back small wages, some of which with luck she could save from being converted into her husband's pints of Guinness. Her reward for this maneuvering was his anger. He would brandish his razor at her while their small son risked injury in an attempt to defend her. No wonder the child had pseudo-epileptic fits.

No wonder, either, that when he needed to write under a pseudonym because he was a county librarian, he reverted to his mother's maiden name of O'Connor. There was a long period during which he would gladly have disclaimed the O'Donovan lineage, yet in later life he found himself less ready to spurn the bluff, foolish man who had begotten him. His first volume of autobiography, *An Only Child* (1961), celebrated Minnie O'Donovan's 'noble nature', his second, though it could not present his other parent in so lyrical a light, indulged the dense mixture in himself by bearing the title *My Father's Son* (1969).

Poverty and talent went together. Frank O'Connor later on would praise the way that Yeats, Lady Gregory and Synge all wrote miracle plays, in which people turned into what they imagined themselves to be. He did as much himself. That he might do so began to be signalled by the time he was six. He was already then a devoted reader, if only of success stories about English public schools. These were as remote as possible from his own primary and Trades School, which he attended until he was fourteen. Yet bad literature, too, can foster ambition. O'Connor would deny later that Madame Bovary could have gone to pieces 'as a result of reading the novels of Scott', and he remained smilingly grateful for the sense of another way of life which his early reading in trashy books had given him. There were also fateful moments in school such as the day when one of his teachers wrote on the blackboard some indecipherable words. They proved to be Irish. The teacher, a little man with a game leg, turned out to be a writer named Daniel Corkery, and this initial impulse from him helped to spur O'Connor to the brilliant translations of Irish poetry which he would make later.

It was his readings in English that had the most immediate influence. Here his mother helped him. Before her marriage, when she had worked as a live-in maid, she had come upon a copy of Shakespeare's works among the unread books in an employer's house. She read them right through. Her son took up her interest, and eventually would write a knowledgeable and shrewd book, *The Road to Stratford* (1948; reissued as *Shakespeare's Progress*). He learned from his mother also to love poetry, first in the sung lyrics of Thomas Moore, then gradually taking in the body of English poetry. In the 1920s he was reading not only Donne but Hopkins. He was also desperate to read poetry in other languages, and learned French and German so he could keep the lines of Ronsard, Verlaine, Heine and Goethe in his head.

But the art of fiction swayed him even more than that of verse. 'To have grown up in an Irish provincial town in the first quarter of the twentieth century,' he said later, 'was to have known the nineteenth-century novel as a contemporary art form.' Around him in real life he began to see the characters he knew in books by Turgenev, Tolstoy, Chekhov, Gogol, Babel, Balzac, Maupassant. He would say later of his youth that it had not been so much lived as hallucinated. He was 'half in, half out of the dream', and saw everything 'through the veil of literature'. The writers whom he loved were all realists, and he always considered himself to be a nineteenth-century realist too. Yet to share his life with their characters was a form of romance.

*

His reverie was only partially interrupted by the rush of Irish nationalism, in which he would take part. He was twelve years old when the Easter Rising occurred in 1916, and he had to watch from the sidelines the Black and Tan War in 1918 and 1919. But when the Civil War broke out, O'Connor, then eighteen, overrode his father's protests and joined the republican forces against the Free State. He knew from Tolstoy and Stendhal the vast confusion of war, and the indistinct battlelines, tactical confusion and conflicting loyalties of the Irish troubles bore out what they had written. Unthinking obedience was not his way. When he was ordered to shoot unarmed Free State soldiers who were walking out with their girlfriends, he brought the matter to higher authority and got the order rescinded. After taking part in some skirmishes he was captured and put in a prisoner-of-war camp. Here too he showed his unwillingness to fit into any stereotype. When the republican prisoners of war throughout the country were ordered by their leaders to go on hunger strike, O'Connor was almost alone in bravely refusing to join in. It was his farewell to obsessional politics. Martyrdom on orders was not the course he had marked out for himself.

The hunger strike collapsed. Instead of vindication for common sense, O'Connor found he had achieved notoriety for standing out against the foolhardy majority. The experience told upon him. It did not make him any the less intransigent; the contrary rather, for he embraced many unpopular causes later. But when his mother saw him on his release, she could see that her child was now a man. A sentence in Gogol's story, 'The Overcoat', summed up O'Connor's state of mind, and he would borrow it later when writing about prisoners: 'And anything that happened to me after I never felt the same about again.' He now had the point of view from which he would write his first book, *Guests of the Nation* (1931). In the first story, the 'guests of the nation' are two British soldiers who have become close friends of their captors. But an order comes for their execution, because the opposite side has executed two men. With this illustration of the cruelty of war, and its absurdity, O'Connor was launched on his literary career.

The implied theme, that flexible people can suddenly become fixed, that the other side may be less the enemy than one's own encrustation, is the theme of many of O'Connor's stories. Hearts or circumstances harden when they might be expected to soften. In 'The Luceys' a father declines to take his brother's hand because of misplaced pride over his dead son. In 'The Mad Lomasneys' a pert young woman who has lived by whim suddenly faces unalterable bleakness because a whim has gone wrong. And yet Frank O'Connor was an obstinate man himself, and could understand being dead set on something. So not every fixity is invalidated. In 'The Masculine Principle' a suitor sticks to his intention of marrying his girl only when he has saved two hundred pounds. Years pass in the process, and he comes near losing her altogether. In the end, though, his stubbornness is respected and rewarded. In 'The Long Road to Ummera', an old woman is determined to be buried nowhere but in the one place, and she has her way, the living being obliged at great inconvenience to obey her wishes. A later story tells how a priest's seemingly bizarre wish to be buried remotely, in 'The Mass Island', is carried out with reluctance, only to be validated when an enormous crowd of mourners gather for the funeral.

If fixity is one pole in the stories, the opposite is accommodation. Ireland is a collusive country, with all sorts of secret understandings that can be invoked when needed. If a curate commits suicide, his priest, 'an old pro', insists that the village doctor certify death from natural causes; when the doctor demurs, a threat of losing his medical practice brings him to heel. In 'Peasants', however, a priest refuses to accommodate a group of peasants who beg him, and then try to bribe him, to leave the police out of a case where a young man has stolen club funds. They for their part are convinced that the priest's obduracy comes only from his having been born and raised in another village, 'fifteen long miles away', and so not of their 'country'. The priest persists in his decision, the young man is tried and given a light sentence. On his release he is provided by his friends with enough money to set up a shop.

What interests O'Connor is not the question of illegality or immorality, but the personal warmth that renders collusion inevitable and implies that most offenses are venial anyway and trivial beside communal bonds. His excellent story, 'In the Train', gathers together the woman who has poisoned her husband, the witnesses who have testified quite falsely on her behalf ('There's never been an informer in my family'), and the police who have not quite persuaded the jury to convict her. After all, everyone knows her husband was a miser and a monster. But when they suggest that she had done the deed out of love for a younger man, she bursts out about the one they name, 'He's no more to me now than the salt sea.' And suddenly we are aware of the intensity of these little lives, capable of rising into poetry as easily as into violence.

Beyond fixities and accommodations is O'Connor's portrait of Ireland with all its quirks and qualities. He did not have much to say about the Ascendancy class which his friend Yeats praised and half chastised, but he knew all the gradations in the middle and lower classes, such as the barrier between a farmer's son and a laborer's daughter. Though for long an unbeliever, he recognized the role religion played in people's lives. He regrets, in an early story, that a woman has become a nun, though he knows that there can be pleasure in having one's life settled, in fearing nothing and hoping for nothing. But in a later treatment of this theme, 'The Star that Bids the Shepherd Fold', he likes the old priest who is trying to save a young woman of his parish from being 'corrupted' by a French sea captain. The captain cannot understand the fuss over two people sleeping together.

As for women, they occupy a subordinate place in the economy, but O'Connor is on their side as they slice through male palaver, and they do not seem submerged or disparaged. He admires them when like himself they are unintimidated. The woman teacher in 'Bridal Night' lies beside her lunatic lover and calms him chastely to sleep in utter indifference to the contumely she may suffer for being in his bed. O'Connor sympathizes with women as they struggle with sexual desire in a country where men are 'death on girls' pasts', and he often deals with the problems of hiding or recognizing illegitimate children. Legitimate or illegitimate, children fascinate him, and he delights in showing their upturned faces as they stare at adults whose behavior is so irrational in comparison with their own. Pervading these and other facets of the country is that extraordinary language, which dots his text with such expressions as 'in the ease of the world', 'while the life was in her', 'giving him the hard word'. The text tingles with these localisms.

Frank O'Connor in the course of his sixty years wrote in most of the possible literary forms: two novels, dramatizations, a biography of Michael Collins, a book of poetry as well as his translations from Irish, some lively travel books, and literary criticism. Some people thought him flamboyant in his views; he did not so regard himself. He thought he was stating conclusions that nobody in his right mind could miss.

The strength of *The Mirror in the Roadway* (1957) and *The Lonely Voice* (1963), which deal with the novel and the short story respectively, comes from this assumptive tone. He begins in close observation but then, in an almost visionary way, renders writers, objects, and themes malleable. Whatever writer he discusses, O'Connor will not release him until he has revealed the network of interconnecting passageways between the external man or woman. If he is bold he is also subtle, as when he says of the mayor's garden in *The Red and the Black*, 'Any real estate agent worth his salt could give us a clearer impression of the property of Monsieur de Renal than Stendhal.'

The burden of his criticism is that fiction has not been faithful to Stendhal's definition of the novel as a mirror dawdling down a road. Instead it has insisted upon going behind the mirror, becoming self-absorbed and indifferent to that crowd which it had once brilliantly particularized. The switch occurred, O'Connor thought, in Henry James, and he depicted it in an enviable figure:

> Somewhere in his work the change takes place between the two; somewhere the ship has been boarded by pirates, and when at last it comes into harbor, nobody could recognize in its rakish lines the respectable passenger ship that set sail from the other side of the water. The passengers would seem to have been murdered on the way, and there is nothing familiar about the dark foreign faces that peer at us over the edge.

On the whole, he regretted this development. What he longed for was candor, not circumlocution, cards on the table rather than held close to the chest. For this reason and others he could not wholly approve of Joyce, feeling that when artistic method had become so dominating life was lost. He liked and practiced a more open confrontation.

Mrs. Yeats used to call him Michael Frank, combining his private and literary selves into one affectionate nickname. There was in fact no hyphen between the two, no impulsion to play artist or reluctance to be man. In him the struggle to express was always involved with a sense of exhilaration, whether he was writing or talking. His friends recognized it not only in his arrowing mind, but in the great bow of his being, now reposeful now taut. For his readers there is the pleasure of catching Ireland as it was changing, and enjoying and cherishing it, flyspecks and all. Nor is it so different from America; continents, after all, are only large islands.

1981

TWO

This view of art may seem more contemporary than the puristic view of the work as an aesthetic object set in the void to burn by its own light.... The void is peopled by works, lives, circumstances, pressures. As the work loses the autotelic privacy which purist critics have sought to ascribe to it, it enters an inter-fusion of art and life.

– 'Love in the Catskills'

Love in the Catskills

During the last year of W. H. Auden's life, I sometimes had the luck to meet him in Oxford. On these occasions he would gradually place me as someone associated with literary biography, and would then inform me kindly but firmly that literary biography was no use. For its only purpose must be to display a relation of life and art, and either this relation – he would say – was obscure and impossible to detect, or else (and here his tone became triumphant) it was obvious and not worth mentioning. The verdict was chastening. But I found a little comfort in the fact that Auden defied his own rules. No one was more curious than he about the underpinnings of artistic careers. He wrote biographical poems about Housman's furtive sexuality and Melville's combat with Nobodaddy, and some of his essays, such as a long article on Oscar Wilde and Alfred Douglas, happily flouted by example his antibiographical precept.

In his will he none the less admonished his friends to destroy his letters with a view to rendering a biography impossible, and this clause is becoming almost standard for writers' testaments. Quite understandably, it is hard to accept that reticence can only last a lifetime. Writers are apt to feel that their biographers, if they do not merely drudge, will prosecute. Few are eager to submit posthumously to the whippings they have more or less 'scaped during life, and the idea of one's corpse lying on the analyst's couch with the analyst for once doing all the talking, and the patient prevented by *rigor mortis* from self-justification, is not fetching.

This aversion to biography is different from that of the structuralists and new critics who, coming from different postulates, agree in trying to clear the work of its creator. They take the view that there is an 'exclusive interdependence of the objective elements which compose the work'. The author's intention, if he had one, cannot be calculated, only miscalculated, and is irrelevant anyway. The intentional fallacy, which biographers are especially prone to commit, is a special case of the old offense, the genetic fallacy, which only Nietzsche among philosophers actively defended.

Still there is an opposite danger, the parthenogenetic fallacy that the text is a virgin birth accomplished without human intervention. 'Look, ma, no hands!' Granted that purging a work of its originator may sometimes be useful and even virtuous, this ritual bath is not obligatory. Writers about whom we know most, those closest to our own day, have usually declined it; Henry Miller even displayed outrage at the suggestion that the Henry Miller in his novels was a fictional character. And most critics have, like William Empson, cheerfully trespassed across the border that separates work and life, and have ransacked letters, journals, first drafts, interviews, and *obiter dicta* for details that might illuminate an author's intentions.

Critical purists often cite Eliot against this procedure, but in fact Eliot turned against them. Though he declared early on, 'The more perfect the artist, the more completely separate in him will be the man who suffers and the mind which creates,' this maxim survived only as long as did the anti-romanticism he learned from Irving Babbitt at Harvard. In later life he began to talk about literature in a way much closer to that of the confessional poets who have held the scene in the second half of this century. It was then he made his famous remark that scouted the interpretation of *The Waste Land* as social criticism, objectively arrived at, and claimed the poem was 'just a piece of rhythmical grumbling'.

Even if we allow for his modesty, Eliot had clearly begun to veer toward the idea of poetry as what Yeats called 'personal utterance'. The repercussions of the change are manifested in *Four Quartets,* where the spiritual struggle of his art is equated with the spiritual struggle of his life, and the pursuit of right words is made tantamount to the pursuit of right feelings. If his early ideal of the art object was the objective correlative of once personal emotions, Eliot's later ideal was parable – the presentation, with as much directness as possible, of the meaning of his experience as a man in the world.

Goethe was in the same mood when he said that all his works were 'fragments of a great confession'. The word 'parable', meaning an illustration of something, is at once personal and representative. It suits the idea of a possibly clandestine yet certainly self-aware purpose. It is different from the attempt to detect unconscious purposes in art. Biographers will continue to look for these as well, but the successes to date in this field have been less encouraging than one hoped. The spread of psychoanalytic criticism has worn thin its tenets; Freud's analyses had an air of the marvellous about them, but his followers have had to wrestle with stereotype.

Because the uncovering of parables in artists' work does not rest upon pre-formulated theory, depending rather upon intimate knowledge of their experience and, so far as available, thoughts about their experience, biographers now are moving in this direction. It can be demonstrated that large works, such as Yeats's *A Vision* or Ruskin's *The Stones of Venice,* were to some extent parables of their authors' experiences, as both Yeats and Ruskin recognized. But I think the same claim may be made for less imposing works.

A convenient example is Washington Irving's 'Rip Van Winkle'. Since its initial publication in 1819, this first American short story has become standard reading outside as well as inside the English-speaking world. In its elegant simplicity, it might seem wonderfully unambiguous, the story-teller delighting disinterestedly in his craft. Yet the circumstances of its composition, and certain elements within it, conduce to the belief that it was a parable, and largely a conscious one, of Irving's life. One paragraph in it is perplexing enough: Rip, as everyone knows, goes off into the Catskills and encounters a silent man dressed in the Dutch fashion who leads him to an amphitheater among the mountains where a group of other men, similarly dressed, including one who appears to be their leader, are playing at ninepins. Though they have funny faces, one all nose, another with pig eyes, the scene is suddenly uncanny. As Irving writes,

> What seemed particularly odd to Rip was, that though these folks were evidently amusing themselves, yet they maintained the gravest faces, the most mysterious silence, and were, withal the most melancholy party of pleasure he had ever witnessed. Nothing interrupted the stillness of the scene but the noise of the balls, which, whenever they were rolled, echoed along the mountains like rumbling peals of thunder.
>
> As Rip and his companion approached them, they suddenly desisted from their play, and stared at him with such fixed countenances, that his heart turned within him, and his knees smote together.

A partial explanation of this terrifying scene is proposed later in the story, when it is said that every twenty years Henry Hudson, the first explorer of this region, and his crew of the *Half Moon* return for a vigil and play at ninepins. Yet they behave neither like ghosts nor like people, and what shakes Rip's knees is the peculiar mixture of the jolly game of ninepins and the 'lackluster' impassivity of their grotesque faces. Rip drinks a magic brew to overcome his fears, and he wakes up twenty years later to find beside him his rusted gun. He returns to the village to learn that in his absence the American Revolution has taken place, and that he, who had gone off in his prime as a British subject, has returned as an American senior citizen.

Irving's biographers have had little to say about this story, in part because Irving borrowed the principal details of the plot from a German story about one Peter Klaus. Yet borrowing is a transaction and what one chooses, or feels obliged, to borrow is an act of decision. In any case, the story of Peter Klaus has no Dutchman but rather some knights, who are anachronistic and formidably bearded, but not otherwise so dreadful. The question remains why Irving was drawn to this particular tale, and why he represented its most intense moment – the game of ninepins – in a manner at once comic and shocking. Such a question may be asked in spite of the story's impersonal surface, and the urbane and amusing, if sometimes arch, manner that Irving could brilliantly sustain. Many of the details lead nowhere. The name Van Winkle was that of a printer in New York whom Irving had employed, and, as he indicates in the story, was that of an early Dutch family in New York. Precise analogues between Rip's life and Irving's are not forthcoming, since Rip suffers from the nagging of his termagant wife, while Irving himself never married. As if to separate himself further, Irving sets the scene in an earlier age, so that Rip awakens from sleep about the time that Irving himself was born.

And yet some connections lurk behind. Irving seems to have been all his life a praiser of times past, as Rip, once his long nap is over, becomes. Irving knew and slightly mocked this proclivity in himself: he signed his most youthful productions, written before he was twenty, in which he nostalgically criticized current customs of marriage and current fashions, with the pseudonym 'Jonathan Oldstyle'. The next pseudonym he adopted was 'Senex'. In later life he devoted himself to chronicles of the dead. The burlesque *History of New York,* meaning its history under the Dutch governors, which he published when he was twenty-six, is represented as having been written by Diedrich Knickerbocker, and at the end of this book Knickerbocker announces that he is withering away in old age and has not long to live. This grim prognosis is confirmed in the story of 'Rip Van Winkle', which has for subtitle 'A Posthumous Writing of Diedrich Knickerbocker', and is represented as having been found among 'the late' Knickerbocker's papers. Irving's sense of himself as an old-timer was constant from early youth.

The fact that Irving used Knickerbocker as author of both the *History of New York* and the history of Rip Van Winkle also indicates that he wished to connect them. In the *History* he had described Henry Hudson and his crew of the *Half Moon* as historical personages, not as absurd-looking creatures with 'lackluster faces' playing at ninepins. Given these connections, perhaps there are others. Irving's early life bears some inspection. As I mentioned, he showed himself a writer at a very youthful age. A career as literary man was what he aspired to, but he needed a more predictable means of support, and so read law. This study was not agreeable; he pursued it with as much truancy as Rip Van Winkle exhibited toward other responsibilities. He bumbled his way through the bar examination, and friendly judges pretended he had passed. But his real interest was in writing a *History of New York*; he began it in collaboration with a brother, but when the brother went into business, Irving proceeded with the book on his own.

Ostensibly he was practicing law in the office of a man named Hoffman, with the aim of establishing himself so he could safely marry Hoffman's daughter. But clandestinely Irving worked on his *History*. Then a most unfortunate event altered all his plans. Matilda Hoffman, in whose household he had been a constant visitor for three years, caught what was first assumed to be a cold, but what was quickly rediagnosed as tuberculosis. Within two months, by April 1809, she was dead. This love story is one of the most affecting in a century distinguished for affecting love stories. Matilda Hoffman died at seventeen, Irving being then twenty-six.

Her death and especially her dying did not fade. 'For three days and nights,' he wrote later in an autobiographical fragment, 'I did not leave the house & scarcely slept. I was by her when she died. ... I was the last one she looked upon.' He remembered 'The last fond look of the glazing eye, turned upon me even from the threshold of existence!' A dozen years later he could still feel almost the same pain.

> I cannot tell you what a horrid state of mind I was in for a long time – I seemed to care for nothing – the world was a blank to me. ... Months elapsed before my mind resumed any tone: but the despondence I had suffered for a long time in the course of this attachment, and the anguish that attended its catastrophe seemed to give a turn to my whole character, and threw some clouds into my disposition which have ever since hung about it.

As a young man Irving had been known for his high spirits. These were now lowered.

In the circumstances it seemed pointless to go on with the law, which he had pretended to accept only to buttress his then impending marriage. He returned instead to his *History of New York*, the broad humor of which could scarcely have been less suited to his new grief.

111

Yet the hope of a profession lay there, and he drove himself on. The book was published in December 1809, about eight months after Matilda Hoffman's death, and gave him a reputation: but as he said, 'the time & circumstances in which it was produced rendered me always unable to look upon it with satisfaction.' As if to confirm this depression of mind, his attempts to continue his work as a writer proved abortive, apart from editing a magazine; in fact, for almost ten years Irving was virtually silent. During this period he was taken into his brothers' business, though he had no head for the work and was not expected to do any. But since the firm had headquarters in England, he traveled there in 1815, arriving just a day or two after the war with Napoleon ended, while the victory bells were still ringing.

Irving recognized the voyage over as momentous, and made it the subject of a chapter called 'The Voyage' in *The Sketch Book,* where 'Rip Van Winkle' appears in close conjunction. 'The Voyage' confirms Irving's lifelong sense of the separation of his life into distinct parts, such a sense of separation as Rip also was to experience. On Irving's way to England, he felt that 'I had closed one volume of the world and its contents, and had time for meditation before I opened another.' 'I stepped upon the land of my forefathers but felt that I was a stranger in the land.' Rip's experience after his nap was cognate to this.

Irving's sojourn in England did not rouse his creative powers. His brothers were sick, he nursed them, and then there occurred a second crisis in his affairs. This crisis was as material as the previous one had been spiritual. His brothers' firm went into bankruptcy, and Irving, though an inactive partner, shared in the disgrace. 'I underwent ruin in all its bitterness and humiliation,' he wrote, 'in a strange land – among strangers. ... I shut myself up from society – and would see no one. For months I studied German day & night by way of driving off horrid thoughts. [This idea had probably been put in his mind by a visit to Sir Walter Scott.] The idea suddenly came to return to my pen. ...'

So in 1817, eight years after the death of Matilda Hoffman, Irving began to make notes for *The Sketch Book,* which was published in installments in 1819 and 1820, with 'Rip Van Winkle' as the capstone of the first installment. His notebook has also been published, and its central entry indicates that in the new grief over financial ruin his old grief over emotional ruin was sharpened. There is a moving passage apostrophizing Matilda Hoffman: 'How lovely was then my life – How has it changed since – what scenes have I gone through since thou has left me. ... The romance of life is past.' The sense of empty, eventless years and of a rude awakening seems comparable to Rip's experience.

I think we can now risk an explanation of the awe-striking jollity of the Dutchmen in 'Rip Van Winkle'. Bankruptcy caused Irving to relive, in the new ruin of his affairs, the old ruin of eight years earlier. The paradox of his life at that earlier time, of which he was acutely conscious, was that he had to write amusingly while feeling funereal, to resurrect with forced animation the dead Dutchmen as figures of fun while bearing always the memory of the glazed last look of Matilda Hoffman, 'on the threshold of existence'. These elements combined and merged into the 'lackluster' gaiety, that incongruous medley which so terrified Rip Van Winkle when he observed it in the dead but very lively Dutch bowlers. And following her death, Irving could look back on long years in which he moved like a somnambulist, alienated by grief in his native America, then by nationality when he became an American in postwar Britain, as Rip was a Briton in postwar America.

When at last he returned, as he said, to his pen, the pen was as rusty as Rip's gun. 'I have suffered several precious years of youth and lively imagination to pass by unimproved,' he wrote to his brother when sending him the manuscript of *The Sketch Book*. Two of his friends have left an account of how Irving wrote 'Rip Van Winkle' in a fever of activity, staying up all one night in June 1818 as he filled and threw aside one page after another. This sense of being seized by the story came from its being a parable of his own monstrous dual vision, in which the history of New York took shape as farce, and the history of his own life took shape as tragedy, a vision followed by years of depression, and then by his reawakening, an artist once again, but a young man no longer.

If this account of Irving's involvement in Rip Van Winkle's career is accepted, the baffling passage in the story ceases to baffle. And it may help to explain the subterranean power of this work which made Rip Van Winkle rather than Peter Klaus one of the great figures of the nineteenth-century imagination. The parabolic value the story had for Irving came from the sifting of his personal emotion through a lighthearted tale. Its pages are, after all, noisy with Rip's termagant wife and with his own recollections, noisy also with chat, with foreseeable stock emotions; but against these elements is the otherness of that scene of the bowlers, its invocation of an emotional plane far different from the rest, a plane where garrulity becomes dumb, conventional feeling is absent, the comic spirit is suddenly challenged by faces devoid of expression, mouths that will not speak, as if in the midst of the festive act of writing Irving could only recall Matilda's glazing eyes and chilling body. It was only by assimilating this experience into a new context that he could resume his literary career. And it was this particular passage, where the fantasy becomes suddenly frightening rather than funny, that raised the story into an unforeseen memorability.

Parables may be motivated in many ways, not only by a desire to put one's affairs in order but by a desire to carry experiences or feelings to limits which they did not actually attain, or perhaps to exorcise them, since what is not there may constitute part of the parable, or to serve other functions. What is illustrated need not be especially moral, but has been subjected to the economy of reflection. The parable may have varying degrees of self-sufficiency, and its meaning is often a trade secret, to be fathomed only on long and close critical association. This view of art may seem more contemporary than the puristic view of the work as an aesthetic object set in the void to burn by its own light. The work appears now less as an object than as a convergence of energies, a momentary delay of forces that come from the individual and from society as well as from the literary tradition. The void is peopled by works, lives, circumstances, pressures. As the work loses the autotelic privacy which purist critics have sought to ascribe to it, it enters an interfusion of art and life. Or as Yeats said in a slightly different context, the stallion eternity mounts the mare of time.

1976

Dorothea's Husbands

A NOVELIST, intent on his art, swallows into it other people along with himself. The living originals of fictional characters are elusive because they have been obliged by the writer to answer purposes not their own. It is as if they were evicted from a universe of free will into a deterministic one. The peril of confusing universes is one to which we have been alerted by fastidious critics and structuralists alike. Yet many novelists are themselves liable to this lapse, and fondly imagine that they have created characters out of people they have known. To follow them a little way is at worst devoted, and at best profitable, since the mode of translating characters from the one universe to the other must be close to basic movements of the mind, and so of critical as well as biographical consequence.

It may be easier to approach George Eliot by way of a writer more patently obsessive. In *Heart of Darkness*, Conrad made avowed use of his own trip to the Congo a dozen years before. Much of the narrative turns out to have an immediate parallel in his experience: Conrad did go to Brussels for his interview, did ship up the Congo River on a steamboat, did rescue a sick agent named Klein who died on the trip back. Yet the story has a quite different feel from the *Congo Diary* and from his letters of the time. And there is an important discrepancy: Klein was no Kurtz, no symbol of spiritual degradation. If anything, he was nondescript. It would seem that the motive power of the story must have come from some other region than the Congo.

This area may be guessed at with the help of a fact first pointed out in Jocelyn Baines's life of Conrad. The correspondence of Conrad's uncle, Tadeusz Bobrowski, discloses that Conrad, at the age of nineteen, did not – as he always said afterwards – fight a duel and suffer a bullet wound. What happened instead was that he gambled away at Monte Carlo some money his uncle had sent him, and then in self-disgust shot himself. This attempted suicide was probably the central event of Conrad's life. In the light of it, the qualities on which Marlow prides himself in *Heart of Darkness* – his rivet-like tenacity, his patience, his coolness under pressure – were the exact opposites of those displayed by the young Conrad. From the moment that he inflicted this wound, Conrad must have regarded it – and its scar – as a sign and symbol of a propensity to give way, to abandon himself. To call his villain Kurtz (German for 'short') was to memorialize this phase of his life when he was not yet Joseph Conrad but still Konrad Korzeniowski – a name prone to be shortened to Korz.

When recovered from his wound, Conrad went to England and sailed on an English coastal vessel. By this time or not long afterwards he had determined to slough off his old life, language, weakness. He decided to present himself no longer as a European but as an Englishman. In the 1880s he took and passed the three examinations which confirmed his navigational skill and executive capacity. If 1875 was the year that he virtually died, 1886 was the year of his virtual resurrection, for during it he qualified as first mate, he became a British subject, and he began to write. Writing was a way of avenging his suicide attempt. Marlow declares, 'mine is the speech that cannot be silenced.' Like Marlow, whose watchword is 'restraint', Conrad must have practiced a conscious self-overcoming.

It would seem likely that young Korzeniowski's suicide attempt was extrapolated as the self-abandonment and moral cowardice of the European Kurtz, and that the confrontation with Marlow, captain of English ships and master of English prose, bearer of an indisputably English name, was symbolically rehabilitative. To commit murder is to yield to the mind's jungle, to write is to colonize with the efficiency so highly regarded by Marlow. Kurtz and Marlow meet in the 'heart of darkness' as in the recesses of Conrad's mind: one dies, the other contrives to be reborn. Conrad did not let this theme rest: his return to it in *Lord Jim* and other works must have been a pricking and stanching of the old wound.

This preliminary example may embolden an enquiry into two characters, and their possible prototypes, in *Middlemarch*. George Eliot, contrary to T. S. Eliot, made no claims for the impersonality of the artist. She confided that her first work of fiction, *Scenes of Clerical Life*, drew upon family reminiscences, and many characters from her other books have been pursued to prototypes in her experience, often with her help. She worked from models then, probably habitually.

Like George Eliot herself, Dorothea had two husbands. Of the two, it is Mr. Casaubon who has deserved and attracted attention. He is a pedant of such Saharan aridity that the temptation to identify him has not often been resisted. Among the proffered candidates, the one most mentioned is Mark Pattison, rector of Lincoln College, Oxford. He had three points of *rapport*: an unhappy marriage with a wife much younger than himself, friendship with George Eliot, and the authorship of a life of the Swiss scholar (of the sixteenth century) Isaac Casaubon. George Eliot obviously borrowed from him the name of his subject, but other resemblances are tenuous, as if the price she paid for the one liberty was not to take others. John Sparrow, the most resolute supporter of Pattison as Casaubon's archetype, has rested his case largely on a passage in Sir Charles Dilke's unpublished autobiography, in which Dilke, later married to Mrs. Pattison, states that Casaubon's marriage proposal and Dorothea's answer were based closely on the equivalent Pattison letters. These letters have not survived. But aside from the flexibility of style and mind so notable in Pattison, so lacking in Casaubon, it is clear from a letter of George Eliot, published in 1971 in the *Times Literary Supplement* by Professor Gordon Haight, that as early as 1846 she was already diverting her friends by concocting the terms of a pedant's proposal of marriage. Casaubon's letter balances precariously on the questions of whether he is seeking a wife or someone to read to him, and of whether he is actuated by love or myopia; the proposal of 'Professor Bücherwurm', which George Eliot pretends to relay to Charles Bray, similarly hinges on the ambiguity of the Professor's securing as his bride someone to translate his books from German. In 1846 George Eliot did not know Pattison, and evidently she had no need to know him in order to evolve Casaubon's letter.

To consider other possible models for Casaubon is to turn up many of George Eliot's acquaintances. Pedantry was not a scarce commodity among them. Ideally the culprit should combine arid learning with sexual insufficiency. This felicitous blend is unexpectedly hard to find. No doubt the laws of Middlemarch, rather than those of experience, demanded that Casaubon's mind symbolize his body, and his body his mind. If George Eliot drew details from models, she used more than one. For sexual low pressure, Herbert Spencer was probably the best example, and Beatrice Webb saw enough resemblance to refer to him as Casaubon. George Eliot knew Spencer well, and may have been perplexed for a time at his failure to marry anyone, herself included. But if his nubility was in doubt for her, his ability was not; it is only a later age that wishes Spencer had been Casaubon enough to finish fewer books. Besides, Spencer came to regard George Eliot as the greatest woman who ever lived, an accolade she would not have so meagrely rewarded.

For the author of the 'Key to all Mythologies', a closer prototype is Dr. R. H. Brabant. It was he whom the novelist Mrs. Eliza Lynn Linton, well acquainted with both him and George Eliot, identified positively as Casaubon. Brabant had similar difficulty in bringing a book to fruition. According to Mrs. Linton in *My Literary Life* (1899), he 'never got farther than the introductory chapter of a book which he intended to be epoch-making, and the final destroyer of superstition and theological dogma'. Under the influence of the German rationalists, Brabant presumably intended to eliminate from all religions that supernatural element which they had eliminated from Christianity. It seems unlikely that he used the word 'key', an inappropriate one for his enterprise. Although Gordon S. Haight, George Eliot's astute and scrupulous biographer, accepts Brabant as the model, there are several obstacles to close identification with him as with Pattison. Brabant's loins were not nearly so exhausted: he did not manifest sexual indifference. He was married, he had a daughter and a son; at the age of sixty-two he squired George Eliot about in a manner which she found happily equivocal in intention, and which his blind wife acutely resented.

Moreover he was a physician, and evidently a good one; his book was a sideline, a token of intellectual community. He had a gift for companionship, and was friends with Coleridge, Moore, Landor, and others. He also had friends in Germany, notably Strauss and Paulus, and it was he who some years later introduced George Eliot, translator of *Das Leben Jesu*, to Strauss, its author. Apparently he could converse more easily in German than she could, and in this respect too he is unlike Casaubon, whose ignorance of German is scored heavily against him. Mrs. Linton describes Brabant as 'well got up and well preserved', while Casaubon is prematurely withered. He was also a man of many interests, in the theatre, art and science, as references in George Eliot's correspondence and John Chapman's diaries confirm. Most of all, he was a man of enthusiasm, generously tendered to the work of others rather than his own.

George Eliot did feel a brief spell of veneration for Brabant, as Dorothea did for Casaubon, but with more semblance of justification. Whatever Brabant's defects as an idol, he was in the same cultural movement as she was. If he dithered, it was not over 'Cush and Mizraim' like Mr. Casaubon, but over what George Eliot also considered the most pressing spiritual problems of the time. She followed his lead with Strauss, she borrowed his copy of Spinoza. If he was dull, he was dull in the swim. So expert a novelist would not have forgotten him – she may have derived from him not only hints for Casaubon but some for Mr. Brooke, a friend of Wordsworth and everyone else. But she was after other game than the Polonius who benignly called her, as his second daughter, 'Deutera' – an improvement on Mary Ann.

Pattison, Spencer and Brabant hang upon Casaubon's coat-tails, but their intellectual interests are far afield. Comparative mythology such as Casaubon's had got off to a heady start in the eighteenth century with Jacob Bryant's *A New System: or, An Analysis of Ancient Mythology* (1774–6). Gordon Haight has pointed out that George Eliot made use of Bryant's theory of 'Chus and Mizraim', Cush (so respelt by Bryant) being represented as the father of all the Scythian nations, and Mizraim as father of the Egyptians. There are further connections that can be offered: Bryant's theory of the Phoenicians (as sons of Esau), of the ancient priests called the Cabiri, and of Dagon the fish god, whom he identified both with Noah and with the Indian god Vishnu, are all behind Mr. Casaubon's researches. It was as if George Eliot had Bryant ready in case she was suspected of deriding a living comparative mythologist, and she could keep him more easily in reserve because his work was evidently a familiar subject for joking between her and her friend Sara Hennell. Her concocted Professor Bücherwurm had offered the notion that Christianity was merely a late development of Buddhism, which was like making Vishnu a prior version of Noah, and Sara Hennell, in reply to her friend's comic letter about Bücherwurm's marriage proposal, quoted Bryant's favorite Egyptian source, Berosus. Yet George Eliot did have a comparative mythologist of her own day, whom she knew well, to fuse with Bryant. This was Robert William Mackay, the author of *The Progress of the Intellect as Exemplified in the Religious Development of the Greeks and Hebrews*, published by George Eliot's friend John Chapman in 1850, and at his request and Mackay's reviewed by her in her first article for the *Westminster Review*.

That Mackay was connected with Casaubon was proposed, as Haight recognizes, by Frances Power Cobbe in her 1894 *Life* of herself: 'Mr. Mackay was somewhat of an invalid and a nervous man, much absorbed in his studies. I have heard it said that he was the original of George Eliot's *Mr. Casaubon*. At all events Mrs. Lewes had met him, and taken a strong prejudice against him.' Miss Cobbe is mistaken about George Eliot's feelings towards Mackay, which were always friendly. Perhaps on this account, Haight dismisses the identification with him as hearsay. But it is not difficult to establish that Mackay contributed a small portion to *Middlemarch*. His book, unlike Brabant's unfinished one, was a revival of comparative mythology. He was more learned even than Bryant, with a dozen footnotes to the latter's one; George Eliot noted his 'industry in research', a virtue constantly claimed by Casaubon. If his search for vegetation

119

gods is difficult to summarize, it is because, as George Eliot complained in her review, much of it seemed mere 'extracts from his
commonplace book', rather than results of 'digested study'. It was
such a book as Dorothea might have compiled after Casaubon's
death. Some of it was manifestly absurd, but George Eliot took a
benign view of his objective, which she summarized in this way:

> It is Mr Mackay's faith that divine revelation is not contained
> exclusively or pre-eminently in the facts and inspirations of any
> one age or nation, but is co-extensive with the history of human
> development.... The master key to this revelation, is the recognition
> of the presence of undeviating law in the material and moral world –
> of that invariability of sequence which is acknowledged to be the
> basis of physical science, but which is still perversely ignored in our
> social organisation, our ethics and our religion.

Here at last is the word 'key', which Mackay himself had not used.
It is his kind of locksmith that George Eliot has in mind in Casaubon's
Key to all Mythologies.

There are further ties. 'Poor Mr. Casaubon himself was lost ... in
an agitated dimness about the Cabeiri' (chapter 20), and poor Mr.
Mackay had followed Bryant to the extent of designating as 'Orphic
or Cabiric' the primitive period of mythology. (She noted in her
article that this was an older view, but refrained from tracing it to
Bryant.) If Mr. Casaubon, in dictating to Dorothea, announces, 'I
omit the second excursus on Crete' (chapter 48), it is perhaps because
Mr. Mackay had devoted a whole chapter to Crete and its god,
'Minos-Zeus', and Mr. Casaubon may well have felt that this first
excursus was enough. If Ladislaw could say of Mr. Casaubon
(chapter 22), 'He is not an Orientalist, you know. He does not profess
to have more than second-hand knowledge there,' it was because
Mr. Mackay had conceded in his preface, 'In quoting from Oriental
sources the writer is under the disadvantage of ignorance of the
languages; but he has taken pains to get the best possible aids.'

Mackay may have had marital designs upon George Eliot; he soon
shifted them to another affective object. The resultant marriage
obviously interested her. After it he appeared 'rather worse than
otherwise', she reported. Following his return from a wedding trip
to Weymouth, she asked him how he and his wife had liked it: 'Not
at all, not at all,' he replied, 'but it was not the fault of the place.'
The barrenness of Rome for the honeymooning Casaubons is at least
glimpsed here.

Mackay served to update Bryant and to fill in details of Casaubon
which other friends could not supply. As ultimate model for the

character, he, like Brabant, is disqualified by his positive qualities. What remains to be found is the source of energy which produces both Casaubon's intensity, and the intensity of contempt, mixed with sporadic pity, which his being arouses in author and characters alike in *Middlemarch*. Gordon Haight, sensible of George Eliot's unusual venom, attributes it to her temporary infatuation with Brabant and later disillusionment with him, but so much feeling after twenty-five years of subsequent friendship, and three years after Brabant's death, seems disproportionate. Brabant was at worst one of her own follies.

Her own follies: putting these Casaubon *manqués* aside, we come to George Eliot herself. F. W. H. Myers related in the *Century Magazine* for November 1881, that when asked where she had found Casaubon, 'with a humorous solemnity, which was quite in earnest, nevertheless, she pointed to her own heart.' This remark deserves to be considered. She meant by it exactly what Flaubert had meant when he said, 'Madame Bovary, *c'est moi*.' Flaubert too had his Brabants and Mackays, and secured a few useful details from actual events and persons, but in his writing he had other things to think about. What must be sought is not a Casaubon, but casaubonism, and this George Eliot found, as Flaubert found *le bovarysme*, in herself. Casaubonism is the entombing of the senses in the mind's cellarage. As a young woman George Eliot was liable to this iniquity, and all her life she was capable of what Myers calls 'almost morbid accesses of self-reproach'.

Casaubon is the only character in George Eliot's work up to this time to have a sexual problem, in the sense of being aberrant. What the problem may be is not easy to say definitely. Whether his marriage is consummated or not is left obscure. Living when she did, George Eliot had reason to be delicate and reticent about such a matter, but her vagueness had literary as well as Victorian causes. Impotence is a disaster, not a vice; if Casaubon cannot consummate his marriage, he is to that extent as pathetic as Ruskin. Too much sympathy would be out of order. George Eliot's fictional universe never allows her men and women to shirk moral responsibility, and Casaubon is no exception. She said that the idea of Casaubon and Dorothea had been in her mind from the time she began to write fiction, and one reason for her long delay in taking up the theme may have been the difficulty of handling Casaubon's sexual insufficiency. She finally solved the difficulty by blending impotence or near-impotence with a choice of chilliness over warmth, in which his culpability would be clear.

This can be traced in terms of one of those recurrent images

which George Eliot used with minute attentiveness. At the center of
Casaubon's situation is the seed. As an image it is evoked three
times. One is at dinner at Mr. Brooke's house before Dorothea's
engagement. In defense of her not going out to ride, Mr. Casaubon
says with sudden fervor, 'We must keep the germinating grain away
from the light' (chapter 2). The association of darkness and seed is
here fixed, with the residual implication that Mr. Casaubon's grain
may not be of the germinating kind. Then in chapter 48 his Key to
all Mythologies is unexpectedly rephrased as 'the seed of all tradition'. His inability to construct a key, or make a seed, might seem
beyond his control. But his blameableness is established in a passage
in chapter 42, to which Barbara Hardy has called attention in
The Appropriate Form (1964). Mr. Casaubon's difficulties are here
explicitly voluntary, not involuntary; as Dorothea is about to take
his arm, he keeps it rigid;

> There was something horrible to Dorothea in the sensation which
> this unresponsive hardness inflicted on her. That is a strong word
> but not too strong. It is in these acts called trivialities that the seeds
> of joy are for ever wasted, until men and women look round with
> haggard faces at the devastation their own waste has made, and
> say, the earth bears no harvest of sweetness – calling their denial
> knowledge.

Mr. Casaubon chooses self-isolation like choosing self-abuse. The
image of Onan is invoked to symbolize his spirit, which in turn is
reflected in his physical denial.

This passage, while bold, is not quite unique in George Eliot's
writings; it has one counterpart, a personal statement, in a letter she
wrote in late adolescence (16 March 1839) to her old teacher Miss
Lewis. The letter is startling because in it the future novelist repudi-
ates novels, on the grounds of their effect upon her fantasy life. In
this burst of candor she declares:

> ... I venture to believe that the same causes which exist in my
> own breast to render novels and romances pernicious have their
> counterpart in that of every fellow-creature.
>
> I am I confess not an impartial member of a jury in this case for
> I owe the culprits a grudge for injuries inflicted on myself. I shall
> carry to my grave the mental diseases with which they have con-
> taminated me. When I was quite a little child I could not be satisfied
> with the things around me; I was constantly living in a world of my
> own creation, and was quite contented to have no companions that
> I might be left to my own musings and imagine scenes in which I

was chief actress. Conceive what a character novels would give to these Utopias.

Not absence of feeling, but deflection of it, appears to be the charge she is leveling against herself. Gordon Haight in his biography advises against taking these statements seriously, although in his 1954–6 edition of the *Letters* he notes that J. W. Cross, in *George Eliot's Life* (1885), omitted the sentence that contains 'contaminated', 'diseases', and 'to my grave'. Evidently Cross took them seriously. To use these weighty words lightly is not in character for George Eliot. If they have any serious meaning at all, then she is declaring that she has been contaminated by novels which have aroused in her erotic fantasies, as opposed to the merely megalomaniac ones of childhood. In *Felix Holt* Mrs. Transome reads French novels and so takes a lover. But George Eliot in adolescence found no such requital. In so far as Casaubon was an expression of her own 'almost morbid accesses of self-reproach' – made vivid by her early evangelicalism – it would seem that his sexual inadequacy was a version of her struggles with adolescent sexuality, and that these struggles stirred in her sensation which remained painful even in memory. The images of darkness which make up Casaubon's mental landscape would then be wincing recollections of 'the mental diseases' which she had predicted she would 'carry to my grave'. Casaubon's sexual insufficiency was an emblem for fruitless fantasies, of which she too fell victim. It was probably in this sense that he drew his strength and intensity from her nature.

The severity with which Casaubon is treated, aside from occasional remissions, would then derive from her need to exorcise this part of her experience. For a woman who prided herself on her plenitude of heart, these early short-circuits of sensual emotion were painful to think on. No wonder that she makes Casaubon die of fatty degeneration of the heart. He is the repository of her inferior qualities, as Dorothea of her superior ones. She instilled her callow misimaginings, suitably shifted in clef, into old Casaubon, and her ripe affirmations into young Dorothea.

The place of Dorothea's second husband, Will Ladislaw, in this drama of George Eliot's mind is not immediately apparent. To a considerable extent Will had to be made congruent with Dorothea, even to the point of sharing or paralleling her traits. Like her, he has a somewhat undirected aspiration to achieve good and useful works, and he has a slight maliciousness to balance her mild vanity. In some ways he too radiates out from George Eliot, even in his person. His rippled nose and strong jaw are an idealization of his creator's features, and are allowed to make him handsome though she felt they made her ugly. In his indictment of Casaubon's mythological researches, he follows closely, as has been noted, George Eliot's review of Mackay and particularly of her strictures on Mackay's predecessors:

> The introduction of a truly philosophic spirit into the study of mythology – an introduction for which we are chiefly indebted to the Germans – is a great step in advance of the superficial Lucian-like tone of ridicule adopted by many authors of the eighteenth century, or the orthodox prepossessions of writers such as Bryant, who saw in the Greek legends simply misrepresentations of the authentic history given in the book of Genesis.

Ladislaw says to Dorothea, 'Do you not see that it is no use now to be crawling a little way after men of the last century – men like Bryant – and correcting their mistakes? – living in a lumber-room and furbishing up broken-legged theories about Chus and Mizraim?' Yet if she modeled Ladislaw a little upon herself, she needed and found another model as well. The choice troubled her. She said that the ending of her novel might disappoint, and perhaps the main reason was that, aside from marrying Ladislaw to Dorothea (like Blake fusing Los with Enitharmon), she could not make him inevitable in the Middlemarch terrain.

Prototype hunters have left Ladislaw alone, on the assumption that George Eliot was too happily fixed in her life with Lewes to have anyone else in mind. Her commitment to Lewes was as much beyond suspicion as it was outside law. If she could not take his last name legally, she took both his last and first names extra-legally. When Harriet Beecher Stowe asked if the Casaubon marriage bore any resemblance to her own, George Eliot replied, 'Impossible to conceive any creature less like Mr. Casaubon than my warm, enthusiastic husband, who cares much more for my doing than for his own, and is a miracle of freedom from all author's jealousy and all suspicion. I fear that the Casaubon-tints are not quite foreign to my own mental complexion. At any rate I am very sorry for him.' (She echoes here her comment as author in *Middlemarch* [chapter 29], 'For my part I am very sorry for him.') Lewes was in fact one of the more engaging minds of his time, willing to tackle scientific, philosophical and literary subjects, and with a gift of sympathy which George Eliot found indispensable to her existence as well as to her writing. If Thomas and Jane Carlyle could not refrain from calling him 'the ape', or Douglas Jerrold from calling him 'the ugliest man in

London', he was not the less likeable; and George Eliot was more indulgent of his ugliness than of her own. He himself sometimes joked about playing Casaubon to his wife's Dorothea, but he had more in common with Ladislaw. He too spent some time as a young man in Germany and knew the language fairly well. He did not have 'a Jew pawnbroker' for his grandfather, an imputation made about Ladislaw, but he had Jewish associations and several times played Shylock on the stage. He had a versatility that smacked of dilettantism, so that he dissected dragonflies one moment and Comtism the next. But like Ladislaw, his variety did not prevent intensity. 'Our sense of duty', says George Eliot in chapter 46, 'must often wait for some work which shall take the place of dilettantism ...'

George Eliot was jealous of her husband as well as notably fond of him. Mrs. Linton quotes her as saying, 'I should not think of allowing George to stay away a night from me.' Yet sporadic deflections of erotic feeling are not inconsistent with marital content or vigilance. In her case a superabundance of amorous sentiment, beyond any immediate object, is suggested by the effusively affectionate correspondence she lavished upon women friends even though, as she had to make clear to Edith Simcox, it was men who interested her. The search for Casaubon begins with others and ends with George Eliot; the search for Ladislaw spreads out from her to her husband and beyond. In this character her critical powers, which enabled her to recognize limitations in Dorothea as in heroes outside of fiction such as Luther and Bunyan, are largely suspended. He occupies a special position in her work, because he is the first character of either sex in her novels to be irresistibly handsome and at the same time good. Early reviewers remarked upon him as constituting a new departure in George Eliot's novels. In *Adam Bede* Hetty is beautiful, but is punished for being so; she is not so good as she looks. The same is true of Tito in *Romola*. Only Ladislaw is treated with utter indulgence, even to being encouraged to toss back his curls on numerous occasions, as if George Eliot feared she had not made him fetching enough. It seems possible that she had herself been suddenly captivated by the image of a handsome young man.

The first important meeting of Dorothea and Ladislaw takes place in Rome, and since George Eliot had been to Rome just three and a half months before she began *Middlemarch*, her sojourn may be scrutinized a little. This was the second visit that she and Lewes had paid to that city, and it did not work out as well as the first. On the way there he had suffered from sciatica, and once arrived he was not in the mood to enjoy Rome. He wrote in his journal, 'I have had enough of it and want to be at home and at work again.' Mr.

Casaubon had similar thoughts. But George Eliot did not share her husband's impatience. 'Here we had many days of unbroken sunshine ...' was her summary. It was now she had the meeting which was to prove so momentous in her life, with John Walter Cross, then twenty-nine.

This meeting had long been in prospect. She had met Cross's mother two years before, thanks to Herbert Spencer, who boasted in later life that he had brought George Eliot into touch with both her husbands. At that time Mrs. Cross's other children were in England, but John was in the United States, carrying on the American side of the family's banking business. He must have been a frequent topic of discussion between the Crosses and Leweses.

On an April day in 1869 George Eliot was walking with Lewes in her beloved Pamfili Doria gardens, when she met by accident Mrs. Cross's oldest daughter and her husband, who like the Casaubons took their wedding trip to Rome. Further meetings were arranged, and when, some days later, Mrs. Cross, her son John, and another daughter arrived, they were invited on 18 April to visit the Leweses in their rooms at the Hotel Minerva – the same hotel they had stayed at on their first Roman visit in 1860. John Walter Cross shared the veneration of all members of his family for George Eliot's writings, and must have testified to that. Thanks to him, one bit of the ensuing conversation has survived: 'And I remember, many years ago, at the time of our first acquaintance, how deeply it pained her when, in reply to a direct question, I was obliged to admit that, with all my admiration for her books, I found them, on the whole, profoundly sad.' Her pain carried over into *Middlemarch*. This conversation is closely paralleled in chapter 22 when Ladislaw admonishes Dorothea, 'Would you turn all the youth of the world into a tragic chorus, wailing and moralising over misery?' She replies, as George Eliot must have replied to Cross, 'I am not a sad, melancholy creature', but he is not so easily put down, and eight chapters later has written her a letter which 'was a lively continuation of his remonstrance with her fanatical sympathy and her want of sturdy neutral delight in things as they were – an outpouring of his young vivacity....'

Cross, nothing if not vivacious, had just returned from the United States, and must have been asked about his travels there. His work had been in New York, where he had invested heavily in the railroads, but, as a magazine article he wrote later confirms, he had also been to California. Something of what he said must have put George Eliot in mind of the penultimate project which she attributes to Ladislaw (before his ultimate one of marrying Dorothea), that of promoting a settlement in the 'Far West'. Cross was in fact excited about what he repeatedly called in print the 'New World'; he praised it because it 'rests on the basis of industrialism as opposed to militarism'. He thought his fellow countrymen wrong to criticize it, and wrote later, in his book with the ragbag title, *Impressions of Dante and of the New World with a Few Words on Bimetallism* (1893), 'One thing is certain, namely, that since all gain of *real* wealth in America *must* be of advantage to England it will surely be the first sign of impending decadence if the business men of this country, instead of putting their shoulders to the wheel to carry their chariot over all obstruction, content themselves with cherishing a vindictive feeling to rivals. . . .' This kind of imagery, natural to Cross, is twitted a little in Ladislaw's projected painting of 'Tamburlaine Driving the Conquered Kings in His Chariot', intended as he says to symbolize 'the tremendous course of the world's physical history lashing on the harnessed dynasties', and to include 'migrations of races and clearings of forests – and America and the steam engine'. Cross's westward travels, the steam engine which drove the trains that carried him, the extension of the railroads to the furthest points of the New World (as he remarked in an article devoted to them), the sympathy for American energy, all found a way into George Eliot's book.

He must have delighted her. The contrast of Ladislaw's youth and Casaubon's age, of the passionate unscholarliness of the first and the uneasy ferreting of the second, would then be an idealized registration of the effect on George Eliot of her meeting with Cross. By implication it promised Dorothea in fiction something better than widow's weeds and good works after Casaubon's death, and so brought the whole of *Middlemarch* into focus. It can only have been a secret tribute to Cross, and one he would have appreciated, that among the misty details of Ladislaw's upbringing one fact stands out clear and is mentioned twice – he went to Rugby. So did Cross.

Momentarily even the beloved Lewes must have appeared to disadvantage beside this taller, handsomer, sharper-sighted, younger banker. Cross was to prove his devotion steadily from this time on, and to be rewarded for it by having conferred upon him the title of 'nephew'. In *Middlemarch* Ladislaw, though actually Casaubon's second cousin, is often taken for his nephew. Cross was regularly and affectionately spoken of as Nephew Johnny, and in the letter George Eliot wrote to him after Lewes's death, in which she asked him to call, she addressed him as 'Dearest N.' Not that she considered for a moment infidelity to her husband; for every reason she was bound to him for life. But she was not averse to making renunciation of another cherished object a part of her bond to Lewes. As she remarks of Mary Garth's loyalty to Fred in *Middlemarch*, 'we can set a watch on our affections and our constancy as we can other treasures.' Certainly as a solution to her problems of ending *Middlemarch*, John Walter Cross had much to offer. She banked this banker in her fictional account.

The friendship of the Leweses with Cross grew deeper over the years. After Lewes's death George Eliot would not receive Cross for a time, but indicated she would do so eventually, perhaps before she received anyone else. And so it was. On the day he was asked to call, her old friend Herbert Spencer was turned away. Since Cross's mother and one of his sisters had died soon after Lewes, he and George Eliot could share each other's grief. As consolation in the next months, they read Dante's *Inferno* and *Purgatorio* together. There was no need to read the *Paradiso*, for the parallel with Beatrice required no enforcement. Cross felt Dantean about George Eliot; she was 'my ideal', 'the best', and to marry her was his 'high calling'. George Eliot did not reprove this exalted feeling; in a letter to Mrs. Burne-Jones of 5 May 1880, she wrote: 'he sees his only longed-for happiness in dedicating his life to me.'

Ladislaw objects to Casaubon's ignorance of the Germans on comparative mythology, but George Eliot is at pains to indicate that he himself has little more than vague acquaintance with these arcane books. No erudition is allowed Ladislaw, only a general interest in art, poetry and politics. His reformist political views are close to those of Cross, who in *Impressions of Dante* . . . espoused a non-revolutionary amelioration of inequity as a liberal goal. A strong hint of George Eliot's sense of Cross as a Ladislaw figure comes in a patronizing (if also matronizing) letter she wrote him on 16 October 1879: 'Best loved and loving one . . . Thou dost not know anything of verbs in Hiphil and Hophal or the history of metaphysics or the position of Kepler in science, but thou knowest best things of another sort, such as belong to the manly heart – secrets of lovingness and rectitude. O I am flattering. Consider what thou wast a little time ago in pantaloons and back hair.' (Back hair was one of Ladislaw's attributes.) By this time Cross was thirty-nine and a settled man in City banking, but he still stood for her as the embodiment of youth, almost of boyhood, with an ignorance that surpassed knowledge. No doubt these feelings had grown in George Eliot over the ten years of their friendship, but the jingled Hebrew of 'Hiphil and Hophal' suggests that from the beginning he had stood as the polar opposite of 'Cush and Mizraim'. He was also the opposite of her husband, and of most of her old friends, in knowing nothing – as she indelicately underlines – of works in ancient languages, in metaphysics, or in science. Marrying Dorothea to Ladislaw had been George Eliot's only adulterous act. Artistically it proved to be a sin. Marrying Cross as Lewes's widow legalized the fantasy. In the same way her own reconciliation with her brother Isaac validated the reconciliation of brother and sister which she had fictionally imagined, in *The Mill on the Floss*.

Now, when they married, there was a strange reversal of roles, with a sixty-year-old Dorothea marrying a forty-one-year-old Ladislaw, a disparity almost as great as that between Casaubon and his bride. Cross's own sentiments could only have been intricate, since he was her nephew, son, pupil and reader, as well as husband. The sense of being a once independently orbited fragment drawn back now into the parent body must have been immensely disturbing. Perhaps more than sexual awkwardness or disparity of age or health was involved in Cross's pitching himself into the Grand Canal at Venice during their wedding trip. It was a solution which George Eliot had never allowed Dorothea to contemplate. Fished out, and restored to the same bedroom, he gave no further trouble.

A final witness is Eliza Lynn Linton. She had known George Eliot as a young provincial, holding her hands and arms like a kangaroo. She had been invited to call just after the decision to live with Lewes, and she met her later on too. Mrs. Linton was jealous of George Eliot's literary pre-eminence, but she acknowledged it. She also wrote a long essay on George Eliot's works, and had this to say about the second marriage of Dorothea in *Middlemarch*:

> And to think that to her first mistake she adds that second of marrying Will Ladislaw – the utter snob that he is! Where were George Eliot's perceptions? Or was it that in Ladislaw she had a model near at hand, whom she saw through coloured glasses, which also shed their rosy light on her reproduction, as that his copy was to her as idealized as the original, and she as ignorant of the effect produced on the clear-sighted?

In *My Literary Life* Mrs. Linton makes clear that she entirely disapproved of the marriage to Cross, as reducing the first marriage to a house of cards, and it is clearly Cross she has here in mind. She is unkind, but she does suggest the fictional complications for George Eliot of modeling Ladislaw on Cross, a man distinguished more for youthful ardor and amorphousness than anything else. (His skill in investment was hard to idealize.) But George Eliot chose well in making him her husband, for he was impeccably discreet in his *Life* of her, and during the more than forty years that he outlived her.

Cross did not allow his photograph to be taken, and in general he effaced himself. But he was not devoid of ambition, and he published two books. His Dante essays in the 1893 *Impressions* ... provide a contrast to the worldly report on American railroads, and indicate that like Ladislaw he loved poetry. The preface perhaps gives a sense of his good-hearted and unassuming but garrulous temperament:

'Don't shoot the organist; he's doing his level best.' This ancient American story of a notice prominently affixed in a church in the Wild West, as a gentle appeal to the congregation, expresses the mildly deprecatory attitude that I desire to assume to my readers – if I have any – or rather the attitude that I hope they will assume to me. 'Don't shoot the essayist; he's doing his level best.' I confess that it is difficult to find a naked excuse for republishing old magazine articles, and in my own case I cannot plead that any host of admiring friends has put pressure on me to collect mine. I take it that the real reason for the republication is always the same – a desire on the part of the writer to leave some print of his footsteps, however shallow, on the sands of time.

This is johnnycrossism, abashed yet candid, the reverse of Casaubon's closed room which no key could unlock. After a lifetime with intellectuals, George Eliot chose a simpler love for herself as she had had Dorothea do after Casaubon's death. The Key to all Mythologies was not so hard to find. Her decision may have been sentimental, but it established the verisimilitude of Dorothea's act.

The two husbands of Dorothea have different functions in *Middlemarch*. The one is all labyrinth and darkness, the other all candor and light. George Eliot was dissatisfied with the book's ending, but she committed herself to Ladislaw in a way hard for most readers to follow. Part of the reason lies in the very different histories of the characters in her internal dialectic. To berate Casaubon, and to bury him, was to overcome in transformed state the narcissistic sensuality of her adolescence. Old feelings of self-reproach could be renewed, and the character, once stirred by this motive power, could be furnished out with details adroitly selected from people she had known either personally or through their writings. The result was a triumph, a new creature. In Ladislaw, a fantasy of middle age, indulged because innocuous, the character is deprived of her usual controls. She allows herself to idealize him, his only imperfection being what is also his chief perfection – youth. He remains a surrogate sun, lacking in energy and heat, no fiction but a figment executed in pastel colours. She had had much time to reflect on the implications of

Casaubon; but, if these speculations are valid, the new image of Ladislaw took her unawares, as a result of the luxuriantly fantasied encounter in Rome with her young admirer and future husband.

1973

Henry James Among the Aesthetes

FEW novelists can have been so reticent as Henry James. Although his letters to a young sculptor give evidence of an inclination towards men, we cannot be sure that he had a sexual life in any customary meaning of that term. Most writers define their characters largely by indiscretions; James appears to define his by discretions. Among writers of the second half of the nineteenth century, such as the Pre-Raphaelites and their successors in England, or the realistic novelists and decadent poets of France, James stands almost alone in being free of scandal. Discretion marked not only his personal life, but his literary confidences as well. His volumes of autobiography, his letters, and his prefaces intimate, without revealing, the mainsprings of his art. Here I will pursue what I suspect to be one of those impulses.

In 1873 Henry James, having turned the poetic year of thirty, decided to do something he had not done before. Up to then he had been, to borrow his own nautical metaphor, 'bumping about, to acquire skill, in the shallow waters and sandy coves of the "short story",' but now he set out to write his first novel. The months during which this book, *Roderick Hudson*, was gathering in his mind are therefore of singular interest. James was quite ready to confide that the 'germ' of a narrative came to him from a Mrs. Anstruther-Thompson at a dinner party, but he was not forthcoming about his bookish impulsions to write. For these the slightest hint may be of use. Such a hint comes in a letter to William James that Henry wrote on 31 May 1873. He was living in Florence, and that day happened to see in a bookseller's window a copy of Walter Pater's new book, *Studies in the History of the Renaissance*. For a moment James was 'inflamed', as he wrote to his brother, to buy it and to compose a notice of it. But he then recognized, he said, that it treated of several things he knew nothing about, and gave up the idea. In any case, he made clear, he was planning to write something quite different.

This letter answered one of William James's, received the same day, in which William pointed out a little reproachfully that by living in Florence Henry was missing out on chances to review such books as Pater's new one on the Renaissance, which their sister Alice had already read and found 'exquisite'. Henry James's answer gives the impression that he never looked at the book, except in the window. But he must have gone inside the shop, and thumbed it, for otherwise he could not have known that some of its contents were on unfamiliar subjects. Since there is evidence that he acquired the book then or soon afterwards, and even reviewed it (though the review was never published and is lost), his silence suggests a writer's *secret d'état*, a discretion adopted to avoid confessing the powerful jolt that the book had given him. I suggest that it played a great part in the composition of *Roderick Hudson*, and that it launched Henry James on what was to be one of his great themes.'

How do we know that he read it? In the 'Florentine Notes' which he sent to a New York weekly, the *Independent*, over several months of 1874 – the very time when he was writing *Roderick Hudson* – he specifically refers to a chapter of Pater's book, that on Botticelli. James speaks of 'an ingenious critic (Mr Pater, in his "Studies in the History of the Renaissance")', which is a reserved compliment, and then says he has written about Botticelli 'more eloquently than coherently'. How back-handed this is we can tell from James's first revision of the passage: instead of Pater's having written 'more eloquently than coherently', he now has written 'more eloquently than conclusively'. In the earliest version James cited Pater's interpretation as 'too fantastic', but by the time he wrote the third and final version, he allowed that this 'fastidious' critic had 'lately paid him [Botticelli] the tribute of an exquisite, a supreme curiosity', and that 'Mr Pater had said all.' The first version is closer to what James wrote to Edmund Gosse after Pater's death in 1894, when he described him as 'faint, pale, embarrassed, exquisite Pater', and as 'a phosphorescence, not a flame'. 'Exquisite', like 'fastidious', is a word that cuts both ways. And when James wrote to his brother that he was momentarily 'inflamed' to read Pater, just as when he called him 'a phosphorescence rather than a flame', he was slighting the most famous line in Pater's book, 'To burn with this hard gemlike flame is success in life.'

James declined to burn this way. There was no doctrine which could have roused in him more revulsion than this one. For reasons which as I have said remain obscure, he appears to have transposed his passions into his characters' lives, and not expressed them in his own. Perhaps, like Paul Overt in 'The Lesson of the Master', it could be said of James that 'nature had dedicated him to intellectual, not to personal passion': on the other hand, Paul Overt in that story feels he may have been hoodwinked into detachment when he wanted immersion. Whatever the cause, James – as measured by Pater – did not achieve success in life. His interior fires were diverted to the lives of his fictional characters. Yet, given his homosexual propensity, he could not fail to observe how Pater's book covertly celebrated such a propensity by dwelling on Leonardo, Michelangelo and Winckelmann. I think that James took alarm, that he heard the incriminating footfalls, that he wished to inscribe himself as neither aesthetic nor homosexual. At the same time, he knew and wanted to portray homosexuals. He could do this by representing them negatively under the guise of aesthetes. Proust would do the same. Pater's manifest relish of men who loved men may also have prompted James to the counter-emphasis in his art criticism of this time on *manliness*, which in context means anything but homosexual love.

Yet his reaction to Pater did not stop in alarm. We must try to see with what eyes he read the celebrated 'Conclusion' of the *Renaissance*. This was the chapter that Pater timidly withdrew in the second edition, then reinstated with cautious qualifiers in the third. It had originally been the concluding pages of an article on 'Aesthetic Poetry' in the *Westminster Review* of 1868. The 'Conclusion' is a kind of manual of seduction of young men, somewhat masked as a manual of instruction for 'aesthetic critics'. James was not easily instructed or seduced. To say that Pater had written more eloquently than coherently about Botticelli was to say that there was more manner than matter – an indictment to be made against aesthetes and aestheticism generally in *The Portrait of a Lady* as 'altogether a thing of forms'. As he wrote in his 'Florentine Notes', 'There are moods in which one feels the impulse to enter a tacit protest against too generous a patronage of pure aesthetics in this starving and sinning world.' (James was himself more interested in sin than starvation.) Although he allows there for 'the heroics of dilettantism', heroics are not heroism.

What Pater urged was an agitated density of taste and savor, both of art and life. Learnedly citing Heraclitus (although Herrick would have served as well), Pater insisted upon the transitoriness of all things, and particularly upon their 'drift' – a word which he celebrated more than he lamented. All things flow like water – a favorite image – or (to take an internal metaphor) like the pulse. Amid this flow, we can only find recourse in the search for passions, impressions, sensations, pulsations, moments – all words which for Pater are doubly charged. 'A counted number of pulses only is given us of a variegated, dramatic life.' We seek 'not the fruit of experience, but experience itself'. With that rhythmical prolongation that characterizes his style, Pater says, 'While all melts under our feet, we may well catch at any exquisite passion, or any contribution to knowledge that seems, by a lifted horizon, to set the spirit free for a moment, or any stirring of the senses, strange dyes, strange flowers, and curious odours, or the face of one's friend ... High passions give one this quickened sense of life, ecstasy and sorrow of love, political or religious enthusiasms, or the "enthusiasm of humanity." ... Only be sure it is passion,' he adds in admonitory afterthought. This famous pronouncement not only offered the aesthetic movement a purpose – it also offered a vocabulary.

Pater's phrases were like caresses, and James shied away from them. His favorite characters are anything but will-o'-wisps in the stream. Solidly contextualizing their passions requires courtships almost endless, engagements prolonged into years, discoveries infinitely delayed. Deferral was for James what instant satisfaction was for Pater. James's most direct comment on the 'Conclusion' comes in his art criticism, where against the Impressionists he insists (in 'The Grosvenor Gallery') that 'A picture is not an impression but an expression'. It was as if he were anticipating a remark that Yeats makes in *Dramatis Personae*, 'The ideal of culture expressed by Pater can only produce feminine souls – the soul becomes a mirror not a brazier.' James also criticizes, in various essays, those narcissistic whims to which Pater gives the more honorific name of passions.

In his preface to *Roderick Hudson*, written for the New York Edition, James avoids any mention of Pater; instead he speaks of how Balzac might have written the opening scenes in Northampton, Massachusetts. Yet these, as he indicates, were peripheral. Though he does not say so, we have only to read beyond them to recognize that the central theme of the novel is a counterstatement to Pater. The plot might almost be an exemplum: Roderick Hudson, a promising young American sculptor, is given three years in Europe by an art patron named Rowland Mallet. The gift is carefully made innocent because both men are represented as in love with the same woman. Its purpose is to enable him to broaden and perfect his art. Roderick Hudson has scarcely arrived in Rome when he begins to speak, not like the Romans, but like Pater. There is a momentous conversation between him and Mallet. In the middle of it, after a long dramatic pause, the Pater patter begins. Hudson asks, 'What becomes of all our emotions, our impressions? ... There are twenty moments a week ... that seem supreme, twenty impressions that seem ultimate ... But others come treading on their heels, and sweeping them along, and they all melt like water into water ...' Here are Pater's moments, impressions, flowings, meltings, and his water images. Rowland Mallet stares askance at his friend Hudson, and thinks: 'His appetite for novelty was insatiable, and for everything characteristically foreign as it presented itself, he had an extravagant feeling; but in half an hour the novelty had faded, he had guessed the secret, he had plucked out the heart of the mystery and was clamouring for a keener sensation...' 'Foreign' is in the context a word like Pater's favorite, 'strange'. Roderick Hudson declares, 'we must live as our pulses are timed', echoing Pater's phrase about our being given 'a counted number of pulses only ... of a variegated, dramatic life'. No wonder then that Roderick's first fortnight in Rome is registered by his friend as 'a high aesthetic revel'. He has fallen into the unheroics of dilettantism.

Unfortunately, the revel soon turns out to be a drift, and the word 'drift', which is picturesque and approved in Pater, is not so in James. Rowland Mallet tells Roderick, 'You have faltered and drifted, you have gone on from accident to accident, and I am sure that at this present moment you can't tell what it is you really desire!' Though James cannot have read Kierkegaard, he was here making the same criticism of aesthetic man that Kierkegaard had made in the 1830s in *Either/Or*. Pater had praised Michelangelo's Adam for its incompleteness; Rowland says with pity, rather, that 'The poor fellow [Roderick] is incomplete.' The 'unlimited experimentation' in which Roderick indulges is only a 'pernicious illusion'. 'Ultimately he doesn't care for anything.' The drift becomes more than a drift, a fall. Roderick falls symbolically, as well as actually, from a Swiss Alp. His collapse is hastened by his pursuit of a new sensation in the shape of Christina Light. Christina, destined to become the Princess Casamassima, is an appropriate object for him, since she has the moral ambiguity that Pater finds in Mona Lisa; in an echo of Pater's furtive admiration for the 'daughters of Herodias', Christina Light is said to 'make a magnificent Herodias'. James felt later that he had stacked the cards too decisively against Roderick, so that the young man collapses too quickly. It was perhaps the result of James's indignation with Pater's formulas. In Roderick he had now created a new character, the aesthete *gloriosus*, who would be the target of his satire, parody and moral reproach. Not that Roderick is drawn entirely without sympathy: he is given an eloquent death among the Alpine crags.

Roderick Hudson was the first stage in an elaborate Napoleonic maneuver that James waged for thirty years. Four years later he wrote, in 1878, a short story, 'A Bundle of Letters'. In this an aesthetic character remarks, 'And what is life but an art? Pater has said that so well, somewhere.' I'm not sure that Pater had said quite this by that time, though he had certainly implied it. In *The Portrait of a*

Lady (1881), James evolves a character who does say it. Gilbert Osmond reminds Isabel Archer, 'Don't you remember my telling you that one ought to make one's life a work of art? You looked rather shocked at first...' He has actually not told her this before in the novel, but his reminder that he is repeating himself indicates that it is his fixed view. For answer, 'Isabel looked up from her book. "What you despise most in the world is bad, is stupid art."' Osmond is saturated with the Paterian heresy. He says of himself, 'I was simply the most fastidious young gentleman living.' He is certainly fastidious – he has tastes, he has sensations; what he lacks is sympathies, and feelings for women. He is all pose, all form without substance, 'a faded rosebud', as Ralph Touchett calls him, and so 'a sterile dilettante'. Pater in his 'Conclusion' had said that the individual is isolated, 'each mind keeping as a solitary prisoner its own dream of a world'. It seems consonant with this metaphor that Osmond should make his house a prison for his wife, and that he should sequester his daughter in the prison of a nunnery. Osmond as artist of life, and Hudson as artist, are trapped in their own selfhood. Osmond's mistress Mme Merle belongs with them, for she treats the 'art of life' as 'some clever trick she had guessed'. By antithesis James pleads for less art, more heart.

When James encountered Pater's book, he recoiled at once. Others responded to Pater with much less dissonance. Oscar Wilde read *Studies in the History of the Renaissance* a little later than James; he was only twenty-one and eager to attach himself to a glamorous doctrine. For him it was always his 'golden book' and 'the book that has had such a strange effect upon my life'. At Trinity College, Dublin, the aesthetic movement was already entrenched. Among the subjects debated at the Philosophical Society in Trinity was one, 'Aesthetic Morality and Its Influence on Our Age', to which Oscar's brother Willie spoke at length. There were also lectures on Ruskin; there was an 'Aesthetic Medal Course'; and privately Wilde was in correspondence with John Addington Symonds, who would play his part as aesthete in Henry James's story, 'The Author of "Beltraffio"'. At Oxford, after he had read Pater, Wilde became a missionary for Paterism. In 1877, for example, he writes a letter to a classmate exhorting him to 'let every part of your nature have play and room'. Unsure in which direction he should point his life, he thought that Pater gave authority to this whirling compass.

Like Christina Light in *Roderick Hudson* he toyed for a time with Catholicism – for him as for her it was 'a new sensation'; and the sonnet which Gilbert Osmond in James's *The Portrait of a Lady* sends to Isabel, with the title 'Rome Revisited', may have been concocted because of the poem Wilde published in 1881 entitled, 'Rome Unvisited'. But it was not only Roman Catholicism which attracted Wilde; he also had simultaneously a new sensation from Freemasonry. And if he responded to Pater's pied piping, he also responded to the moral chiding which he simultaneously received from John Ruskin's lectures and conversation. At moments his own proneness to change distressed him: he wrote to a friend, 'I need not say, though, that I shift with every breath of thought and am weaker and more self-deceiving than ever.' In this mood he wrote his poem 'Hélas!' in which he represents himself, like Pater and Roderick Hudson, as adrift:

> To drift with every passion till my soul
> Is a stringed lute on which all winds can play...

But in another mood, in 1886, he defended himself: 'I would go to the stake for a sensation and be a sceptic to the last! Only one thing remains infinitely fascinating to me, the mystery of moods. To be master of these moods is exquisite, to be mastered by them more exquisite still. Sometimes I think that the artistic life is a long and lovely suicide, and am not sorry that it is so.' To some extent Wilde sought to enact the man of many parts – connoisseur of art as of life – whom Pater's *Renaissance* had characterized trait by trait.

It was inevitable that Wilde, in his early days loyal to the 'Conclusion' of Pater's book, should be in a different corner from James. They may well have met on 30 April 1877, at the opening of the Grosvenor Gallery in New Bond Street, which both attended. We don't know how James was attired, but we do know that Oscar Wilde wore a coat that had the shape and color of a cello because a dream of such a coat had come to him. The new gallery was particularly well disposed towards the Pre-Raphaelites, and both writers, in separate notices for different journals, praised Burne-Jones, though Henry James feared he detected a want of manliness in him. By chance both men described the first important painting in the show, one by G. F. Watts entitled *Love and Death*. James writes gracefully and to the point:

> On a large canvas a white draped figure, with its back to the spectator, and with a sinister sweep of garment and gesture, prepares to pass across a threshold where, beside a rosebush that has shed its flowers, a boy figure of love staggers forth, and, with head and body reverted in entreaty, tries in vain to bar its entrance.

The same elements make Wilde gush; he perceives

a marble doorway, all overgrown with white-starred jasmine and sweet briar-rose. Death, a giant form, veiled in grey draperies, is passing in with inevitable and mysterious power, breaking through all the flowers. One foot is already on the threshold, and one relentless hand is extended, while Love, a beautiful boy with lithe brown limbs and rainbow-coloured wings, all shrinking like a crumpled leaf, is trying, with vain hands, to bar the entrance.

Judicious and cautious James finds that the painting 'has a certain graceful impressiveness'; aesthetic and incautious Wilde ranks it with Michelangelo's 'God Dividing the Light from the Darkness'. When they come to the beautiful boy, Wilde is all atremble, James all aslant. In his essay on George Du Maurier in 1888 Henry James blamed the 'excessive enthusiasm' of the aesthetes on their 'lack of real aesthetic discrimination'. James's own discriminations of the time were weighted on the side of morality, like Ruskin's; he was like Ruskin in disapproving strenuously of Whistler, in whom he thought he saw Pater's impressionism at work. But Wilde, though he jested a little about the painting of bursting rockets, recognized Whistler to be a great artist. Twenty years later Henry James came round to this view.

Probably neither James nor Wilde saw each other's review of the Grosvenor Gallery opening, since James's appeared in America and Wilde's in Ireland. But they were to confront each other directly on James's home ground, during Wilde's year-long tour of America in 1882. By this time Wilde, like Pater, was less naïvely sensationalist in his point of view. His aestheticism had had to become more profound because of attacks upon it, by W. H. Mallock in *The New Republic*, by various parodic plays, by Du Maurier's sketches for *Punch*, and by Gilbert and Sullivan's *Patience*. But the absurdities of those who cried absurd were those to which Wilde addressed himself. He was forming what might be called post-aestheticism, or reconsidered aestheticism. He firmly denied in a review that art for art's sake was in any sense a statement of the final cause of art; instead it was 'merely a formula of creation', the condition or state of mind in which the work is actually composed. As for beauty, he continued to celebrate it, but as something to be sought not merely by the artist and his appreciators but by society in general. He would eventually move towards a brand of socialism, a doctrine to which Pater was not at all attracted, but which enabled Wilde to outmoralize the moralists. In extolling 'The English Renaissance' as his lecture topic in America, Wilde had quite emerged from the prison of isolated appreciation of moments that Pater had pictured so longingly. This renaissance, unlike Pater's, was not for connoisseurs but for everyone, involving changes in dress, architecture and home decoration.

Wilde's tour took him to Washington, and it was here, in January 1882, that he and Henry James, who had been in the city for a month, were first thrown together. They had met first at the house of Judge Edward G. Loring, where Wilde appeared in kneebreeches and with a large yellow silk handkerchief. James avoided him. But he was unexpectedly pleased by a newspaper interview that Wilde gave, in which he said that no contemporary English novelist could compare with Howells and James. Such compliments were not so frequent that James would ignore them. He went to Wilde's hotel to thank him. It was not a successful visit. James remarked, 'I am very homesick for London.' Wilde could not resist putting him down. 'Really?' he said, no doubt in his most cultivated Oxford accent. 'You care for *places*? The *world* is my home.' He felt himself to be a citizen of the world. To a writer like James, for whom the international theme was so important, this was offensive. Wilde said also to James, 'I am going to Bosston; there I have a letter to the dearest friend of my dearest friend – Charles Norton from Burne-Jones.' James knew both men well, too well to be pleased to have their names dropped. We must imagine Henry James outraged by Wilde's kneebreeches, contemptuous of his self-advertising and pointless nomadism. He informed Mrs. Henry Adams, who had refused to meet Wilde because she did not like 'noodles', that she was right. ' "Hosscar" Wilde is a fatuous fool, tenth-rate cad, an unclean beast.' The images are so steamy as to suggest that James saw in Wilde a threat which he did not find in Pater. Pater's homosexuality was covert, Wilde's was patent. Pater could be summed up as 'faint, pale, embarrassed, exquisite', but for Wilde James found other epithets embracing his mind, manners, and probable sexual proclivities ('unclean beast'). It was as if Henry James, foreseeing scandal, was eager to put himself on record as totally without regard for Wilde. Mrs. Adams spoke knowingly of Wilde's sex as 'undecided'. James seems so vehement as to suggest that this meeting had made him queasy by stirring up his own equivocation about sexuality.

He returned in 1884 to the aesthetic theme. This was in one of his best stories, 'The Author of "Beltraffio"'. In his preface James declared that he had got the idea of the story from hearing about an English aesthete whose wife disapproved of his writings. This man has been identified as John Addington Symonds. It has been said that James did not learn till later that Symonds was homosexual. There was, however, good reason for not going into that question in the story, for James wanted to mock and anatomize aestheticism without extraneous concerns.

'The Author of "Beltraffio"' carries its critique further than James's earlier writings do. The book Mark Ambient has written, *Beltraffio*, is said to be 'the most complete presentation that had yet been made of the gospel of art; it was a kind of aesthetic warcry'. But just before James wrote the story, exactly such a book had been published, which went far beyond faint, pale, embarrassed, exquisite Pater. This was Huysmans's *A Rebours*. However sardonic its intent – and parts of it are obviously sardonic – it became, the moment it was published in May 1884, the Bible of aestheticism. James's friend Paul Bourget thought it wonderful, Whistler went to congratulate the author the day after publication, Wilde thought it the best thing he had seen in years. James had a copy of the first edition, but thought it monstrous. That he read it at once seems to be established by the atmosphere he devised for this story, 'The Author of "Beltraffio"', of artifice and disease. Huysmans's hero Des Esseintes, it will be recalled, after trying artificial flowers that look like real ones, decides instead to have real flowers that look artificial; in Mark Ambient's garden, James tells us, 'certain old brown walls were muffled in creepers that appeared to me to have been copied from a masterpiece of one of the pre-Raphaelites'. (Huysmans too refers to the Pre-Raphaelites.) Ambient's house seems to be copied from a prose description of a house in one of Ambient's books. Ambient's sister looks like a copy of a symbolic picture, and his son is 'like some perfect little work of art'. Only Mrs. Ambient objects to being aestheticized: 'I don't in the least consider that I'm living in one of his books at all.' The illness from which Ambient's aestheticized son suffers brings death into this scene where no one is quite alive. In Huysmans a tortoise, encrusted with jewels, dies of artifice, and at the end Des Esseintes is obliged to give artifice up if he is to survive. James has evolved a quite different story, and yet it seems clear that he has profited from *A Rebours* here as he did from Pater's *Renaissance* in *Roderick Hudson*.

During the next four years, from 1884 to 1888, James, Wilde and Pater could scarcely have failed to meet occasionally in the inbred society of London. Certain things happened in this period that might prompt James to reconsider his earlier view of Wilde. One was that Wilde put aside his kneebreeches and married. A possible scandal had been averted. Another was that he began to publish something besides aesthetic poetry – reviews of books first and a book of fairy tales. Very likely Wilde succeeded in charming James, as he charmed so many of his sometime detractors. That this happened is borne out by the fact that when in 1888 Wilde was put up for membership in the Savile Club, Henry James inscribed his name among those who supported him.

For his part, Wilde criticized James's novels in print, but always with respect. There are veiled references in his reviews of the late Eighties to a new school of fiction writing, which 'is not native, nor does it seek to reproduce any English master. It may be described as the result of the realism of Paris filtered through the refining influence of Boston. Analysis, not action, is its aim; it has more psychology than passion, and it plays very cleverly upon one string, and that is the commonplace.' This remark comes from the *Woman's World*, of which Wilde was editor, in 1888. Then in January 1889 he referred to James again, in 'The Decay of Lying'; this time he said that James 'writes novels as if it were a painful duty and wastes upon mean motives and imperceptible "points of view" his neat literary style, his felicitous phrases, his swift and caustic satire.' This may not sound generous, but was as favorable an account as Wilde gave of any contemporary novelist, and James did not show any sign of resenting it. It has been suggested, however, that it may have encouraged him to take up again the character of the aesthete, in *The Tragic Muse* which he wrote the same year.

In this novel Gabriel Nash disdains the title of aesthete, but is one. He is a much more attractive representative of the type than Roderick Hudson or Gilbert Osmond or Mark Ambient. He has no need to fall from a cliff or, being a bachelor, to be beastly to a wife. Still, he has his jargon: for him the only 'duty' in life is to recognize 'our particular form, the instrument that each of us carries in his being' and to play that instrument 'in perfection'. (Both Pater and Wilde use musical metaphors for the soul.) But there is a nomadic quality about Nash which fits Wilde much better than stay-at-home Pater. So when Nick Dormer asks Nash, 'Don't we both live in London, after all, and in the Nineteenth century?' Nash replies, 'Ah, my dear Dormer, excuse me. I don't live in the Nineteenth Century. *Jamais de la vie!*' 'Nor in London either?' 'Yes – when I'm not in Samarcand.' Gabriel is always represented as on his way 'somewhere else'.

Probably James was here recalling his Washington conversation with Wilde, and the latter's insistence that he was a citizen of the world. But instead of dismissing him as cad, fool and beast, James allows Gabriel Nash to be catalytically useful in starting Dormer on a new career as a painter, and acknowledges that Gabriel has good taste. Gabriel's career is as amorphous as at that time Wilde's must have appeared to be. He has written a novel, said to contain good things, but is mostly idle. His reflections are said to be 'more ingenious than opportune'. Although other models for Gabriel Nash have been proposed, and other men were no doubt idle, still no one writing about aestheticism in 1889 could have failed to bear that supreme idler Wilde in mind. Moreover, James specifies that he is 'not English', and since he is clearly not American, the chances are very good that he is Irish. James specifies as well that Nash's manner of speaking shows 'a conspicuous and aggressive perfection', a quality which Yeats and many others remarked in Wilde. Like Wilde, too, Nash remains the center of conversation even when he is absent. James allows his aesthete to defend himself with spirit against two charges that were frequently made against Wilde. The first was that he was a mere *farceur*; so reproached, Gabriel Nash replies, 'One has the manner that one can, and mine moreover's a part of my little system.' The other is that Wilde promulgated aestheticism but provided no workaday example of its achievements (he would provide examples later). On this point Gabriel replies, 'Oh having something to show's such a poor business. It's a kind of confession of failure.' Wilde would tell André Gide about this time, 'I have put all my genius into my life; I have put only my talent into my works.'

The aesthetic theory that Gabriel Nash proffers is a Paterian one, with no sign that he has caught up with Wilde's post-aestheticism. Here are old chestnuts already run through by Roderick Hudson and 'The Author of "Beltraffio" ': 'We must feel everything, everything that we can. We live for this.' Gabriel goes through 'phases', 'shades of impression'. 'My feelings direct me – if such a life as mine may be said to have direction. Where there's anything to feel I try to be there!' The result is that he is a balloon without ballast: 'I rove, drift, float', he declares, joining Pater, Wilde, and the drifters in James's earlier fiction, but without apology or fictional punishment.

James's divergence from Gabriel becomes apparent towards the end of the book. Gabriel is persuaded to sit for his portrait to Nick Dormer, but after one sitting he fails to turn up for the next. No one knows where he has gone. And then a strange thing happens. He fades from the novel altogether, and even from the portrait, where his painted image begins to vanish as if magically from the canvas. What James implies is that Nash, being all unsituated sensation, does not really exist at all. The perceiver of shades without substance fades into impalpability, the citizen of the world is a citizen of nowhere.

It does not seem likely that Wilde would have failed to read *The Tragic Muse*. He kept up with everything, and he read Henry James all his life; *The Ambassadors* was on his last bookseller's bill. In fact, the novel which Wilde wrote in the following months shows some signs of profiting from Henry James's work. Like *The Tragic Muse*, *The Picture of Dorian Gray* has for three of its main characters a painter, an aesthete, and a tragic actress. The portrait of Gabriel Nash is like the portrait of Dorian in its capacity to change emblematically. One of the stage names that Miriam Routh, the tragic muse of James's title, adopts is Gladys Vane; it seems scarcely accidental that Wilde's actress should be called Sibyl Vane. Miriam Routh is Jewish, Sibyl Vane is not, but, as if the ingredient had to be included somehow, Sibyl works for a Jewish manager.

Dorian Gray is often misinterpreted. This book is as critical of aestheticism as James in *The Tragic Muse*. The old adages from Pater are dusted off and brought out again, only to be discredited. Lord Henry Wotton is full of them – his worst fault in the book is not profligacy, of which he is innocent, but plagiarism from early Pater, for which he is fully culpable. What Lord Henry fails to recognize, as Pater himself said in a review of the book (for Pater sober appealed from Pater drunk), was that the life of mere sensation is anarchic and self-destructive. Dorian Gray is his experiment; the experiment fails. Wilde's intention in the novel has been overlooked because the bad characters talk like him, and the good characters like you and me. But the book is his parable of the impossibility of leading a life on aesthetic terms. Dorian cannot isolate himself. Self-indulgence leads him eventually to vandalize his own portrait, but this act proves to be a reversal of what he intends; however unwillingly, he discloses his better self, though only in death. He has pushed through to the point where extremes meet. By suicide Dorian becomes aestheticism's first martyr. The text: Drift beautifully on the surface, and you will die miserably in the depths.

To James, though he made no public comment on *Dorian Gray*, the book can only have seemed another of those loose fictions that people around him insisted upon writing. Wilde made the book elegantly casual, as if writing a novel were a diversion rather than 'a painful duty'. No one could mistake it for a workmanlike job: our hacks can do that for us. The underlying legend, of Faust trying to elicit more than life can give, arouses deep and criminal yearnings; the contrast of these with the polish of English civilization at its verbal peak makes for more tension than the plot appears to hold.

To James's irritation, the early 1890s proved to be the age of Dorian. His old contempt for Wilde reasserted itself. Yet he found himself to be in the position of a rival. This was particularly true because both men took up playwriting at the same time. Wilde did not write aesthetic plays, but James disliked them no less for that. He pronounced *Lady Windermere's Fan* 'infantine ... both in subject and form'. He conceded that it contained 'so much drollery – that is "cheeky" paradoxical wit of dialogue' that it might go. Some epigrams he thought good enough to quote in letters. (He had long before borrowed Wilde's remark in Washington that the city had too many bronze generals.) To a mutual friend of his and Wilde's, Henrietta Reubell in Paris, James wrote that 'the unspeakable one' (he hated to name him) had responded to the curtain calls by appearing 'with a metallic blue [it was green] carnation in his buttonhole and a cigarette in his fingers'. He thought Wilde's remark, 'I have enjoyed myself immensely', quite inadequate, though the audience seems to have been greatly amused by it. '*Ce monsieur* gives at last on one's nerves,' James confided. Not naming Wilde here, as later in his correspondence with Edmund Gosse, may indicate his renewed sense that association with Wilde might prove dangerous.

Wilde's next play, *A Woman of No Importance*, fared no better with Henry James. He thought it '*un enfantillage*', 'a piece of helpless puerility'. Yet he was not altogether uninfluenced by Wilde's example. In the play he now himself wrote, *Guy Domville*, there are occasional speeches that sound remotely Wildean. Guy Domville says, when accused of making his aunt jealous by putting the Church first, 'I don't know what I could that I haven't done, to set such jealousy at rest. There's scarcely a rule I haven't utterly abjured – there's scarcely a trust I haven't rigidly betrayed – there's scarcely a vow I haven't scrupulously broken! What more can a man do for conscience?' The stage history of *Guy Domville* has often been told, but it may be salutary to consider it under the aspect of Wilde. It was James's most important effort as a playwright. When Alexander was to produce it, James felt timid of attending his own first night. He decided to attend Wilde's *An Ideal Husband* at a nearby theatre instead. He expected inadequacy, and found it. It was 'so helpless, so crude, so bad, so clumsy, feeble, and vulgar'. Yet the audience liked it. So much the worse for the audience, then. And yet there was that in *An Ideal Husband* to give him pause. For the theme of renunciation entered into both plays. Guy Domville's is of a basic kind: he is about to renounce the world and enter the Roman Catholic priesthood. At the crucial moment, however, the death of a relative makes him the last of the Domvilles, and he is persuaded to carry on the name and to seek a wife instead. But as events turn out, he gives up on his claim to one prospective bride, and then to another, and returns to his original renunciation of the world. Highmindedness can go no further.

What could particularly annoy Henry James was that in *An Ideal Husband*, Sir Robert Chiltern – the ideal husband of the title – is faced with a comparable decision. He is guilty of having sold a Cabinet secret in his youth, and though the world will never know it, his wife persuades him that he must in all conscience renounce politics. But in the end he is persuaded, as is she, that the renunciation is not necessary. Wilde offers the indulgence of comedy, where James, himself a great renunciant, had offered only sturdiness of purpose. Wilde had tossed off a play that was better than the one James had laboriously wrought. Worst of all Alexander decided to take James's play off the boards, and to put on *The Importance of Being Earnest* instead. Henry James had to suffer the indignity, though only after a decent month's run, of having the arch-aesthete's play take over his theatre.

No doubt this was bitter to him. His biographers tell us that Henry James, after witnessing the audience enthusiasm for Wilde's *An Ideal Husband*, walked over to the theatre where his own play was just ending. George Alexander somewhat maliciously brought James out of the wings for a curtain call. James thought for a moment there was cheering, when it fact there was jeering, and he had to retreat in keen embarrassment. It has been said that this incident plunged James into a 'black abyss'. But we must not underestimate his sense of himself. After all, he was fifty-two, famous, infinitely clever. He had just seen the *ignobile vulgus* praise a play he knew to be bad; why then accept their adverse judgment of one he was convinced was good? His behavior after the performance was stoical: he had promised the cast a dinner, and gave them one. He wrote to his brother of his humiliating experience at the theatre, but added, 'Don't worry about me. I am a Rock.' The next day he gave a luncheon for some friends, and he attended the second performance of *Guy Domville* and saw the play received with respect. The reviews were mixed, but William Archer, Geoffrey Scott, H. G. Wells and Bernard Shaw all praised it. There was comfort in them. Among the friends who spoke reassuringly was Ellen Terry, who asked him to write another play for her. This James agreed to do three days after he supposedly entered the slough of despond.

He had in fact too much self-esteem, too much contempt for the London audience and for the plays it admired, to be in any abyss. We can see something of his spirit in that he did finish the play for Ellen Terry a few months later. It was called *Summersoft* and was about courtship. A bit of the dialogue indicates that James had seen Wilde's *The Importance of Being Earnest*: Cora tells Mrs. Gracedew of her lover, 'He's clever, and he's good, and I know he loves me.'

'Then what is the matter with him?' 'His name.' 'What is it?' 'Buddle.' Mrs. Gracedew ponders and then says, 'Well – Buddle will do.' There is a touch of Bunbury, as well as a reminiscence of the sparring about the name Ernest, in this byplay – though James's point is perhaps different, that Buddle, besides being uneuphonious, is irretrievably middle-class. No matter, such light touches did not make Ellen Terry envisage herself in Cora's part. Henry James went to see Edmund Gosse and his wife, and complained that Ellen Terry had commissioned *Summersoft* and then refused to play it. Mrs. Gosse, to smoothe him down, ventured, 'Perhaps she did not think the part suited to her?' James turned upon them and (as Gosse told it) replied thunderingly, 'Think? *Think?* How should the poor toothless chattering hag THINK?' I cannot believe that a writer in the 'black abyss' would speak with such arrogance.

Whatever resentment James felt – and he did feel some – of Wilde's superior success as a playwright was suddenly rendered meaningless by Wilde's trial. He was appalled at the 'little beasts of witnesses'. 'What a nest of almost infant blackmailers!' he commented. But the letter he wrote to Edmund Gosse shows little sympathy:

> Yes, too, it has been, it is, hideously, atrociously dramatic and really interesting – so far as one can say that of a thing of which the interest is qualified by such a sickening horribility. It is the squalid gratuitousness of it all – of the mere exposure – that blurs the spectacle. But the *fall* – from nearly 20 years of a really unique kind of 'brilliant' conspicuity (wit, 'art', conversation – 'one of our 2 or 3 dramatists etc.') to that sordid prison-cell and this gulf of obscenity over which the ghoulish public hangs and gloats – it is beyond any utterance of irony or any pang of compassion! He was never in the smallest degree interesting to me – but this hideous human history has made him so – in a manner.

This letter was James's way of showing, by not showing, his involvement. Another letter from him, to Paul Bourget, commented that the sentence, when it was handed down, was cruel; instead of the two years of hard labor meted out by the judge, James proposed that solitary confinement would have been more humane. In fact, Wilde suffered both. Only once did James venture that if Wilde should recover after his prison sentence, 'what masterpieces might he yet produce!' But this seems *pro forma* sympathy, as if for the record. James did not relent later: in 1905 he said on a lecture tour in America that Wilde was 'one of those Irish adventurers who had something of the Roman character – able, but false'. His life had been 'abominable' before and after imprisonment, his death James pronounced to be 'miserable'.

With Pater dead since 1894, and Wilde virtually so from his trial a year after that, James returned to the subject of aestheticism. When he came to write *The Spoils of Poynton* in 1897, he perhaps had in mind a lecture Wilde had delivered around England in 1883, 'The House Beautiful'. Originally James intended to call his new novel by that name, a vile phrase that Pater had also used in *Appreciations*. In this novel aestheticism is exemplified by Mrs. Gereth, who feels an acute suffering brought on by the 'aesthetic misery' of Waterbath. James is interested in other issues, possessing and collecting, sacrificing and exploiting, but at least part of the book is directed against the valuing of sensations that arise from good taste over more basic emotions. Connoisseurship is not so much attacked as put in its place, as part of James's continued presentation of the shortcomings of aestheticism when isolated from the rest of life.

Then in *The Ambassadors*, in 1903, Strether arrives from Woolett, Massachusetts, wearing his puritan glasses, but under the vivid impression of Paris puts on aesthetic ones. Then aestheticism fails him as, contemplating a country scene as if it were a painting, he is jarred by the sight of two compromised lovers, neither of them painted. His moral sense now returns in force. Strether had urged Little Bilham to 'Live all you can; it's a mistake not to'. But at the end of the book Strether is obliged to recognize that this aesthetic advice is too partial, that beauty loses its attraction when founded on deceit, that morality cannot be dismissed simply because it is gloomily unaesthetic. For himself, both his aesthetic and his moral sense preclude Strether's staying longer. He is no longer pleased in either way. In these novels there is no villain, and a general compassion seems to be accorded both to aesthetes and to non-aesthetes. James was no longer so vehement.

He came back to aestheticism for the last time in 1904, in his essay on D'Annunzio. Here he speaks in friendly retrospect of how some years before society had been roused 'as from some deep drugged sleep, to the conception of the "aesthetic" law of life ...'. But all its exponents, until D'Annunzio, were inadequate. What aestheticism offered was 'beauty at any price', but James contends that in so doing it promoted taste at any price and sexuality at any price. He found D'Annunzio's work to be characterized by an 'exasperated sensibility'. Its ultimate defect is to see the sexual relation in isolation from the rest of life, when only in the rest of life does it have its 'consummation and extension'. Apart from that it is merely 'zoological'. James holds out the hope that aestheticism will yet find a more convincing advocate, as if Pater and Wilde, Huysmans and D'Annunzio had all written in vain. By this time he had been having an affair, or an approximation of an affair, with the young sculptor Henrik Andersen, to whom he wrote letters full of endearments and references to caresses.

It isn't fanciful to suggest that Henry James probably thought of himself as that more convincing advocate. The year he wrote on D'Annunzio was also the year in which he wrote *The Golden Bowl*. James might well feel that in this novel he was remixing the ingredients of aestheticism to show how they might be more gainfully employed than they had been in the past. The four principal characters in the novel are exquisite in their various ways: their taste buds and other antennae are developed as fully and subtly as a Walter Pater could wish. Their sexual relations are as central as in D'Annunzio, but it is the rearrangement of these by thought that provides the interest. The object of the heroine is, *tout court*, to win back her husband from his affair with her father's wife. This can only be done by the effect of imagination working upon life, transforming its ugliness into beauty, a beauty consistent with morality but not primarily moral in intent. The golden bowl of the title is an emblem of her quest, yet the bowl described in the book is a bowl with a crack in it, which must be smashed to pieces so that a new golden bowl of the mind can be created. The ultimate refinement is directed not towards the accumulation of choice external objects but towards the eliciting of latent personal qualities for the sake of love. The result is beautiful, but it is not beauty merely that is being sought.

So aestheticism did not come to an end. It continued to command a following as a series of writers attempted to redefine it. In its more primitive form it awoke Henry James to write his first novel as a criticism of it. Although he had other subjects he never left this one alone for long. At the end of his writing career he saw more clearly that he had used the movement as a stalking horse because it enabled him to represent people like himself under the guise of disclosing their shortcomings. In *The Golden Bowl*, mellowed and emboldened, James makes the fastidiousness of aestheticism and its insistence upon beauty central to life's concerns rather than opposed or peripheral to them. In other words aesthetes, like homosexuals, may have their place in the scheme of creation.

1983

Two Faces of Edward

VICTORIA stayed too long, Edward arrived too late. By the time the superannuated Prince of Wales became king, it was evident that a change would take place in literature; it took place, but Edward has somehow never received credit for it, and the phrase 'Edwardian literature' is not often heard. We have to fall back on it, though, because there is no neat phrase in English, like 'the Nineties', to describe the first ten years of a century. The word 'Edwardian' has taken its connotations from social rather than literary history. Just what it means is not certain, beyond the high collars and tight trousers which flouted Victorian dowdiness then, and which later became for a time the pedantic signs of juvenile delinquency. Perhaps 'pre-war courtliness' is the closest we can come to the meaning of Edwardian outside literature, sedate Victorianism in better dress. The meaning was present enough to Virginia Woolf for her to declare that 'on or about December 1910', that is, in the year of Edward's death, 'human character changed.' Edward 'the Peacemaker' had to die before the world could become modern, and she pushed the dead Edwardians aside to make room for the lively Georgians. The distinction was more relevant, however, for describing Virginia Woolf's own accession to purposiveness than George's accession to rule.

While the late Victorians seem to have relished the idea that they were the last, the Edwardians at once declined to consider themselves as stragglers, ghostly remains of those Englishmen who had stretched the Empire so far. The Edwardians had, in fact, a good deal of contempt for the previous reign, and an odd admiration for their own doughtiness. In the midst of the general melancholy over Victoria's death, her son said sturdily, 'The King lives.' To Virginia Woolf the hated Edwardian writers were Bennett, Galsworthy, and Wells, yet even these writers labored under the apprehension or misapprehension that they were trying something new. Lascelles Abercrombie, in one of the few essays on Edwardian literature, finds the period to be only the decorous extension of tradition, and in his essay is detectable that faintly patronizing note which occurs also in biographies of Edward that prove the king was a worthy man. So for Abercrombie the writers of this time were engagingly discreet; they drew in literature, as Edward in life, upon an ample wardrobe, and perhaps dared to go so far as to leave unbuttoned the lowest button on their literary waistcoats.

That the Edwardians have been discounted is understandable, I think, because of the prevalence of a sociological assumption. If the birth of modern literature is dated back to the century's first decade, what happens to our conviction that it was the Great War which turned the tables? At any cost we have to confine the beginning of the century to the infancy or adolescence of modern writers, so that only when the guns boomed did they become old enough to discern the nature of the world. The admonitory fact, however, is that most of the writers whom we are accustomed to call modern were already in their twenties or older when King Edward died. In 1910 Eliot was twenty-two, Lawrence and Pound were twenty-five, Joyce and Virginia Woolf were twenty-eight, Forster was thirty-one, Ford Madox Ford thirty-seven, Conrad fifty-three, Shaw fifty-four, Henry James sixty-seven. Bennett, Galsworthy and Wells were in their forties. To dismiss most of the writers I have named as either too young or too old to be Edwardians, as if only men of middle age counted in literary fashion, is one of those historical simplicities like denying that the Twenties were the Twenties because so many people didn't know the Twenties were going on. Neither age nor self-consciousness determines the private character of a period; if anything does, it is the existence of a community between young and old experimental writers. Such a community existed in the Edwardian period. It was a community which extended not only across the Irish Sea but, spottily at least, across the Channel and the Atlantic; so, if I extend Edward's dominions occasionally to countries he did not rule, it is only to recover the imperial word 'Edwardian' from an enforced limitation.

If a moment must be found for human character to have changed, I should suggest that 1900 is both more convenient and more accurate than Virginia Woolf's 1910. In 1900, Yeats said with good-humored exaggeration in his introduction to *The Oxford Book of Modern Verse* (1936), 'everybody got down off his stilts; henceforth nobody drank absinthe with his black coffee; nobody went mad; nobody committed suicide; nobody joined the Catholic Church; or if they did I have forgotten.' That there was pressure upon them to change was something that the writers of this time were distinctly aware of; it is not only Yeats whose attitudes take a new turn; it is also lesser writers. Even John Masefield was once asked how it had happened that his poetry had moved from the nostalgic rhythms of his early work to the more athletic ones of 'The Everlasting Mercy', and he replied simply, 'Everybody changed his style then.' The Edwardians came like Dryden after Sir Thomas Browne, anxious to develop a more wiry speech. Their sentences grew more vigorous and concentrated. I will not claim for the Edwardians' work total novelty – that can never be found in any period, and many of their most individual traits had origin in the Nineties or earlier. But in all that they do they are freshly self-conscious. What can be claimed is that there was a gathering of different talents towards common devices, themes, and attitudes, and King Edward at least did nothing to impede it.

What strikes us at once about Edwardian literature is that it is thoroughly secular, yet so earnest that secularism does not describe it. It is generally assumed that in this period religion was something to ignore and not to practice. Edwardian writers were not in fact religious, but they were not ostentatiously irreligious. In the Victorian period people had fumed and left the churches; in the Edwardian period, becalmed, they published memoirs or novels describing how strongly they had *once* felt about the subject. This is the point of Gosse's *Father and Son* (1907) as well as of Samuel Butler's *The Way of All Flesh* (written earlier, but published in 1903). It was also part of the subject of Joyce's *A Portrait of the Artist as a Young Man,* much of it written in 1907–8, as it is of Yeats's first autobiographical book, *Reveries over Childhood and Youth,* written just before the war. In all these books the intensity of rebellion is past, an incident of an unhappy childhood (and the vogue of having had an unhappy childhood may well have begun with the Edwardians) succeeded by confident maturity.

Because they outlived their passionate revolt, writers as different as Yeats and Joyce are sometimes suspected now of having been reverted Christians or at least demi-Christians. Certainly they no longer make a fuss about being infidels. And they are suspected of belief for another reason, too. Almost to a man, Edwardian writers rejected Christianity, and having done so, they felt free to *use* it, for while they did not need religion they did need religious metaphors. It is no accident that the Catholic modernists, with their emphasis upon the metaphorical rather than the literal truth of Catholic doctrines, became powerful enough in the first years of the century to be worth excommunicating in 1907. There were other signs of a changed attitude towards religion: the comparative mythologists tolerantly accepted Easter as one of many spring vegetation rites; William James's *The Varieties of Religious Experience,* published in

1902, made all varieties equally valid.

In creative writers, this new temper appears not in discussion of religion, which does not interest them, but in vocabulary. Religious terms are suddenly in vogue among unbelievers. Yeats calls up God to be a symbol of the most complete thought. Joyce in *A Portrait* allows the infidel Stephen to cry out 'Heavenly God!' when, seeing a girl wading, he experiences 'an outburst of *profane* joy'. Elsewhere, as in *Ulysses*, he asks what difference it makes whether God's name be Christus or Bloom, and Jesus is allowed into *Finnegans Wake* as one of Finnegan's many avatars. Ezra Pound, newly arrived in London in 1908, immediately writes a canzone to celebrate 'The Yearly Slain', a pagan god, and then a ballad to celebrate the 'Goodly Fere', who turns out to be Christ made into a Scottish chap. All deaths of all gods roused Pound to the same fervor. There was no need to attack with Swinburne the 'pale Galilean', or to say with Nietzsche that 'God is dead'; as a metaphor God was not dead but distinctly alive, so much so that a character in Granville-Barker's play *Waste* (1906–7) asks sardonically, 'What is the prose for God?' T. S. Eliot, if for a moment he may be regarded as an Edwardian rather than as a Rooseveltian, in 'Prufrock' (written in 1910) used John the Baptist and Lazarus as if they were characters like Hamlet, and even in his later life, after becoming consciously, even self-consciously Christian, he used the words 'God' and 'Christ' with the greatest circumspection, while unbelievers used the words much more casually, their individual talents more at ease in his tradition than he himself. D. H. Lawrence, the same age as Pound, writes his 'Hymn to Priapus' in 1912, yet remains attracted by images of Christ and is willing enough, in spite of his preference for older and darker gods, to revise Christianity and use its metaphors. In *The Rainbow* (begun the same year), Tom Brangwen and his wife, when their physical relationship improves, experience what Lawrence variously calls 'baptism to another life', 'transfiguration', and 'glorification'. In later life Lawrence would give Christ a new resurrection so he could learn to behave like the god Pan, and in poems such as 'Last Words to Miriam' the cross becomes emblematic of the failure to cohabit properly, an interpretation which I should like to think of as Edwardian or at least post-Edwardian. Even H. G. Wells played for a time with the notion of a 'finite God', 'the king of man's adventures in space and time,' though by 1934, in *Experiment in Autobiography*, he granted, too unimaginatively, that he had been guilty of 'terminological disingenuousness'.

To accept Christianity as one of a group of what Gottfried Benn calls 'regional moods', or to rewrite it for a new, pagan purpose, seemed to the Edwardians equally cogent directions. For the first time writers can take for granted that a large part of their audience will be irreligious, and paradoxically this fact gives them confidence to use religious imagery. They neither wish to shock nor fear to shock. There is precision, not impiety, in Joyce's use of religious words for secular processes. About 1900, when he was eighteen, he began to describe his prose sketches not as poems in prose, the fashionable term, but as 'epiphanies', showings-forth of essences comparable to the showing-forth of Christ. *Dubliners* he first conceived of in 1904 as a series of ten *epicleseis*, that is, invocations to the Holy Spirit to transmute bread and wine into the body and blood of Christ, a sacramental way of saying that he wished to fix in their eternal significance the commonplace incidents he found about him. To moments of fullness he applied the term 'eucharistic'. When Stephen Dedalus leaves the Catholic priesthood behind him, it is to become 'a priest of eternal imagination, transmuting the daily bread of experience into the radiant body of everlasting life.' One did not have to be a defected Irish Catholic to use terms this way. Granville-Barker's hero in *Waste* wants to buy the Christian tradition and transmute it. Proust, searching for an adjective to express his sense of basic experiences, calls them 'celestial'. Yeats, a defected Protestant, wrote in 1903 that his early work was directed towards the transfiguration on the mountain, and his new work towards incarnation. The artist, he held, must make a Sacred Book, which would not be Christian or anti-Christian, but would revive old pieties and rituals in the universal colours of art instead of in the hue of a single creed.

The re-establishment of Christianity, this time as outer panoply for an inner creed, was not limited to a few writers. In the Edwardian novels of Henry James the words he is fondest of are 'save' and 'sacrifice', and these are secular equivalents for religious concepts to which in their own terms he is indifferent. In the novels of E. M. Forster, mostly written before Edward died, there is exhibited this same propensity. Forster usually reserves his religious imagery for the end of his novels. In the last pages of *Where Angels Fear to Tread*, his first novel (1905), Forster writes of Philip, 'Quietly, without hysterical prayers or banging of drums, he underwent conversion. He was saved.' *The Longest Journey* (1907) concludes with Stephen Wanham undergoing 'salvation'. In *A Room with a View* (1908), there is a 'Sacred Lake', immersion in which, we are told, is 'a call to the blood and to the relaxed will, a passing benediction whose influence did not pass, a holiness, a spell, a momentary chalice for youth'. At the end the heroine derives from Mr. Emerson, who has 'the face of a saint who understood', 'a sense of deities reconciled, a feeling that, in gaining the man she loved, she would gain something for the whole world'.

Even allowing that writers always incline to inflated language for their perorations, Forster obviously intends his words momentously, almost portentously. He is not for Christ or Pan, but with profoundly Edwardian zeal, for the deities reconciled. Some of the same images appear with much the same meaning in his contemporaries. A character in Granville-Barker calls for 'A secular Church'. Shaw's *Major Barbara* (1905) makes similar use of the theme of salvation with its earnest fun about the Salvation Army. Let us be saved, Shaw says, but with less Christian noise and more Roman efficiency. Forster's 'chalice' is like the chalice in Joyce's 'Araby' (written in 1905), which is a symbol of the boy's love for his sweetheart. The 'Sacred Lake' with its subverting of Christian implication is like *The Lake* in George Moore's novel (1905), in which the priest-hero immerses himself in the lake not in order to become Christian, but to become pagan. Forster's deflection of familiar Christian phrasing in having his heroine feel that, in gaining the man she loves she gains something for the whole world, is cognate with Joyce's heroine in 'The Dead' (written in 1907), who says of her pagan lover, 'I think he died for me,' a statement which helps to justify the ending of that story in a mood of secular sacrifice for which the imagery of barren thorns and spears is Christian yet paganized. I do not think it would be useful to discriminate closely the slightly varying attitudes towards Christianity in these examples: the mood is the same, a secular one.

Yet to express secularism in such images is to give it a special inflection. The Edwardians were looking for ways to express their conviction that we can be religious about life itself, and they naturally adopted metaphors offered by the religion they knew best. The capitalized word for the Edwardians is not 'God' but 'Life': 'What I'm really trying to render is nothing more nor less than Life,' says George Ponderevo, when Wells is forty-three; 'Live,' says Strether to Little Bilham, when Henry James is sixty; 'O life,' cries Stephen Dedalus to no one in particular when Joyce is about thirty-four; 'I am going to begin a book about Life,' announces D. H. Lawrence, when he is thirty. It does not much matter whether life is exciting or dull, though Conrad is a little exceptional in choosing extraordinary incidents. Arnold Bennett is more usual in his assurance that two old women are worth writing *The Old Wives' Tale* (1908) about. The Edwardians vied with each other in finding more and more commonplace life to write about, and in giving the impression of writing about it in more and more common speech. In Ireland there is the most distinct return to simple men for revelation, in the peasant drama, in Lady Gregory's collection of folklore, in Moore's and Joyce's short stories; but there is a good deal of it in England too, in Arthur Morrison for example. It is connected with an increasing physicality in writers like Lawrence and Joyce, as if they must discuss the forbidden as well as the allowed commonplace. In Lawrence and in Yeats there is the exaltation of spontaneous ignorance, the gamekeeper in the one and the fisherman in the other held up as models to those who suppose that wisdom is something that comes with higher education. In 1911 Ford Madox Ford calls upon poets to write about ash-buckets at dawn rather than about the song of birds or moonlight. While Henry James could not bring himself to joy in ash-buckets, he too believed that by uninhibited scrutiny the artist might attract life's secrets.

The Edwardian writers granted that the world was secular, but saw no reason to add that it was irrational or meaningless. A kind of inner belief pervades their writings, that the transcendent is immanent in the earthy, that to go down far enough is to go up. They felt free to introduce startling coincidences quite flagrantly, as in *A Room with a View* and *The Ambassadors*, to hint that life is much more than it appears to be, although none of them would have offered that admission openly. While Biblical miracles aroused their incredulity, they were singularly credulous of miracles of their own. As Conrad said in his preface to *The Shadow-Line*, 'The world of the living contains enough marvels and mysteries as it is; marvels and mysteries acting upon our emotions and intelligence in ways so inexplicable that it would almost justify the conception of life as an enchanted state.' The central miracle for the Edwardians is the sudden alteration of the self; around it much of their literature pivots. In 1907 Yeats began work on *The Player Queen*, a dramatic statement of his conviction that, if we pretend hard enough to be someone else, we can become that other self or mask. That was the year, too, when Joyce planned out the miraculous birth of his hero's mature soul as the conclusion of *A Portrait of the Artist*, and when J. M. Synge, in *The Playboy of the Western World*, represented dramatically the battle for selfhood. At the end of Synge's play, Christy Mahon is the true playboy he has up to now only pretended to be, and his swagger is replaced by inner confidence. In *The Voysey Inheritance* (1905) Granville-Barker brings Edward Voysey to sudden maturity when, like the hero of that neo-Edwardian novel of James Gould Cozzens, *By Love Possessed*, he discovers the world is contaminated and that he may none the less act in it. Lawrence's heroes must always shed old skins for new ones. In Conrad's *Lord Jim* (1900), the struggle for selfhood is the hero's quest, a quest achieved only with his death. In Henry James's *The Ambassadors* (1903), the miracles among which Strether moves at first are phantasmagoric, but there is no phantasmagoria about the miracle which finally occurs: the release of Strether from ignorance to total understanding. Though the dove dies in another of James's novels of this time (1902), her wings mysteriously extend beyond death into the minds of the living, to alter their conduct miraculously. The golden bowl (1904) is cracked and finally broken, but by miracle is recreated in the mind.

Miracles of this sort occur in surprising places, even in H. G. Wells. In *Kipps* the hero is transformed from a small person named Kipps into a bloated person named Cuyps and finally into a considerable person named Kipps. He is himself at last. Less obviously, such a change takes place in George Ponderevo in *Tono-Bungay*. It is part of Wells's favorite myth of human achievement, and trying to express that George Ponderevo says, 'How can I express the values of a thing at once so essential and so immaterial?' To do so he falls back upon the words 'Science' or 'Truth', words as reverberant for Wells as 'chalice' for Forster or 'eucharist' for Joyce. Selfhood – the crown of life, attained by a mysterious grace – forced the Edwardians into their grandest metaphors. It will not seem strange that Bernard Shaw's mind hovers continually about it, as in *Man and Superman* (1901–3) and *Pygmalion* (1912), where miracles as striking and as secular as those in Synge, Joyce or Yeats take place. Perhaps we could distinguish two kinds of such miracles: the kind of Shaw and Wells, in which a victory in the spirit is accompanied usually by some material victory, and the kind of James, Lawrence, Conrad, Yeats, and Joyce, in which a victory in the spirit is usually accompanied by some defeat. Shaw complained vigorously to Henry James that James's kind of miracle was not 'scientific'.

If the secular miracle is usually the climax of Edwardian writings, there is also a thematic center, usually some single unifying event or object, some external symbol which the Edwardians bear down upon very hard until, to use Conrad's unprepossessing phrase, they 'squeeze the guts out of it'. So Forster's *A Room with a View* is organized round the title; Lucy Honeychurch, viewless at first, must learn to see; Forster plays upon the word 'view' at strategic points in the novel, and at the end Lucy attains sight. In Conrad's *Nostromo* (1904) the central motif is silver, established, by Conrad's custom, in the first chapter: silver civilizes and silver obsesses, a two-edged sword, and the different attitudes that silver inspires control the action of the book. The meaning of the hero's name, Nostromo, becomes as ambiguous as silver; a lifetime of virtue is balanced against an ineradicable moral fault, and Nostromo dies an example of Conrad's fallen man, partially at least saved by misery and death. In *The Man of Property* (1906), John Galsworthy, somewhat under Conrad's influence, developed the very name of Forsyte into a symbol, and as if fearful we might miss it, he keeps reminding us that the Forsytes were not only a family but a class, a state of mind, a social disease. The use of a symbolic nucleus in these books seems to justify itself by its public quality, a whole society being measured in terms of it. In *The Golden Bowl*, one of those demonstrations of method which Forster found too extreme, Henry James not only invokes the bowl itself several times in the novel, but keeps invoking its atmosphere by repeating the words 'gold' and 'golden'. Verbal iteration is a means by which Edwardian novelists make up for the obliquity of their method, the complexity of their theme, and give away some of their hand. So Conrad in *Lord Jim* speaks of his hero's clothing, on the first page, as 'immaculate', and at the last he is 'a white speck', all the incongruities of the book pointed up by the overemphasis on stainlessness. Joyce plays on a group of words in *A Portrait*, 'apologise', 'admit', 'fall', 'fly', and the like, expanding their meaning gradually through the book. The pressure of this Edwardian conception of novel-writing is felt even in the work of Lawrence. In his first book, written in 1910, Lawrence is still rather primitive in his use of key words. He changed his title from *Nethermere* to *The White Peacock*, and then laboriously emphasized his heroine's whiteness and introduced discussion of the pride of peacocks. By the time he started *The Rainbow* two years later, he had developed this technique so far as to use the words 'light' and 'dark', and the image of the rainbow itself, obsessively, and he does not relax this method in *Women in Love* or his later books. He even does what most Edwardians do not do, writes his essay 'The Crown' to explain what light, dark, and rainbow signify.

A good example, too, is Joyce's transformation of *Stephen Hero* (1904–5) into *A Portrait of the Artist as a Young Man* (chiefly 1907–8). Between writing the two books he read a good deal of Henry James, George Moore and others, and quite possibly caught up Edwardian habits from them. *Stephen Hero* was to a large extent a Victorian novel, with an interest in incident for its own sake; so Joyce was particularly pleased when he composed the scene in which Stephen asks Emma Clery to spend the night with him. But two or three years later he expunged that scene: it had become irrelevant to his central image. For by then he had decided to make *A Portrait* an account of the gestation of a soul, and in this metaphor of the soul's growth as like an embryo's he found his principle of order and exclusion. It gave him an opportunity to be passionately meticulous. In the new version the book begins with Stephen's father and, just before the ending, it depicts the hero's severance from his mother. From the start the soul is surrounded by liquids, urine, slime, seawater, amniotic tides, 'drops of water' (as Joyce says at the end of the first chapter) 'falling softly in the brimming bowl'. The atmosphere of biological struggle is necessarily dark and melancholy until the light of life is glimpsed. In the first chapter the foetal soul is for a few pages only slightly individualized, the organism responds only to the most primitive sensory impressions, then the heart forms and musters its affections, the being struggles towards some unspecified, uncomprehended culmination, it is flooded in ways it cannot understand or control, it gropes wordlessly towards sexual differentiation. In the third chapter shame floods Stephen's whole body as conscience develops; the lower bestial nature is put by. Then, at the end of the penultimate chapter, the soul discovers the goal towards which it has been mysteriously proceeding – the goal of life. It must swim no more but emerge into air, the new metaphor being flight. The last chapter shows the soul, already fully developed, fattening itself for its journey until at last it is ready to leave. In the final pages of the book, Stephen's diary, the style shifts with savage abruptness to signalize birth. The soul is ready now, it throws off its sense of imprisonment, its melancholy, its no longer tolerable conditions of lower existence, to be born.

By making his book the matrix for the ontogeny of the soul, Joyce achieved a unity as perfect as any of the Edwardians could achieve, and justified literally his description of the artist as like a mother brooding over her creation until it assumes independent life. The aspiration towards unity in the novel seems related to the search for unity elsewhere, in psychology for example, where the major effort is to bring the day-world and the night-world together. Edwardian writers who commented on history demonstrated the same desire to see human life in a synthesis. In 1900 Joyce announced in his paper on 'Drama and Life' that 'human society is the embodiment of changeless laws', laws which he would picture in operation in *Finnegans Wake*. H. G. Wells insisted later that 'History is one', and proceeded to outline it. Yeats said, 'All forms are one form,' and made clear in *A Vision* that the same cyclical laws bind the lifetime of a person, a civilization, or an idea; and this perception of unity enabled him, he said, to hold 'in a single thought reality and justice'.

When they came to state their aesthetic theories, the Edwardians bore down hard on the importance of unity. To choose one among a multitude of their sources, they were to some extent making English the tradition of the *symbolistes* of whom Arthur Symons had written in 1899. Aggressively and ostentatiously, the Edwardians point to their works as microcosms characterized by the intense apprehension of the organic unity of all things. They felt justified in subordinating all other elements to this node of unity. Events of the plot can be so subordinated, for example, since, as Virginia Woolf declares, life is not a series of gig lamps symmetrically arranged but a 'luminous halo'. Short stories and novels begin to present atmospheres rather than narratives; and even when events are exciting in themselves, as in Conrad and often in James, the artist's chief labor goes to establish their meaning in a painstaking way, and he will often set the most dramatic events offstage or, rather than present them directly, allow someone to recollect them. Time can be twisted or turned, for unity has little to do with chronology. What subject-matter is used becomes of less importance because any part of life, if fully apprehended, may serve. As Ford Madox Ford says in *The English Novel* (1929), describing the novel of this period, 'Your "subject" might be no more than a child catching frogs in a swamp or the emotions of a nervous woman in a thunderstorm, but all the history of the world has gone to putting child or woman where they are. ...'

Since characters are also subsidiary to the sought-after unity, there is a tendency to control them tightly. Few Edwardian characters can escape from their books. Galsworthy's plays are called *Strife* (1909) or *Justice* (1910), as if to establish the pre-eminence of theme over character. The heroic hero is particularly suspect. He is undermined not only by Lytton Strachey in *Eminent Victorians* (begun in 1912), but by Joyce, who calls his first novel *Stephen Hero* on the analogy of the ballad 'Turpin Hero', as if to guard by awkwardness against Stephen's being thought too glibly heroic; Granville-Barker writes plays in which the heroes do not deserve the name. The Edwardian male, as he appears in the books of this time, is often passive and put upon, like Maugham's Philip in *Of Human Bondage* (published in 1915 but drafted much earlier) or James's Strether, not only because this is the period of the feminist movement, but because it is the period of the hero's subordination. Concurrently, there is a loss of interest in what the hero does for a living – the emphasis comes so strongly upon their relatively disinterested mental activity that the occupations of Strether, Birkin or Bloom become shadowy and almost nominal.

The amount of unity which the Edwardians instilled in their work is one of their extraordinary accomplishments. As Edith Wharton aggressively and seriously declared in the *Times Literary Supplement* in

1914, 'the conclusion of [a] tale should be contained in germ in its first page.' Conrad said in his preface to *The Nigger of the 'Narcissus'* that a work of art 'should carry its justification in every line'. There were occasional signs of revolt against this zealous 'desire and pursuit of the whole' (the title of Frederick Baron Corvo's novel, written in 1909). So Wells found Henry James's insistence upon what he aptly called 'continuous relevance' to be objectionable. 'The thing his novel is about is always there,' he said disapprovingly, probably remembering how Joseph Conrad had irritatingly asked several times what Wells's own novels were really *about*. Wells thought himself later to be in favor of irrelevance, but he himself said that 'almost every sentence should have its share in the entire design,' and his best books are not thoughtlessly constructed; they are unified, as I have suggested, by the myth of selfhood.

The Edwardian aesthetic is fairly closely related to the Imagist movement, or part of it. T. E. Hulme had interested Pound and others in his theory of intensive manifolds, that is, of wholes with absolutely interpenetrating parts instead of aggregates of separate elements. Hulme instructed them to place themselves 'inside the object instead of surveying it from the outside'. This position was that which Yeats also insisted upon when he said that the center of the poem was not an impersonal essence of beauty, but an actual man thinking and feeling. He threw himself into the drama because he saw in it a rejection of externality, even of scenery, and an invitation to the writer to relinquish his self. Henry James was also convinced that the 'mere muffled majesty of irresponsible "authorship"' must be eliminated, and entered the consciousness of his most sensitive characters so thoroughly as to make possible disputes over where *he* stood.

What is confusing about the first Imagist manifestos is that this theory has got mixed up with another, a notion of objectivity and impersonality which, though it receives passing applause from Stephen in *A Portrait*, is not Joycean or Edwardian. Most Edwardian writing is *not* aloof, and the poems Pound praised for their Imagist qualities were poems like Yeats's 'The Magi', or Joyce's 'I hear an army', in which the writer is not at all removed from his image. Pound found a more congenial version of the Edwardian aesthetic in the Vorticist movement, for that was manifestly based upon the absorption of the artist into his work, rather than his detachment from it. The word 'vortex' was something of an embarrassment. Pound said, with an obvious allusion to its female symbolism, 'In decency one can only call it a vortex.' But it had the advantage of implying the death of the poet in his poem: the ultimate arrogance of the artist is to disappear. This was the point of view of James and of Yeats as well as of Joyce; Edwardian writers were not much concerned with the artist as were writers of the Nineties; they were concerned only with the art. They began to put away their flowing ties. Yeats could never understand the reluctance of some writers to let him improve their poems for them, since to him the work was all. The Edwardian writer is an artist not because he proclaims he is, as Wilde did, but because his works proclaim it. There is much less time for affectation and eccentricity, the point being to get on with the job. As Conrad said in his preface to *The Secret Agent,* 'In the matter of all my books I have always attended to my business. I have attended to it with complete self-surrender.'

Having yielded up his own identity to write his work, the Edwardian wished the reader to make comparable sacrifices. The *hypocrite lecteur* whom Baudelaire had arraigned was the reader who thought he might observe without joining in the work of art. This was to pass through the house like an irresponsible tenant, and the Edwardian novelist was too good a landlord for that. The reader must become responsible, must pay his rent. The sense of the importance of what their books were doing, the sense that only art, working through religious metaphor, can give life value, made the writers free to ask a great deal of their readers, and the literature of the time moved towards greater difficulty, the revival of Donne in 1912 being one of its manifestations, or towards greater importunacy, as in Lawrence. As Henry James remarked to a writer who complained that a meeting of authors was dull, 'Hewlett, we are not here to enjoy ourselves.'

It may seem that, though I have offered to exhibit two faces of Edward, I have in fact shown only one, and that one staring urgently towards the age of anxiety. Yet modern as Edwardian literature was, it was not fully modern. There was a difference in mood, which Yeats hinted at when he said that after 1900 nobody did any of the violent things they had done in the Nineties. Can we not detect in this period, so distinguished in many ways, its writers so strict with themselves and with us, a sensible loss of vigor and heat? The Edwardians managed to retain much of the stability of the Victorians, but they did so only by becoming artful where their predecessors had seemed artless. The easy skill of Victorian narrative disappears, and while the Edwardians have good reasons for trying for more awesome effects, their work does not escape the charge of being self-conscious, almost *voulu*. It is the age of prefaces and of revisions. Their secular miracles, which they arranged so graciously, seem too easy now, and the modern equivalents of them, in Malamud or Bellow, for example, are deliberately wrought with far greater restraint. Writers of social protest like Galsworthy seem, as Esmé Wingfield-Stratford points out in *The Victorian Aftermath* (1934), resigned to their own helplessness. H. G. Wells, though so energetic, seems when he is not at his best too devout towards science, towards popular mechanics, and the later history of his writing of novels makes us wonder if even earlier he was quite so energetic as he appeared. Bennett presents his slices of life with the assurance of a good chef that life is appetizing, yet he has mastered his ingredients without much flair. *A Portrait of the Artist* is a work of genius, but wanting in gusto; and even Yeats is for much of this time more eloquent than implicated, not so much passionate as in favor of passion. Conrad achieves his effects, yet so laboriously, and with awkward narrators like Marlow who, in spite of his laudable artistic purposes, is a bit of a stick. The repetition of words and images, while helpful to the creation of unity, gives an air of pedantry to this aspiring period; the bird flies, but with leaden wings. I should like to find in George Gissing's book, *The Private Papers of Henry Ryecroft* (1903), a reflection of this diminution of vitality in a period that prided itself on its life. Gissing lived turbulently enough, but in this autobiographical fiction he is at pains to seem full of calm; a writer today might live calmly, but would want his books to be distraught.

The war, for I will not deny that it took place, made everything harder. The Edwardian confidence in artistic sensibility was broken down; the possibility of nothingness seems to replace the conviction of somethingness. Those Edwardian writers who lived through the war found stability less easy to come by. Before the war Yeats could write 'The Magi', with its longing for violence; after the war he wrote 'The Second Coming', in which violence inspires horror. Forster, who had accomplished his secular miracles rather handily in his early books, as by the trick of sending his thinner-blooded characters to lush Italy, descends lower to *A Passage to India,* where there is more brutality, and where the realizations to which he brings his personages are less ample, less reassuring. Pound, content with his troubadours before the war, turns upon himself in *Mauberley* with a strange blend of self-destruction and self-justification. Eliot, after politely mocking Edwardian politeness in 'Prufrock', becomes impolite in *The Waste Land.* Lawrence becomes strident, frantic, exhortatory, almost suffocating his own mind. Virginia Woolf, unable to find herself before the war, discovers at last a tense point round which to organize her books, and this is not so much unity as the threat of the breakdown of unity. Joyce, content to stay in the conscious mind in his earlier work, descends to a fiercer underworld in the *Circe* episode of *Ulysses,* where Edward VII appears, appropriately now turned to a nightmare figure babbling hysterically of 'Peace, perfect peace'. The miracle of birth was accomplished in *A Portrait of the Artist* without much resistance, but the comparable miracle in *Ulysses,* Bloom's rescue of Stephen in a world where gratuitous kindness seems out of context, is described by Joyce with great circumspection, as if humanistic miracles now embarrassed him. The religion of life keeps most of its Edwardian adherents, but it has begun to stir up its own atheists and agnostics.

1959

Lawrence and His Demon

LAWRENCE wrote his poems for the usual literary public as well as for the congregation of the faithful. Consequently, even when they are bad they are readable; and Eliot's remark about Lawrence's prose, that he had to write often badly in order to write sometimes well, is applicable to his poetry too. He has much more skill, and more interest in skill, than many – even among his adherents – will claim for him. Their moderation is based upon the impression that while many of the poems are poems, others are naked and personal records of pains caused by blows to Lawrence's solar plexus, his *soi-disant* nub of thought and feeling.

Even these records are, however, symbolic and representative rather than merely personal and autobiographical. Describing the revisions of his early work, Lawrence wrote: 'A young man is afraid of his demon and puts his hand over the demon's mouth sometimes and speaks for him. And the things the young man says are very rarely poetry. So I have tried to let the demon say his say, and to remove the passages where the young man intruded.' R. P. Blackmur, understandably impatient with Lawrence, puts a hostile interpretation on these admissions; he takes 'the young man in the quotation to be just what Lawrence thought he was not, the poet as craftsman, and the demon ... exactly that outburst of personal feeling which needs the discipline of craft to become a poem.' But surely this was not what Lawrence meant. He was distinguishing the archetypal self, purged of everyday accidents, from the self-consciousness of an inhibited young man bound by a particular space and time. His revisions necessarily improve upon form as well as content.

The early poem, 'Lightning', published in 1913 in *Love Poems*, demonstrates Lawrence's poetic character in both its unrevised and revised versions. Blackmur has pointed out how full it is of Hardy; the diction does, in fact, often suggest him: 'the lurch and halt of her heart', 'the hot blood's blindfold art', and 'the clips of my arms'. But the situation could hardly be more essentially Lawrence's. Like most of his early love poems, 'Lightning' is scarcely a love poem at all; rather it is an accusation. With the fervor of a Sordello he accuses his lady of coldness, a coldness brought up-to-date by identifying it with frigidity masking itself as virtue: 'Almost I hated her, she was so good'. The defect of this version of the poem is not that it is like Hardy, a master whom Lawence might have studied even more carefully, but that it is often like lesser poets: 'And the sense of her clinging flesh was sweet' sounds like Dowson; 'Pale love lost in a snow of fear' sounds like Swinburne; 'And claim her utterly in a kiss' sounds like Rossetti or any poet of little consequence.

If we compare three stanzas from each of the two versions, it becomes evident that Lawrence had more linguistic sensitivity than he has usually been credited with:

> I leaned me forward to find her lips,
>   And claim her utterly in a kiss,
> When the lightning flew across her face,
> And I saw her for the flaring space
>   Of a second, afraid of the clips
> Of my arms, inert with dread, wilted in fear of my kiss.
>
> A moment, like a wavering spark,
>   Her face lay there before my breast,
> Pale love lost in a snow of fear,
> And guarded by a glittering tear,
>   And lips apart with dumb cries;
> A moment, and she was taken again in the merciful dark.
>
> I heard the thunder, and felt the rain,
>   And my arms fell loose, and I was dumb.
> Almost I hated her, she was so good,
> Hated myself, and the place, and my blood,
>   Which burned with rage, as I bade her come
> Home, away home, ere the lightning floated forth again.

The final version, completed fifteen years later, is not flawless, but is greatly improved:

> I leaned in the darkness to find her lips
>   And claim her utterly in a kiss,
> When the lightning flew across her face
> And I saw her for the flaring space
>   Of a second, like snow that slips
> From a roof, inert with death, weeping 'Not this! Not this!'
>
> A moment there, like snow in the dark
>   Her face lay pale against my breast,
> Pale love lost in a thaw of fear

And melted in an icy tear,
    And open lips, distressed;
A moment; then darkness shut the lid of the sacred ark.

And I heard the thunder, and felt the rain,
    And my arms fell loose, and I was dumb.
Almost I hated her, sacrificed;
    Hated myself, and the place, and the iced
    Rain that burnt on my rage; saying: Come
Home, come home, the lightning has made it too plain!

Lawrence has made the imagery of the storm, with its rain, snow and ice, more continuous and fused. The language is generally more direct, natural, forceful and concrete; so 'the iced rain that burnt on my rage' replaces a trite with a sharp phrase, and the queerly broken two last lines seem emblematic of the lovers' parting. The power of the poem comes not from the passion of love, but the passion of critical insight.

When Lawrence revised his poems for the 1928 collection he did not touch the poems published after 1916 and generally written after May 1912. For from the time he was twenty-seven, when he and Frieda ran off together, he assumed a firmer control of his material. If stanzaic pattern was never a primary interest with him, diction was; if rhyme did not bother him much, rhythm did. Lawrence rid himself of Victorian diction and rhythm at about the same time as Eliot, Yeats and Pound; it has even been suggested that, since the Imagists published his work in their anthologies, he was under their influence. What evidence is available, such as Lawrence's own disavowal of Imagist intentions and the individual character of his subject matter, suggests a parallel development rather than a derivation. Lawrence, like Pound, never completely purified his diction, but he made remarkable changes in it. His early poems dwell like 'Virgin Youth' upon 'the soft ripples below my breasts' and 'my beautiful, lovely body'. But by *Look! We Have Come Through* (1917) his body, and his attitude, are tougher and no longer androgynous. So, in his later revisions, Lawrence takes such a stanza from 'The Wild Common' as this:

What if the gorse flowers shrivelled and kissing were lost?
Without the pulsing waters, where were the marigolds and
    the songs of the brook?
If my veins and my breasts with love embossed
Withered, my insolent soul would be gone like flowers
    that the hot wind took,

and supplies a new diction:

> What if the gorse-flowers shrivelled, and I were gone?
> What if the waters ceased, where were the marigolds then,
>   and the gudgeon?
> What is this thing that I look down upon?
> White on the water wimples my shadow, strains like a dog
>   on a string, to run on.

The speaker's veins and breasts are no longer embossed with love, for the emphasis must come on his abundant life rather than his amorous contours. Similarly, Lawrence removes the sentimental identification of nature with kissing; by replacing the conventional 'songs of the brook' with the arresting 'gudgeon', he imparts an energy to nature which was not present in the early version. The substitution of the shadow, an obviously transitory phenomenon, for the 'insolent soul,' whose mortality was less apparent, makes for a stronger contrast of abundance and nothingness. The change is not only thematic and verbal; it is also rhythmical. He breaks up the mainly anapestic rhythm, particularly in the conversational third line; he cuts short the loose second line, and interrupts the fourth with separate phrases instead of the breathless extended clause of the previous version. The rhythm is less prettified, the diction less sentimental, the attitude less eccentric.

Many of Lawrence's alterations are of the kind (if not altogether of the quality) that Yeats made. In 'Monologue of a Mother', 'a strange white bird' becomes 'a thin white bird', as if Lawrence had looked more closely at the object, and in 'Week-Night Service' 'the dim old church' becomes 'the droning church'. He comes to be more sparing in his use of words like 'pale' and 'beautiful'; 'The still, pale floor of the sky' in 'Troth with the Dead' is turned to 'the low, still floor of the sky', while in 'Lotus and Frost' the line, 'And sensitive beautiful blossoming of passion', is somewhat restrained to 'And sensitive, bud-like blossoming of passion.' He is also more specific: in 'Dreams Old and Nascent: Old', 'the great, uplifted blue palace' is later named as 'the great blue palace at Sydenham'. He is apt to substitute the concrete statement for the abstract even when the abstraction is more sensational; in 'Malade', he changes 'I am choking with creeping, grey confinedness' to 'Ah, but I am ill, and it is still raining, coldly raining.' Generally his images become bolder and barer. He first compared the church bells in 'Week-Night Service' to 'spattering showers from a bursten sky-rocket dropping / In splashes of sound, endlessly, never stopping'; his later substitution is less grandiose and facile: 'spattering shouts of an orator endlessly dropping / From the tower on the town, but endlessly, never stopping.' And in 'The Enkindled Spring', he took the last stanza, which originally began:

> And I, what fountain of fire am I among
> This leaping combustion of spring? My spirit is tossed ...

and wrote instead:

> And I, what sort of fire am I among
> This conflagration of spring? the gap in it all–!

The rhythm and diction are much more convincingly natural.

These revisions are proof that he knew, almost as well as his critics, the difference between a good line and a bad one. They do not indicate subservience on his part to the theory that content is all-important and that form will take care of itself. If any theory of composition is implicit, it is that form should not be sought in isolation; form and content arise together in the demon, the archetypal self, and their emergence in consort reflects that self's inner order. As he wrote of *Pansies*, 'Each little piece is a thought; not a bare idea or an opinion or a didactic statement, but a true thought, which comes as much from the heart and the genitals as from the head. A thought, with its own blood of emotion and instinct running in it like the fire in a fire-opal, if I may be so bold.' Mental constructs are not, or should not be, merely mental: 'The profoundest of all sensualities', Lawrence said, 'is the sense of truth/And the next deepest sensual experience/is the sense of justice.' If the head, heart and genitals in Lawrence's poetry are not often perfectly joined, they sometimes reach a magnificent accord.

The best poems, the best passages, are bursts of such unified perception. They have a brutal honesty of observation. Lawrence pries open the lid, whatever the box may hold. It is the honesty of a man with a *parti pris*, not of an impartial observer. He disturbs whatever he touches; he goads and is goaded. It is a poetry of exacerbation, in which sometimes anger and sometimes love provides the motive force. 'Last Words to Miriam', which deals with the same situation as 'Lightning', but more confidently and freshly, is a good example:

> You had the power to explore me,
>   Blossom me stalk by stalk;
> You woke my spirit, you bore me
> To consciousness, you gave me the dour
>   Awareness – then I suffered a balk.
>   .   .   .   .   .

> Now who will burn you free
>   From your body's deadness and dross?
> Since the fire has failed in me,
> What man will stoop in your flesh to plough
>   The shrieking cross?

The mixture of love and hate, both for Miriam and for the sexual act, reaches a climax remarkable for Lawrence, who was not often good at climaxes. The metaphor of the cross is one of the most dramatic and successful images, for it implies the sacredness, terror and pain which were for him essential parts of the sexual experience. In a retrospective, particular and personal pattern Lawrence expresses an unadorned insight that might have come from *Songs of Experience*.

Honesty does not necessarily make for artistic merit. When Lawrence is being merely honest, his diction is sometimes slack – curiously, 'slackness' was a favorable term for him – and sometimes insufficiently restrained. The protagonist of 'Snake' suffers from these qualities:

> The voice of my education said to me
> He must be killed,
> For in Sicily the black, black snakes are innocent,
>   the gold are venomous.
>
>   .   .   .   .   .
>
> Was it cowardice, that I dared not kill him?
> Was it perversity, that I longed to talk to him?
> Was it humility, to feel so honoured?
> I felt so honoured.

The self-searching is morally commendable but poetically tedious. On the other hand, his best poem about his mother, 'Hymn to Priapus', is a triumph of self-examination, so harsh that it almost ridicules his sorrow. It begins with the thought of his dead mother, then describes his love-making with a live country girl, and ends by considering the limits and checks which have been put upon human grief:

> She fares in the stark immortal
> Fields of death;
> I in these goodly, frozen
> Fields beneath.

Something in me remembers
And will not forget
The stream of my life in the darkness
Deathward set!

And something in me has forgotten,
Has ceased to care.
Desire comes up, and contentment
Is debonair.

I, who am worn and careful,
How much do I care?
How is it I grin then, and chuckle
Over despair?

Grief, grief, I suppose, and sufficient
Grief makes us free
To be faithless and faithful together
As we have to be.

The struggle to express a complicated state of mind increases the
interest of this poem; the language, while not especially distinguished,
holds tightly together and gathers at the end into an intricate knot.
The honesty of this poem, unlike that of 'Snake', is highly dramatic.

Aside from that occasional slackness, Lawrence's mature work is
impressive. If at one moment he is all thumbs, at the next he tells us
something which we ignore at our peril. His earlier defects are almost
gone; sentimental, trite, and vague words are carefully excluded. He
tries to present an experience or mood as cleanly as possible, and in
rewriting his early poems he reveals a great increase in self-discipline.
While his authority is not always unchallengeable, he is master of
his own house. His demon offered him more and more help as he
grew older. In those poems where all Lawrence's powers emerge, his
verse shines, as he wished, like 'a fire-opal'.

1952

Wallace Stevens's Ice-Cream

IN CONTEMPLATING the poetry written by executives of large insurance companies, it is hard not to be curious about their treatment of the great fact of death upon which their ample livelihood depends. Lugubrious as the subject is, it offers a way into the obliquities of Wallace Stevens. Death appears importunately several times in Stevens's first volume, *Harmonium* (1923), and less frequently thereafter, but a better beginning is his early play, *Three Travellers Watch a Sunrise*, because in it the principal bit of stage property is a corpse. It is the corpse of a dead lover, murdered by his girl's father; and the question in the play is how the three Chinese travellers, who have come out to watch the sunrise and not to look at corpses, will take the discovery of the body. It soon becomes apparent that they do not mind it a bit; they sympathize with the grief-stricken girl, but the corpse itself they treat as one more matter to be included in their surveyal of the scene. The sun, they say, will shine on the corpse as on another new thing:

> Red is not only
> The color of blood,
> Or [*indicating the body*]
> Of a man's eyes,
> Or [*Pointedly.*]
> Of a girl's.
> And as the red of the sun
> Is one thing to me
> And one thing to another,
> So it is the green of one tree
> And the green of another,
> Without which it would all be black.
> Sunrise is multiplied,
> Like the earth on which it shines,
> By the eyes that open on it,
> Even dead eyes,
> As red is multiplied by the leaves of trees.

They have no horror of death and no fear of it; but rather they take it as part of some larger order which they have long since learned to accept as essential. The green of life, and the red of grief or death, are both preferable to blackness. The sun shines not indifferently but intimately upon death as upon life. A corpse contributes to the variety of the landscape. Probably Stevens put this point of view, which is his own, into the mouths of three Chinese, because it seemed to him vaguely Oriental. But his setting is not China but eastern Pennsylvania, his Chinese are Chinese Americans, and we would be wrong to follow his equivocal hint in assuming that he advocates that the West accept the acceptance of the East.

If we look at his poems about death, we will find that he has decisive personal views about it. The early poems are even a little truculent. In 'The Death of a Soldier', he tells us that the soldier 'does not become a three-days personage, / Imposing his separation, / Calling for pomp', and in 'Cortège for Rosenbloom', a more difficult poem, he defends the view of death which he has labeled Chinese by challenging its opposite, by challenging, that is, the notion that death is something apart and isolated. The ceremony of conventional mourning, its stilted decorum, its withdrawal of the dead man from the natural world, its figmental afterlife, are all satirized here. *Que faites vous dans ce galère*, what are *you* doing in this mortician's heaven? the poet seems to be asking the wry Rosenbloom' whose body is so absurdly apotheosized. The name of Rosenbloom suggests both an ordinary man and someone who springs like a flower out of nature and should not be separated from it.

> Now, the wry Rosenbloom is dead
> And his finical carriers tread,
> On a hundred legs, the tread
> Of the dead.
> Rosenbloom is dead.

The finical mourners are made buglike.

> They carry the wizened one
> Of the color of horn
> To the sullen hill,
> Treading a tread
> In unison for the dead.

(Horn is death's color in Stevens's verse.)

> Rosenbloom is dead.
> The tread of the carriers does not halt

173

> On the hill, but turns
> Up the sky.
> They are bearing his body into the sky.

The next stanza makes quite clear what the poet thinks of this extraordinary ascent from the *ground*, from the solidity of the real, towards nothingness and nebulousness:

> It is the infants of misanthropes
> And the infants of nothingness
> That tread
> The wooden ascents
> Of the ascending of the dead.

The mourners are infants because their concepts of man are undeveloped and founded on a dislike of man's real nature; hence they love their extra-human illusions.

> It is turbans they wear
> And boots of fur
> As they tread the boards
> In a region of frost,
> Viewing the frost;

These are the tripsters of mourning; here they come with their conventional accoutrements, viewing death as an isolated, frigid country.

> To a chirr of gongs
> And a chitter of cries
> And the heavy thrum
> Of the endless tread
> That they tread;

again they are insect-like, ant-like, their absurd noises adding to their general absurdity.

> To a jangle of doom
> And a jumble of words
> Of the intense poem
> Of the strictest prose
> Of Rosenbloom.

> And they bury him there,
> Body and soul,
> In a place in the sky.

> The lamentable tread!
> Rosenbloom is dead.

The real nature of man, Stevens is suggesting to us, is comprehended only in terms of an adult, human culture; Rosenbloom himself is an intense poem, is strictest prose, and prose and poetry are set against infants and insects. No wonder the mourners jumble the essence of Rosenbloom.

This cortège, then, in the simplest terms, is the wrong way to conduct a funeral. What is the right way? 'The Emperor of Ice-Cream' is the right way. Here the poet is hortatory, not descriptive, and his tone is buoyant and defiant. It defies the mourners of Rosenbloom, who would like to treat this corpse with the usual ceremony, but the poet will have none of their services. Instead he summons the living, and, to emphasize his point, he makes clear that everyone living is welcome, and especially those who proceed by nature with scant ceremony; this time the season is summer, as favored in Stevens's verse as winter is disfavored.

> Call the roller of big cigars,
> The muscular one, and bid him whip
> In kitchen cups concupiscent curds.
> Let the wenches dawdle in such dress
> As they are used to wear, and let the boys
> Bring flowers in last month's newspapers.
> Let be be finale of seem.
> The only emperor is the emperor of ice-cream.
>
> Take from the dresser of deal,
> Lacking the three glass knobs, that sheet
> On which she embroidered fantails once
> And spread it so as to cover her face.
> If her horny feet protrude, they come
> To show how cold she is, and dumb.
> Let the lamp affix its beam.
> The only emperor is the emperor of ice-cream.

The way to treat death is to wear ordinary clothes, not turbans or boots of fur. It is to whip up some ice-cream in the kitchen, not to be finical; it is to spread flowers, not to toll the bell or ululate. Death, as we learned from the Chinese, is not horrible. The horny feet may protrude, and if they do, it is just as well. Do not call the embalmers. 'Let be be the finale of seem' – that is, away with the panoply of empty conventional mourning and empty conventional myths of death and afterlife. Let us accept being, which like the sun's rays comprehends death with life.

The last battlement before us is the line, 'The only emperor is the emperor of ice-cream.' There are two going interpretations of this line, one that the emperor is life, the other that he is death. When Stevens was informed of this difference of critical opinion, he said, in effect, 'So much the better!' and refused to judge between them. If we take the emperor to be life, and the poet's whole sympathy to be with the living, then why does the poem deal so precisely and deliberately with the corpse in the second stanza? Why not push it out of the way instead of displaying it? And can a wake, even an ice-cream wake, be completely detached from death? On the other hand, if the emperor is to be identified with death, why bring in the cigar-rolling, ice-cream-mixing muscular man? Is concupiscence desirable at funerals?

I think we may reach a little nearer if we remember that the characteristics of ice-cream are that it is tasty, transitory and cold. Life may be tasty and perishable, but it is not cold. Death may be cold but scarcely transitory, unless we assume that Stevens believes in an afterlife, which he doesn't, or tasty, unless we assume he has a death-wish, which he doesn't. Whoever the emperor is, he is realer than the run-of-the-mill emperors, the kaisers and Erlkönige, and his domain seems to include both life and death. The coldness of ice-cream suggests the corpse, as its sweetness suggests life's concupiscence. Stevens has said that his only daughter had a superlative liking for ice-cream, and is reported to have said also that she asked him to write a poem about it. Whether she did or not, there is a childlike quality about the poem – its absence of taboo, its complete, simultaneous, unruffled acceptance of conventional contraries – party food and horny feet. The child examines both without distaste. Both are included in the imperial domain. Ice-cream then is death and life.

But we must not think of death and life as a dual monarchy loosely joined by an indifferent ruler. The emperor is more than his ice-cream empire; he is the force that inspires and makes it one. Here again I call Stevens for my rather uncommunicative witness. He commented of the poem that it contained something of the essential gaudiness of poetry; this gaudiness must affect our estimate of the emperor. It is the more appropriate when we remember that in the poem 'Metaphor as Degeneration', Stevens asserts that 'being' includes death and the imagination. My candidate for the emperor of ice-cream, then, is the force of being, understood as including life, death, and the imagination which plays in this poem so gustily upon both. The emperor creates ice-cream, expresses himself through death and life, conceives of them as a unity, and is immanent in both of them.

If the volume *Harmonium* has an integrating theme, it is this deliberate acceptance of death with life. Stevens will have none of heaven or immortality; these fictions, always of questionable value, are worn through. In both 'Sunday Morning' and 'Le Monocle de Mon Oncle' Stevens endeavors to show just what place death has in being. The first is an argument with a woman who, on Sunday morning, is prompted to think of Christ's sacrificial death and of the heaven which Christ opened to man by dying for him. The poet asks, 'Why should she give her bounty to the dead?' and calls to her mind the beauty of the landscape. But when she continues to long for some imperishable bliss as contrasted with the cyclical, seasonal landscape, he advises her:

> Death is the mother of beauty; hence from her,
> Alone, shall come fulfilment to our dreams
> And our desires. Although she strews the leaves
> Of sure obliteration on our paths,
> The path sick sorrow took, the many paths
> Where triumph rang its brassy phrase, or love
> Whispered a little out of tenderness,
> She makes the willow shiver in the sun
> For maidens who were wont to sit and gaze
> Upon the grass, relinquished to their feet.
> She causes boys to pile new plums and pears
> On disregarded plate. The maidens taste
> And stray impassioned in the littering leaves.

The threat of something contrary to love, of obliteration, is what gives love its force. If there were no door there would be no room, but we are interested in the room, not the door. Then the poet mocks heaven and its attempt to abstract life from being and leave death behind:

> Is there no change of death in paradise?
> Does ripe fruit never fall? Or do the boughs
> Hang always heavy in that perfect sky,
> Unchanging, yet so like our perishing earth,
> With rivers like our own that seek for seas
> They never find, the same receding shores
> That never touch with inarticulate pang?

Why set the pear upon those river-banks
Or spice the shores with odors of the plum?
Alas, that they should wear our colors there,
The silken weavings of our afternoons,
And pick the strings of our insipid lutes!
Death is the mother of beauty, mystical,
Within whose burning bosom we devise
Our earthly mothers waiting, sleeplessly.

It is in the context of death that we see our earthly mothers of beauty – our loves, who are waiting sleeplessly because, like the heroine, they are anxious with the problem of perishability.

Supple and turbulent, a ring of men
Shall chant in orgy on a summer morn
Their boisterous devotion to the sun,
Not as a god, but as a god might be,
Naked among them, like a savage source.
Their chant shall be a chant of paradise,
Out of their blood, returning to the sky;
And in their chant shall enter, voice by voice,
The windy lake wherein their lord delights,
The trees, like serafin, and echoing hills,
That choir among themselves long afterward.
They shall know well the heavenly fellowship
Of men that perish and of summer morn.
And whence they came and whither they shall go
The dew upon their feet shall manifest.

Here, in more mellifluous phrases, are the same elements as in 'The Emperor of Ice-Cream'; the men are supple, in the other poem muscular; here they are turbulent, boisterous, in orgy, there they are eaters of concupiscent curds. The sun to which they chant cannot be taken only as the power which creates life, for Stevens emphasizes that the singers are men who perish like dew; it has to be also the power that moves in death. Let us say tentatively that it is what Dylan Thomas calls the force that through the green fuse drives the flower and blasts the roots of trees. Here we not only accept being, we worship it. And because life is such a good thing, death, upon which it depends, must be a good thing too. But death is only a small part of being; instead of speaking of life and death as if they were equals, we might speak of a god whose death is no more than a cue for his instant rebirth.

Stevens returns to the problem of death in another fine poem in

Harmonium, 'Le Monocle de Mon Oncle'. It is characterstic of this poet, who wrote English as if it were French (just as Carlyle wrote English as if it were German), that he puts his most serious thoughts into a courtly dialogue between a man and a woman. The poem begins in a wilfully pretentious style:

> 'Mother of heaven, regina of the clouds,
> O sceptre of the sun, crown of the moon,
> There is not nothing, no, no, never nothing,
> Like the clashed edges of two words that kill.'

The first two lines, which echo the litany, are pseudo-religious, in violent contrast with the next two. The lethal quality of two words is itself illustrated by the jarring double negatives of the third line. But there is more to the third line than that. It has been suggested that this is just one of Stevens's playful linguistic tricks, but the real reason will become clear as we proceed:

> And so I mocked her in magnificent measure.
> Or was it that I mocked myself alone?
> I wish that I might be a thinking stone.
> The sea of spuming thought foists up again
> The radiant bubble that she was. And then
> A deep up-pouring from some saltier well
> Within me, bursts its watery syllable.
>
> A red bird flies across the golden floor.
> It is a red bird that seeks out his choir
> Among the choirs of wind and wet and wing.
> A torrent will fall from him when he finds.
> Shall I uncrumple this much-crumpled thing?
> I am a man of fortune greeting heirs;
> For it has come that thus I greet the Spring.
> These choirs of welcome choir for me farewell.
> No Spring can follow past meridian.
> Yet you persist with anecdotal bliss
> To make believe a starry *connaissance*.
>
> Is it for nothing, then, that old Chinese
> Sat titivating by their mountain pools
> Or in the Yangtse studied out their beards?
> I shall not play the flat historic scale.
> You know how Utamaro's beauties sought
> The end of love in their all-speaking braids.
> You know the mountainous coiffures of Bath.

> Alas! Have all the barbers lived in vain
> That not one curl in Nature has survived?
> Why, without pity in these studious ghosts,
> Do you come dripping in your hair from sleep?

The repetition of 'nothing' in the third stanza makes clear that the word nothing is one which he has borrowed from her and therefore repeated so mockingly in the first stanza. We have to imagine the dialogue as beginning before the poem starts, when the woman, having left her bed with her hair in disarray, says to the poet that now that she is middle-aged there is 'nothing' left for her but old age and death and after that, she hopes, heaven – that starry *connaissance* for lovers once young. The problem of the poem then is to win her over to accepting death and denying an afterlife. The speaker begins by associating himself with her feeling of age and regret, but ends by insisting that we should concern ourselves, even in old age, with life rather than with death.

> This luscious and impeccable fruit of life
> Falls, it appears, of its own weight to earth.
> When you were Eve, its acrid juice was sweet,
> Untasted, in its heavenly, orchard air –

So long as we remain immortal in Eden, we long for life, and pluck its apple even if death comes with it:

> An apple serves as well as any skull
> To be the book in which to read a round,
> And is as excellent, in that it is composed
> Of what, like skulls, comes rotting back to ground.

The poet then offers a series of parabolic instances, the first of which proves that

> The honey of heaven may or may not come,
> But that of earth both comes and goes at once,

for this honey, like ice-cream, is vested in perishability. He next establishes that life and love continue even though individuals depart, and finally demonstrates that life, which has offered strong passions to the young, offers to the aged the power to value its ephemeral, perishing moments.

In his later poetry Stevens continues his efforts to make death subordinate to life. His attitude does not alter, but his emphasis in later poems falls less on rebuking others for erroneous ideas of death than on attempting to portray his own idea. He endeavors to find a picture of death which will not terrify us and will not separate it from life. Some of these treatments of death, such as 'The Owl in the Sarcophagus', where he finds death to be made up of three modern mythological personages – peace, sleep, and memory; 'The Airman's Death', where the airman sinks into a profound emptiness which yet is somehow made close and a part of us; and 'Burghers of Petty Death', where actual death seems a little thing beside the feeling of death that sometimes pervades the mind, are not so seductive as his early arguments. In 'Esthètique du Mal', Stevens tries in the seventh section to come to grips with the problem entirely in pictorial form, and this poem is more winning. Like 'Cortège for Rosenbloom', it begins by anchoring the hero in nature like a rose:

> How red the rose that is the soldier's wound,
> The wounds of many soldiers, the wounds of all
> The soldiers that have fallen, red in blood,
> The soldier of time grown deathless in great size.
>
> A mountain in which no ease is ever found,
> Unless indifference to deeper death
> Is ease, stands in the dark, a shadows' hill,
> And there the soldier of time has deathless rest.
>
> Concentric circles of shadows, motionless
> Of their own part, yet moving on the wind,
> Form mystical convolutions in the sleep
> Of time's red soldier deathless on his bed.
>
> The shadows of his fellows ring him round
> In the high night, the summer breathes for them
> Its fragrance, a heavy somnolence, and for him,
> For the soldier of time, it breathes a summer sleep,
>
> In which his wound is good because life was.
> No part of him was ever part of death.
> A woman smoothes her forehead with her hand
> And the soldier of time lies calm beneath that stroke.

This death is deathless in the sense that it is close to nature, close to life, close to the community of men living and men dead. It has nothing to do with the great looming abstraction of capitalized Death. The woman smoothing her hair might seem altogether detached from the soldier, but the soldier has never left the living and her gesture is a part of his being. This conception begins with the physical nearness of living and dead, but implies a metaphysical bond as well.

In Stevens's later verse there are many suggestions that death is what we make of it. 'Madame la Fleurie' is a poem about a man who read horror into nature, and instead of seeing her as a lady with flowers conceived of her as a bearded queen, wicked in her dead light. He died in this falsification, and the result is that there are no bluejays for him to remember, now that he is dead; he is not like the soldier whose death is merely an extension, in a different tempo, of his life.

I suggested earlier that to Stevens the sun is the primal force which, as in Dylan Thomas, creates and destroys. I think we should correct this now to indicate that the destructive force is much less important for Stevens than for Thomas, that they are nearly opposites. For in Thomas, who sees the body as a shroud, and life as either a rapturous ignorance of death or a knowing horror of it, the main revelation is that death pervades life, while in Stevens it is that life pervades death. In Thomas the glory of life is stolen from death. Stevens's vision, for it is almost that, is of living and unliving – a term which seems closer to his ideas than dead – men joined together in admiration, whether vocal or mute, of being. Being is the great poem, and all our lesser poems only approximate its intensity and power.

The sun is this primal force of being, reflected alike by living and unliving, by people and by things. Our dualisms disguise their single origin. It can be called God or the Imagination ('Final Soliloquy of the Interior Paramour'), though these terms are also only metaphors for what is ultimately a mystery to be worshipped rather than fathomed. The beauty that the sun creates antedates human life; long before we came on the earth the sun was covering the rock of reality with leaves, but once arrived here, we too participate in it. The sun is the Ulysses to which we and the world are the faithful Penelope. Its force is constant, and anchors in repetition all the changes which occur in the world, as the everchanging gleams of sunshine stem always from the same burning source. It is bodiless, unreal in that sense, yet it fills bodies with light and inspirits them. 'It is the ever-never-changing-same,' Stevens writes in 'Adult Epigram', and elsewhere he says it is the will to change which underlies all changes. We are, he writes in 'An Ordinary Evening in New Haven', in a permanence composed of impermanence.

Many of Stevens's poems can be read as accounts of the interaction of imagination and reality, but they have a theme which underlies that. 'Peter Quince at the Clavier', for instance, seems to be about an Abt Vogler building up a mountain of music from a few hints in experience, but the theme which was, I think, even more important to Stevens, is summarized in the lines,

> The body dies, the body's beauty lives.
> So gardens die, in their green going
> A wave interminably flowing.

The wave is a frequent metaphor for the force elsewhere saluted as the sun. As Stevens says in one of his essays, 'A wave is a force and not the water of which it is composed, which is never the same.' Sometimes he epitomizes this force as a river called Swatara, or simply as an unnamed river in Connecticut that flows nowhere like the sea; sometimes it is a changing giant ('Things of August'), sometimes a bodiless serpent ('St. John and the Back-Ache', 'The Auroras of Autumn'). But the force can also be found in a creature like the blackbird in 'Thirteen Ways of Looking at a Blackbird', a poem which we would be well advised to read not as a declaration that there are thirteen ways of looking at a blackbird but that there is a blackbird behind all these impressions. I do not think it has been remarked that Stevens is unsympathetic to only one of the thirteen ways, Number 11, in which the protagonist is not 'I' but 'He'.

> He rode over Connecticut
> In a glass coach.
> Once, a fear pierced him,
> In that he mistook
> The shadow of his equipage
> For blackbirds.

The error of the man in the glass coach – and glass is almost always a bar to sight in Stevens's poems – is that he sees the blackbird merely as death; the further proof of his error is that he has *not* seen the blackbird, has seen only his own dark mind, the shadow of his equipage. And so, like the man in 'Madame la Fleurie', he abstracts the blackbird from nature and sees only fear in it.

Most of Stevens's poems are based upon images which somehow participate in this primal force of being, and it is the existence of the force in them that he is concerned to demonstrate. The sense of 'The Worms at Heaven's Gate' is almost destroyed by its isolation in anthologies, where it seems to mean that the sardonic worms are handing up bits of a corpse with ironic comments on their deterioration. For Stevens the beauty does continue, it survives corruption, and the worms, not sardonic at all, can only talk of beauty, not of death.

183

In the individual person, the self, as Stevens says in 'The Planet on the Table', is the sun. This self should be dominated by the imagination, a solar light within the mind. In expressing our imagination we express the force of being. But in the individual man the light may be deflected. The imagination may look not upon the rest of being, but only upon itself; so like Chieftain Iffucan, it may disparage the world of nature, or, like the other bantam in pine woods, solipsistically fail to recognize that we are all parts of a common world and bound together by the shared light of the sun. The danger of such narcissism is that it leads to empty hallucinations, such as that denial of being which is heaven, that denial of beauty which is modern religion, that denial of the imagination which is reason, that denial of life which is nostalgia. The trouble with all these is that they are petrifying, they produce bad statues instead of men, the creative fire is thwarted in them. The imagination should queen it over the mind, with reason as her obsequious butler and memory as her underpaid maid-of-all-work. But she must always see the teeming earth, not the empty sky, as her domain. If she doesn't, the world becomes fixed and inert instead of malleable and suffusable. The imagination is constantly re-shaping and reforming reality; it is not the poet's exclusive preserve – everyone has it – but the poet uses it more steadily and powerfully and with more recognition of its value. It is the imagination, like the sun, which keeps the world from being black. Memory and reason can aid instead of impeding it, by confirming the imagination's felt bond with all existence.

We can see why Stevens's poetry is so different from that of Eliot. Although Stevens occasionally takes note of our age as a leaden time, this is not at all a principal theme. In no sense does Stevens sigh for lost beliefs; rather he is elated that old hallucinations are over now so that the imagination can get a fresh start. They have prevented us from living in the physical world, and the great poverty for man is not to live there. The major man – Stevens's modest version of the superman – is the man who brings most sunlight to most rock, most imagination to most reality, and is closest to the primal force.

Although there is an obvious similarity between Stevens and Yeats in that they worship in the church of the imagination, Stevens conceives of the primal force as existing independent of man and prior to him, while Yeats often suggests that it begins with man and is altogether human. In Stevens the imagination is impersonal and anonymous; it reminds us of Ortega y Gasset's contention that much modern art is dehumanized; but for Yeats the imagination works always through proper names. I find, more brashly, a second imperfect parallel in Stevens and his fellow American, the muscular one, Ernest Hemingway. When we think of Hemingway's stories about death, and particularly of 'The Snows of Kilimanjaro', what strikes us is that the rather ignoble hero is given in the end a noble hero's death, and for a moment we may be baffled and ask why this man who has made such a mess of his talents and of his marriages should be treated by his creator so well. It is because, with all his defects, he has remained true to his eye; the great virtue in Hemingway is not to live the good life, but to see, as the great virtue in Stevens is to imagine. Even if the hero of 'The Snows' has not done anything else, he has seen, and so mastered reality. In Wallace Stevens, the soldier, wounded also by life, is also saved by what he has found in it. Death, in both Stevens and Hemingway, comes beneficently to those who have expressed the primal force of vision, who have lived in the sun.

Most of Stevens's poetry is an essay in the intricacies of contentment, the mind and nature conspiring to render more lovely and awesome the force of being. There are sensual poems about plums, and philosophical poems about the mind's embrace of the plum, and a few, but only a few, poems about plumlessness, a state which depends upon plums for recognition. Stevens objects to those poets who make their pleas to the night-bird, who dwell upon discontent. His interest in grief, anger, and other unpleasant emotions is cursory. He does not evade tragedy, but he does not regard it as very important. An atmosphere of elation pervades his work as he surveys the marvels of the world; he insures us against death by assigning it so minor and integral a place in being. He is too fascinated by the endless procession of beauties to pay much mind to the retirements of particular individuals. He confronts us with a table of fragrancies and succulencies, solemnly reminds us that all of these, like us, are islanded between the nothingness that precedes form and the rot that ends it, and then urges us to fall to.

1957

The Ductile Universe of Henri Michaux

READING Michaux makes one uncomfortable. The world of his poems bears some relation to that of everyday, but it is hard to determine what. If we try to reassure ourselves by calling it fantasy, we have to ignore the scalpel which is playing about our insides. On the other hand, the term 'satire' at first seems equally inappropriate, for the point of reference is hidden, and no obvious appeal to law, convention, or common sense provides a focus for an attack on human ways. And to call Michaux's world obsessive or neurotic, as we may also be tempted momentarily to do, is to disregard the pervasive wit, a wit which is too keen, and implies too much control, to confirm a psychiatric explanation.

What makes his writings so difficult to categorize is not his concern with the self's wobblings and grapplings, though he is very good at these; rather it is his habit of casting psychological insights into physical instead of mental terms, or into a system of images which at first appear arbitrary. The frame of reference is subtly displaced. For example, these two brothers fighting in the mud: are they real or are they some wave of brutality in the mind, and therefore perhaps more real? This man who is turned into a whale: what stirrings of anxiety does he represent? These people who cannot stay still for an instant, who are always on horseback, always galloping: are they from 'Great Garaban', as Michaux calls one of his mythical lands, or from next door, or do they live in our brains? He will not tell us, and however accustomed we may be to reading poetic metaphor, we are thrown off guard.

Michaux resembles allegorical writers in that he finds the internal world more important than the external one; he differs from them, however, in being unable or unwilling to keep the two separate. They merge disconcertingly. Then too, he comes upon the reader unawares, aiming at that part of the mind where daytime habits of thought are least possessive. With dreams and nightmares to corroborate him, he has seemed to suggest that if any formula can be elicited from experience, it is that the unexpected happens to the unready. Working independently of a writer like Kafka, he has arrived at a view of life which at many points is comparable. The same veneer of logicality overlies *The Space Within* (*L'Espace du Dedans*, 1945) as *The Castle* or *The Trial*. While both authors exert literary control over their material, that material is nothing if not the uncontrollable. Unknown or scarcely known forces dominate helplessly resisting or unresisting characters; yet the bleak landscape is relieved by the steady light of a sardonic humor, which restores a kind of equilibrium, a kind of normalcy, imparts detachment, and in the end suggests that man is more than a creature thrown into a mine without tools, flashlight or map.

So dislocating a picture has not obtained easy acceptance. When Michaux began to write in the 1920s, his detractors said that his writing was not literature and that his language was not French. He paid no attention to them. The Surrealists attempted to claim him as one of their own, but he resolutely went his own way. Not until the last war did he become well known. He did not set himself up as a war poet or, like Aragon, as spokesman for his times. But his poems leaped into credibility; the preposterous or monstrous events which he had been describing for years, if they had no exact correlative in contemporary events, were no longer remote from them. He at last won recognition as one of the most original and important writers of his generation.

We cannot satisfy our curiosity as to how he happened to take his unusual direction. The details of his life are for the most part unknown. He was born in Namur, Belgium, in 1899, in a respectable middle-class family. His childhood, if we can interpret his reticent and ambiguous accounts of it, was astonishingly perverse. 'I clenched my teeth against life,' he says. He was a stranger to his parents. 'No sooner could I talk than I said I was a foundling.' As a small boy he isolated himself; he probably describes his own anarchic self-sufficiency in the 'Portrait of A.':

> Up to the threshold of adolescence he kept forming a hermetic and self-sufficient ball, a dense and personal and dim universe where nothing came in, neither parents, nor affections, nor any object, nor their image, nor their existence, unless they used force against him. In fact he was detested, they said he would never be a man. . . .

Other information is scattered and less startling. There are hints about ill health, about an absurdly self-effacing father, about a Jesuit school. He says that he read omnivorously, but does not tell what books. A later poem mentions Ruysbroeck, the Dutch mystic, as one of his masters; other sources add Pascal, Ernest Hello and Lao-tse. A considerable part of his reading must have been in mystical literature, which made a permanent impression on him as it did on many contemporary poets. He searched in books, he writes, 'the same fugitive and contourless universe' that he found inside him; they gave him 'revelations' which made him 'superior to himself'. At the age of twenty came a sudden illumination: he became aware all at once of the 'anti-life' he was leading, and decided to break free of it. The change was characteristically abrupt: he signed on board a collier at Boulogne as a sailor, and went on the first of many voyages. The 'Portrait of A.' suggests that the several months he spent sailing about North and South America were a period of intense suffering.

Soon after his return, he went to Paris. It was probably at this time that he came upon the gloomy, violent, angry rhetoric, with its bursts of satanic laughter, of Lautréamont's *Chants de Maldoror,* a book that led him to believe for the first time that literature might serve him as a medium of expression. He came in contact, too, with the painters Paul Klee, Max Ernst, André Masson and others, and some years later began to paint in a manner which shows his familiarity with them although it is his own. During the Twenties he also satisfied what had grown into a passion for travel, and went, as a passenger this time, to South America, where he wrote *Ecuador* (1929). A subsequent trip to the Far East resulted in the wholly original travel book, *A Barbarian in Asia* (*Un Barbare en Asie,* 1933). Between 1937 and 1939 he was editor of the review *Hermès,* which endeavored to bring together poetry, philosophy and mysticism. He was in Brazil for a few months after war broke out, but returned to Paris in 1940 and spent the war there and in the South of France. In 1941 André Gide planned to give a lecture on him in Nice, but was discouraged by the Vichy authorities. The lecture was published later that year under the title *Découvrons Henri Michaux,* and helped to win the poet a larger audience. Even the more conservative critics began to acclaim him, but fame proved more embarrassing to him than pleasurable. He remained aloof from most of the world, did not go to cafés, and refused to be photographed out of a fear that people might recognize him on the Métro. If his 'dense and personal and dim universe' established connections with the world outside, some of the old barricades have remained intact.

It is characteristic of him to have maintained a similarly intransigent attitude towards literature. He has nothing to say about the dignity of letters, though he attaches what he calls a 'hygienic' value to them. While obviously a skilled and conscientious craftsman, he has insisted upon a kind of amateur standing in the writing profession; his work must always be spontaneous, never *voulu.* Of one of his books, *My Properties* (*Mes Propriétés*, 1929), he comments in a 'postface': 'Nothing [there] of the wilful imagination of the professionals. Neither themes, nor development, nor construction, nor method. On the contrary, only the imagination of the powerlessness to conform.'

Formality disturbs and oppresses him. 'Oh how I hate you, Boileau,' he cries in one poem. He writes in free verse, prose poems, and prose, and the distinction between them seems to him of no consequence. He accentuates their informality by occasionally odd syntax, by frequent shifts between conversational and literary tenses, by idioms invented *ad hoc* and used as if known to everybody, by a colloquial over-use of the neuter gender, by an unusual concentration of verbs at the expense of other parts of speech, by exclamations, slang terms, and sentence fragments. But his iconoclasm is not so great as to prevent his occasionally introducing a formal note with remarkable results. In 'The March into the Tunnel', for example, he revives the Homeric simile:

> As a comparison, sailing negligently, as it seems, in a distracted mind, goes off fishing for a still obscure reality in a still more obscure area and brings it to light for you, all of a sudden, stamped with significant words, so the unhappy epoch, stupefied by incessant blows, prepares some important thing which is going to make intelligible the tremendous confusion where millions are fighting each other to the death, without being able to stop, caught in the straps of evil.

The total effect is not one of disarray, for in spite of his disclaimers the writing is always purposeful, never a mere stream of consciousness. But he will not let literature gain power over him. The statement of poetic method which he made in René Bertelé's *Panorama de la jeune poésie française* (1942) is typically insubordinate:

> I write as I can, the first time after a bet or rather a rage. I was very surprised by the result of the explosion which was called a poem. That repeated itself. I am not used to it yet. ...
> I write with transport and for myself,
> a) sometimes to liberate myself from an intolerable tension or from a no less painful abandonment.
> b) sometimes for a companion whom I imagine, for a kind of *alter ego* whom I would honestly like to keep up-to-date on an extraordinary transition in me, or in the world, which I, ordinarily forgetful, all at once believe I rediscover in, so to speak, its virginity.
> c) deliberately to shake the congealed and established, to invent.
> Readers trouble me. I write, if you like, for the unknown reader.

The first of these purposes, the liberation from an intolerable tension, is one which Michaux has emphasized several times. It is almost identical with Eliot's statement, in *The Use of Poetry and the Use of Criticism,* that writing a poem is to him 'a sudden relief from an intolerable burden'. The insolence with which Michaux states his position arises not from any indifference to literature, but from a sense of its awe-striking, mysterious power. He defines it more clearly in the preface to *Ordeals, Exorcisms* (1944), which like most of his manifestos deals chiefly with the effect of the poem on the author rather than the reader. Here, where he again makes a ball the symbol of unification of self, Michaux makes poetry a magical agent of that unification:

> One of the things to do: exorcism.
> Exorcism, reaction in strength, in a ram-like attack, is the veritable poem of the prisoner.
> Into the very spot of suffering and of obsession you introduce such exaltation, such magnificent violence, together with the hammering of words, that the pain, gradually dissolving, is replaced by an ethereal and demoniacal ball – wonderful state!

The conception of the self implicit here is not usual in Western thought. 'Our body', said Nietzsche, who in many ways stands outside the tradition, 'is a social structure composed of many souls.' Michaux also declares that we are multiple, carried this way or that by influences of different intensity from various sources, 'born', as he puts it, 'of too many mothers'. 'There is no one self. There are no ten selves. There is no self. SELF is only a position of equilibrium. (One among a thousand others continually possible and always ready.)' To follow through anyone's thinking, even that of an Aristotle, is to find that he is ill-informed about his own thought and its components:

> His intentions, his passions, his *libido dominandi,* his mythomania, his nervousness, his desire to be right, to triumph, to seduce, to astonish, to believe and to compel belief in what he likes, to deceive, to conceal himself, his appetites and his disgusts, his complexes, and his whole life, harmonized without his knowing it, in organs, in glands, in the hidden life of the body, in his physical deficiencies, all this is unknown to him.

When this fluid, elastic self attempts to come to grips with the world of objects, it is necessarily incapable of dominating them; they slip away. The attitude in the poems is one of non-acceptance of the world, of constant struggle against disintegration by the world. As

André Rolland de Renéville has pointed out in his essay on Michaux in *Univers de la parole* (1944), the two most frequent expressions of a basic *dépaysement* are travels and diseases. The protagonist is a traveler in strange lands because there he is expatriated and can look on with an unconcern impossible to him at home; or else he is a sick man because in disease, too, alienated from the crowd, he wages a conflict both spiritual and physical with an enemy who has no face, and under the pressure of fever drastically distorts reality. But there is irony in both. In the first the exotic countries have an indissoluble, even if tormentingly undefined, connection with the world the traveler has left behind, for as Michaux says in the preface to *Ailleurs* (1948), 'He who wants to escape the world translates it'; and further, the traveler's impartiality is a figment, events force him to take sides, to express opinions. And in diseases the feverish distortions of reality that are possible to the sick man are mockeries of his desire to invent his own reality. The world and the self are forever at loggerheads; subject and object can neither be separated (as in Boileau's world view) nor fused (as in Ruysbroeck's ecstasy). Hence the pathos and, too, the wry humor.

The selected poems which made up the volume, *The Space Within*, written over a twenty-year period, are expressions of this incompatibility. Their posture is nearly always one of attack. In some of the poems the attack is directed, as Michaux says, against all that is 'congealed and established' – the Parthenons, the Arabian arts, the Mings, the multimillennial order and the acceptance of it. In others the attack is directed against words themselves. It is not waged in behalf of chaos, but of something beyond man which the present set-up of things does not make room for. Somewhere there is a 'Big Secret', somewhere the millennium is waiting which will be the epoch of the visionaries, the moment when the Jack Pot in the heavens will erect 'in an instant upon my diarrhea' His 'straight and insurmountable cathedral'.

This total liberation can only be discussed ironically, but it forms a recurrent theme in Michaux's writings, and has become explicit in such poems as 'Ecce Homo', where, after describing man's present shortcomings, he concludes:

> And these were the philosophies of the least philosophical animal of the world, the *ies* and the *isms* burying young bodies in old clothes, but something alert was there too and this was the new man, the unsatisfied man, with caffeined thought, hoping indefatigably, holding out his arms. (Towards what can arms not be held out?)

The millennium – existence at its highest peak – is one theme, its converse, nothingness, is another. Night, unstratified space, peaceful or desolate landscapes, death, silence, and emptiness have a persistent fascination for him. One of his finest symbols is 'Icebergs', which he singles out because they are without personality, without man: 'Icebergs, Icebergs, Solitaires without cause, countries barred-up, distant, and free of vermin.' They participate magnificently in the isolation of non-being.

Nothingness and the millennium have this in common: in both man is finally at one with the universe, by unconsciousness if, like the 'Clown', he is 'drained of the abscess of being somebody', and by hyperconsciousness if he is a visionary. Between being nothing and being everything lies, as Michaux knows, most of human life, which may even be thought of as the nerve-racking tensions between the two poles. There is nostalgia for nothingness, ironic hope for the millennium, and between them the life of the chameleon which struggles hopelessly to keep one color. So the search for being, for fixity, for communication which implies fixity, is Michaux's search. His characters try to express themselves (in both senses of the term), seeking as in the poem 'Heads' for their autonomy. One of the most telling accounts of this quest is the series 'I Am Writing to You from a Far-Off Country', where that country's conditions are bafflingly like yet unlike those we know, and the anonymous letter-writer is in constant fear of being misunderstood, of failing to explain, of never meeting her silent correspondent; she is on the verge of hysteria, but why? Are her letters ever delivered? It is as if the recesses of the being were attempting to communicate with the outer layers. In a nostalgic poem like 'The Jetty' or a horrifying one like 'My Properties' or 'And More Changes Still', the effort either to change the universe or to come to terms with it is undermined on the one hand by an insufficiency of creative power, and on the other by a 'prodigious incapacity for adaptation'.

The characters in the poems are usually anonymous, but they often fall loosely into one of three categories. The first is Plume, a simple-hearted, tractable man who has much in common with Charlie Chaplin. He never resists, and is forever abused or forced to participate in nightmares. He submits to circumstances as if he were the anti-self of the bellicose poet. Beside him is the second-rate magician, who cannot quite fit reality into his mold, or achieve a free, independent act of choice. There is a point at which reality resists. The third character is the unconstrained observer, who simply comments on the distortions of reality which he observes, as in the *Voyage to Great Garaban* (1936) or *In the Land of Magic* (1942).

The Ductile Universe of Henri Michaux

None of these characters is round or full. Plume might be an American as easily as a Frenchman; the details which could single him out have been resolutely cut away. For Michaux deals in flat planes, never in the third dimension. His people and situations alike come out of nothingness; they have no background and exist in a narrow space which cannot contain the multiplicity of ordinary experience. They inhabit what is essentially an artist's arrangeable world. The mythical scene – the land of magic, for instance – is an aesthetic area where Michaux can justifiably manipulate characters and settings. Just as Klee, by simplifying the human figure into a few lines, excludes the confusion of many particulars, centers attention on the rudimentary, and forces us to think of the figure only in terms of the essence incorporated within the lines, so Michaux anatomizes a small and carefully selected part of experience. Like Klee he is arbitrary in his choice of the facts he wants us to consider; he presents a logical extension or intension, overstatement or understatement. In 'Cries' he describes a fever as an orchestra emerging noisily from his skull, in *Great Garaban* he dismisses some atrocity as a mere trifle. Focussing on only a few facts, he imparts a heightened sensitivity to what he portrays. As Gide remarks, Michaux 'excels in making us feel intuitively both the strangeness of natural things and the naturalness of strange things'.

His words are as severely constricted in their meaning as his pictures in their detail. It should be noticed that, for all his stylistic freedom, he rigidly disavows those metaphorical connotations and allusions that most contemporary poets insist upon. With Michaux the poetry is not in the metaphor of words, but of situations. The statement itself is prosaic, but the tensions created are ultimately equivalent to those created by poems.

These tensions are never fully resolved. Michaux does not step out of his scene to reach formal conclusions about it. He diverges from Kafka by implying no general guilt; he posits no god or devil to explain what is going on in the world. Instead he clearly and clinically presents the algebra of suffering; in spare, almost antiseptic terms, he works out the equation: man being man, here is what happens. He does not enquire whose fault it is, for his concern is with data, not with speculations. The parodic element which results from his scientific coolness in examining highly emotional situations is firmly grounded in human experience. It is not misanthropic but, by the very fact of parodying, recognizes a value in the thing parodied.

Bookstores today are full of attempts by others to render the new vision of the world which Michaux initiated, and of which he remains

193

the primary exponent. In reaction against those who find the arts sublime, Michaux disavowed the role of writer or of artist; if he fell into it, he did so for none of the standard reasons. Art was not artifact, at most it might be self-liberation. As for communication, he wrote for no readers except perhaps the unknown one. To approach literature with suspicion, doubt, repugnance even, to regard the act of writing as involuntary; to compare it not with *la haute magie* of the Sar Peladan but with a lower form born out of desperation and savage wile: these are, if not precisely Michaux's attributes, at least the signs of his presence.

The attempt of many writers to detach their work from their lives is not his. The reason is not that he objects to wearing a false face – he likes false faces – but that the notion of art as stasis will no longer serve. On the other hand, his work is autobiographical only if that word is sufficiently contorted. Surface events in life are just light shocks far from the electrical center – the internal being. That being is not stable but allotropic, or rather, it is a series of momentary adherences of confluent elements which are themselves changing and unforeseen. The world of action, decision, and control, regarded from this perspective, is too remote to be of interest even as hallucination. On the other hand, Michaux's interest in unseen and perhaps mystical reality has not taken him to the *au-delà* but to the *du dedans*. He does not escape the world but deciphers the original manuscript underlying the palimpsest.

Though below the surface, we do not drown; we are preserved in the whale's belly, examining with attentiveness (the one virtue which Michaux allows) that anatomy, Jonahs at once enclosed and relentlessly, frenziedly scientific. Or, to use abstract terms which he avoids, we measure collision, encroachment, surrender and insubmission, disorder masked as custom, the unimaginable pretending to be inevitable.

Much of what Michaux describes, or rather exfoliates, in what Blake called 'minute particulars', is brutal, some is agonizing. Without offering help, he discloses a curious, at times ludicrous formality in separate anguishes that is so out of place as to change their pitch. Horror, at first magnified by specification, then diminishes, as if to verbalize was to redeem from the unspeakable. As Michaux uncovers the vast practical joke of which we constitute ourselves the victims, we begin to apprehend, we wince, grimace, we even snicker.

Thus, as he has himself declared, his work which appears so egoistic is really social. Put him next to Rabelais and his extraordinary men and animals seem in place; put him next to Swift and his voyages, his uninhibited exposures, his angers almost have a tradition. He is less explicit than Swift or Voltaire in describing what man might be. He pictures no Houyhnhnm-land or El Dorado. But his standards are, like theirs, medicinal; good and evil fall into place. The mind's inner workings are exposed in a way that is modern but compatible with tradition. Unawed by form or fashion in society or literature, he has waged his battle not against social or literary values, but, with a new tone and from a new perspective, against the tyranny of conventional experience.

1952/1968

THREE

The springs of any act are complicated, and perhaps especially of acts of writing; still, this intricate relationship tempts explorers as surely as F.6. Peaks are for climbing.

– 'Getting to Know You'

The Hemingway Circle

AT THE end of August 1944, an exultant Hemingway was lolling in the breastworks of the Paris Ritz when André Malraux, ostentatiously the colonel, paid him a visit. Malraux came straight to the point: 'How many men have you commanded?' '*Dix ou douze*,' said Hemingway; then, seeing his modesty was lost on this rival, '*Non, plus – deux cent.*' Malraux's face twitched. '*Moi – deux mille.*' Hemingway replied, untwitchingly, '*Quelle dommage* that we did not have the assistance of your force when we took this small town of Paris.' A Hemingway hanger-on then volunteered in a low voice, 'Papa, *on peut fusiller ce con?*' But Hemingway grandly offered a *fine* instead.

That this incident probably didn't happen this way, being available only *ex parte* Hemingway, is a problem that heavily engages Carlos Baker in *Ernest Hemingway, A Life Story* (1969). Hemingway had that propensity to lie which Tolstoy finds as inevitable in soldiers as Plato in poets. Even as a small child he fell into braggadocio, and to his mother's coy question, 'What are you afraid of?' lisped back his stock response, 'Fraid o' nothing,' a boast made more ridiculous by his inability then and later to pronounce an *r*. And yet he probably had some right, in some fashion, to several of the virtues he claimed. To pretend to more he practiced one or two, and this complication of his subject is lost in Carlos Baker's excessive, linear skepticism. In an early chapter, he brands as 'only another of his exaggerations' Hemingway's tale of having thrown an axe at another man with intent to kill, but on the page before he has conceded that the axe was thrown, and by Hemingway, and at another man, the only quibble being that it was thrown at night against an unknown prowler. In the annals of axe-heaving this is still axe-heaving. In the same way, Baker doesn't want anybody to think that Hemingway really took the small town of Paris, but the evidence marshaled indicates that, with OSS cronies and other irregulars, he did at least infiltrate it in a private war game which amused everyone except General Le Clerc. If not exactly high heroism, it was at least high jinks. As he told the last of his four wives, he was a braggart but not a phoney. Disallowing a quarter of each story, we still have more left than Captain Pistol. Hemingway could even be or pretend to be self-ridiculing, as when in high school he adopted the playfully anti-Semitic nickname, Hemingstein, though his friends had to submit to being nicknamed with comparable absurdity. But his more usual manner was to swashbuckle and so to dominate. Stronger characters than he, such as Gertrude Stein and William Faulkner, resisted by calling him a coward. In sports and wars the charge was false, and yet, as he knew, it expressed their basic feeling that in literary concerns – the only ones that mattered to them – they were the Quixotes, and Hemingway, riding a small talent, a limited vocabulary and a showy success, was only an Oak Park (Illinois) Sancho Panza with big feet.

In his early work Hemingway was more modest, and made his warriors underplay their achievements. Avid for medals himself – he old-soldiered General Lanham into giving him one at the close of the Second World War – he makes his characters ostentatiously forget what medals they have and what for. They flaunt their modesty. In one of his best stories, 'Big Two-Hearted River', he originally planned to end with a monologue divulging the hero's wartime experiences, but with sudden boldness expunged this ending, leaving the heroism formidably unmentionable. Count Mippipopolous in *The Sun Also Rises* [*Fiesta*] exhibits his arrow wounds; asked by Brett whether he got them when in the army, he replies, 'I was on a business trip.' Arrow wounds received in war are obvious enough, but received on a business trip may still surprise a lady and so impress her more. Hemingway prided himself as author on this restraint: when Harold Loeb objected to the way he had been depicted as Robert Cohn, in the same novel, Hemingway replied, 'I let you knock me (Jake) down, didn't I, when everybody knows I could beat the hell out of you.' But afterwards this inability to keep his life and his work separate was to undo him.

In his later writing, the parade of prowess becomes more insistent, what was left out tends to be thrust in, and the characters function as Hemingway's self-defenses and self-aggrandizements. There is pathos in this decline, which after *For Whom the Bell Tolls* becomes steady. Baker's account misses this prevailing rhythm, I think, because he overvalues *The Old Man and the Sea* as Hemingway resurgent. (Hemingway wanted it overvalued; on being told by Baker that Santiago was like Lear, he allowed that *Lear* was indeed a wonderful play, but declared that the sea was already 'quite old' when Lear was king. Shakespeare, no angler, never dealt with this archaic force.) Suicide was a means of arresting a movement he knew to be downward. Its immediate provocation was the shock treatments to which he was subjected; these destroyed his memory, a memory out of which he had 'invented' those characters who, by contrast, mostly live without memories, existentially. He had, however, as Baker shows, brooded on suicide at intervals throughout his life, and now he knew he had covered all the available sports (individual, not team) and battles in his narrow syntax to the extent possible. He could also acknowledge a latent bond with his father, whom he himself had described as a coward and whose suicidal gun he had persuaded his mother to let him have as a keepsake.

This anxious unsuccess hangs about many of Hemingway's exploits, sometimes inclining them towards comedy rather than tragedy. Carlos Baker tells more fully than has been done before how Hemingway, during the Second World War, fitted out his fishing boat, the *Pilar*, with secret armament, so as to trick and sink the German submarines that were supposed to be near Cuba. After two years aprowl, the *Pilar* had yet to get close to a sub, and a suspicion grew that instead of being a naval vessel disguised as a fishing boat, it was, quite simply, a fishing boat. As such, it enabled Hemingway to make ferocious anti-Nazi gestures while he spent his silly time catching marlin. At this point the then Mrs. Hemingway, Martha Gellhorn, piqued him into not missing out on the latest war, and, so aroused, he managed in a taurine rush to beat her to the front lines as war correspondent. One is sickened by both of them and their appetite for turning the horror of others into journalese.

On such matters as these Carlos Baker provides a good deal more information than discrimination, though the familiar lines of Hemingway's career remain unchanged. The notes indicate how sedulously material has been gathered. The book is, none the less, conceived with what seems needless timidity. It would have been helpful to have Baker's judgments of many matters where he labors to remain neutral, such as Hemingway's repeated evaluation of his mother as a bitch. For the most part he lets us drown in Hemingway, drown in events which, deprived of shape, are only half-events. Baker offers to disarm criticism by stating that his biography isn't definitive and that no biography can be until the year 2000 because 'many lines of investigation remain to be followed out, as they will be, by generations of scholars'. Such reliance upon the future is misguided; even if more letters are unearthed and more memoirs written by Hemingway brothers-and-sisters and Hemingway henchmen, the future biographer will have no more chance of being definitive. After all, what is wanted is not more incidents, or more prunings of incidents, but evaluation of relationships, comprehension of motives, depiction of persons. In the year 2000, no biographer will be able to

talk with Hemingway's friends and with three of his relicts, as Carlos
Baker has done, or to remember personally 'the way it was' in
Hemingway's time. Baker seems to dismiss interpretation as mere
pedantry: 'This is not a thesis biography.' Instead of a thesis he
offers a series of untutored pictures that show 'the man of many
contradictions'. For example, Hemingway was 'the man of action,
harnessed to the same chariot as the man of words'. But every writer,
perhaps every man, is platitudinously that. Hemingway was also
'the man who once admitted that he would have liked to be a king',
an admission that might be wrung once from the rest of the human
race as well. Another instance adduced of complexity is that:

> He could be thrown into a slump by weather that was cold and damp
> or hot and sticky. He could be lifted from the depths by early
> morning, the time of sunset, breezy sunlight, crisp cold, hills and
> mountains, and the sea.

To this much complexity all simple men can aspire. Hemingway
disliked, Baker informs us, the use of 'false bosom-builders'. Bold,
original judgment! Because of a lack of thesis, of conception, these
details offer not the singularity which Hemingway possessed, and
which the biographer has a duty to elicit, but only reasons for
thinking him nothing special.

The book tends to become archival, with all its pictures, and the
details within them, of just about equal emphasis. So a paragraph
will contain, without warning, sudden breaks of sequence:

> He held the child tenderly in his arms and told Ramon that he had
> always wanted a daughter. Although he later assured Ralph Ingersoll
> that Hong Kong was well defended, this was only public propaganda.

Attempts at describing relationships come down to gratuitous simul-
taneities:

> Just as they [Scott Fitzgerald and Marjorie Rawlings] were winding
> up their conversation in Asheville, Ernest was drinking an evening
> whiskey in the Sidley cabin on the Nordquist ranch.

Or a burst of concreteness will begin a section, 'At a quarter past six
on the Friday evening of January 8, 1954, the Hemingways were at
peace in the familiar surroundings of their camp at Kimana,' but
the next sentence lapses into a too easy foreboding, a shabby old
cloud over Fridays to come: 'Not many such evenings now remained.'
Or a chapter concludes: 'He did not know what the future held, but
he knew it would hold something.' This might have been extracted
from Hemingway's famous, cruel parody of Sherwood Anderson,
The Torrents of Spring.

The Hemingway Circle

Carlos Baker has written so much better in the past (in *Hemingway: The Writer as Artist*, 1952) that it seems possible he may have been impeded here by certain special problems. He quotes hardly at all from Hemingway's correspondence, while constantly paraphrasing it, and perhaps, as has been rumored, permission to quote more than occasional sentences has been denied him. If so, the interdict is most unfair to him and to his subject. Hemingway can't be put into indirect discourse without sounding foolish, and phrases which must once have stung are subdued here into bathos. At the same time, this writer's style is easily overwhelming, and it affects the biographer's, until one longs for a Henry James suspended sentence instead of this play-by-play chronicle. Not that Hemingway's style can be easily assimilated: Baker doesn't always sense its difficulties. In the first sentence of the book, 'As soon as it was safe for the boy to travel, they bore him away to the northern woods', he practices a Hemingway-like archness in not naming the boy, but loses the effect by the poeticality, 'bore him away'. The next paragraph begins, 'It was the closing year of the old century', a sentence redolent of Wardour Street rather than of the northern woods.

The pathos of Hemingway seems to have come from a sharp sense of his limitations, which drove him to claim greater excellence than he had in both writing and living. His success consisted in drawing around himself a tight circle, characterized by reticence, a winnowed vocabulary and simplified syntax, and a capacity to encompass nicknamed persons, practiced gestures, thoroughly known objects. If he changed his location it was only to become papa of the next one. Occasionally he protected the circle by flailing fists or words at people outside it, whether or not they were encroaching. Sometimes, if the outsiders accepted subordination as wives, defeated sparring partners, or just as listeners, he let them in. Seemingly the most international of American writers, he was in fact the most confined. In this circle the arc of courage is not easily distinguishable from that of cowardice, and perhaps neither term is much use. Hemingway hoped that his circle, if totally controlled by him, might pack a magical force. The language of his spells gradually became routine, however, and ceased to bind; it became an idiom of proprietorship rather than of comprehension. In his last days he could no longer keep the circle intact, and wife, friends and illness forced him into alien squares such as the Mayo Clinic, which he could not liberate, as he had Paris, by making it into Hemingwayville. At the last he reconstituted his circle with his shotgun.

1969

How Wallace Stevens Saw Himself

IN HIS *Principles of Psychology* William James recalls from the Martinus Scriblerus papers that Sir John Cutler owned a pair of black worsted stockings; these his maid had darned so often with silk that they became at last a pair of silk stockings. If they had been endowed with consciousness throughout the darning, they would at the end have thought of themselves as still a pair of worsted stockings, even though not a thread of the original material was left. The self is equally subject to change, bound chiefly by memory to its earlier stages, and always very difficult to define. David Hume points out that nothing in one's experience quite answers to the word 'I', and William James finds the self to be 'only a loosely construed thing'.

Yet that there is, as Wallace Stevens said in 'Le Monocle de Mon Oncle', 'a substance in us that prevails' is an assumption that can hardly be renounced. It may well be that biographers are wrong to assume, as they generally do, that their subjects have essences or characters that flow liquidly in childhood and jell in youth, and perhaps petrify in old age. There may be almost as much discontinuity as continuity. The child may father a man who scarcely resembles him, in defiance of Freudian theory, which holds that the character is formed by the age of five, or of cultural rituals which defer the moment until the onset of puberty. Existential biographers like Jean-Paul Sartre prefer to see the self as faced with a series of dramatic choices, none of which presupposes those that follow, while a writer like Michel Leiris in *L'Age d'homme* (1966) sees the self as by nature fitted and forced to pass through a series of mythical identifications.

With most lives, documentation is sparse for the years of childhood, so not much can be said about them anyway. Writers do, it is true, often speak of their early years in autobiographies, but they see childhood chiefly in terms of the elements that proved fit to survive. Those elements that were sloughed off, and why, they rarely remember, or at least rarely confide to us. What a biographer would like to do is to enter the cloud of unknowing that precedes knowledge, of indecision that precedes choice. If only we could return to those fits and starts, vaguenesses and blurs, small humiliations and anguishes and small efforts to cope with them, we might recover the atmosphere in which a being seeks and measures its place among other beings. Long before anything occurs that could qualify as an event, there must be preliminary stirrings. Events are only residues. If we could, we would go back behind history to prehistory, searching for primitive tools and weapons, even though the pygmies who used them have long since disappeared into the giants who took their places.

As a biographical subject, hardly anyone offers more difficulties than Wallace Stevens. He was born four years after Robert Frost, whom he does not resemble, and well before Pound and Eliot, who do not resemble him. His life presents, like that of Shakespeare and those of most literary men, an image of attentive boisterousness in youth and boisterous discrimination in age. Not much is known about his life in either period, and perhaps not much is to be known. He had, for example, a great appetite for travel, but like the young Parisian in Joris Karl Huysmans's *A Rebours*, who reveled in the prospect of a trip to England, then suddenly anticipated its discomforts and remained in Paris instead, Stevens mostly stayed home. He resembled also his Crispin, whom he described in prose as 'an every-day man who lives a life without the slightest adventure except that he lives it in a poetic atmosphere as we all do'. From nine to five each day he applied himself to insurance dossiers at the Hartford Indemnity and Insurance Corporation, an occupation he shared with Charles Ives and Franz Kafka, though they worked for rival concerns. 'At night', he said, 'I strut my individual state once more.' Stevens prided himself on the disconnection of his two careers. Has there been since Shakespeare a poet who made himself so impenetrable? Hartford might be Stratford for all we know of it from him. If Stevens called his friend William Carlos Williams anti-poetic, he was himself anti-autobiographical. Instead of the urge to confess or at least to confide, which, happily for biographers, most of their subjects evince, Stevens displays a counter-urge to conceal and fall silent.

Notoriously uncomfortable with his fellow poets, he chose as his boon companions men who were anything but memoir writers by temperament. They vindicated his appraisal by leaving no records. Other friends, including some of his principal correspondents, he never or rarely met, and they remained Mr. and Mrs. Such incidents as are reported remain of uncertain reliability, such as Witter Bynner's statement that Stevens left Harvard under a cloud, possibly because of his mock-rape of a waitress, or of uncertain significance, such as Ernest Hemingway's slugging Stevens and giving him a black eye. It might have been expected that his letters to his wife, especially during their five-year courtship, would reveal the inner Stevens, but, tender and considerate as the letters are, they thwart the biographer's longing for lapses of decorum. Holly Stevens, the poet's daughter, reports (*Souvenirs and Prophecies: The Young Wallace Stevens*, 1977) that her mother disliked seeing Wallace Stevens's books because they contained poems that she regarded as having been written solely to her. But the poems she so regarded seem scarcely private at all.

That such a man should have kept a journal might appear a contradiction, especially since he titled the journal, 'The Book of Doubts and Fears'. Yet intimacies are exactly what it does not contain. Perhaps there were some at one time, since passages have been excised, though whether by Stevens or by his wife is uncertain. But a reference backward to one such excised passage indicates that even there he did not give up all reserve. His entry of 28 March 1900 says, 'I find that in the early part of this book I have written that I could never be a great poet except in mute feeling.' (The entry referred to is not to be found.) He then, at the age of twenty-one, challenges this self-estimation that dated from his nineteenth year as 'silly and immature'. (Yet a certain muteness in feeling went with his lifelong articulateness.) Another characteristic statement comes from 1900: 'Personality must be kept secret before the world'. He would later, in 'The Figure of the Youth as Virile Poet', find authority for his view in Aristotle: ' "The poet should say very little in *propria persona*." ' Still, while disavowing direct egotism, he insists there that 'without indirect egotism there can be no poetry. There can be no poetry without the personality of the poet. . . .' His letters (ed. Holly Stevens, 1966) are equally at cross-purposes on the subject: 'one struggles to suppress the merely personal,' he told Harvey Breit, but, at the same time, the personal is the 'origin' of poetry. Similarly, he confessed that he read little verse by other poets for fear of echoing them, yet he declared more proudly, 'While, of course, I come down from the past, the past is my own and not something marked Coleridge, Wordsworth, etc. I know of no one who has been particularly important to me. My reality-imagination complex is entirely my own even though I see it in others.' In fact, no contemporary poet seems less derivative.

Stevens's projections of himself in his verse are mostly ironical; he would not have described himself, as Yeats did, as 'one who ruffled in a manly pose / For all his timid heart.' In a letter Stevens spoke of his friend Thomas McGreevy as 'an inhabitant of the world of names', perhaps because he thought of his own world as essentially a nameless one. ('Our Stars Come from Ireland', in which McGreevy is named, was an exception, a tribute to a name from a consciousness that automatically excluded such identification.) Stevens preferred to use names like Peter Quince or Crispin or Jocundus or Mrs. Alfred Uruguay. When, as in 'The Idea of Order at Key West', he did use an actual name, Ramon Fernandez, he immediately disclaimed any relation between the critic named Ramon Fernandez and the character in the poem. There are, none the less, occasional references in his later verse to Freud, Nietzsche, Claude, Whitman, or to places like New Haven, and these are all quite startling in context, like the sudden incursions of an Arctic explorer into Africa.

If, then, we look to Stevens to find early stirrings of his character, suppression of personal circumstances and feelings is clearly an attribute, even if an unhelpful one. In a letter written to Elsie Moll two years before his marriage to her in 1910, he speaks of having written for an hour in his journal, only to emphasize that he has left out a great deal: 'it did not seem desireable to disclose so much of my own spirit,' he says, then hastens to add, 'I cannot pretend to any mystery'. There must have been enough mystery to warrant reticence. Not to disclose his own spirit is a curious motto for a poet in any age, but especially if the poet is a lyrical one and writes in the age of Yeats, Pound and Eliot, whose works he knew well. None of these was confessional in the present-day mode, but each told us overtly a good deal more about himself than Stevens did.

The delineation of Stevens's idea of himself is then something he purposely impeded. Still, the difficulty may serve as a spur to explore his 'mind's native land', to use a phrase of Mallarmé. In the absence of much in the way of external incident, there are still hints, almost enough to enable us to map that native land, establish some of its contours, surmise its weather conditions, and perhaps speculate on the eruptions that brought it into being. In *Wallace Stevens: The Poems of Our Climate* (1977), Harold Bloom denies that Stevens 'ever underwent an intense crisis of an intellectual variety', but it is just that area that I propose to trace. Stevens's early materials are scarce and were written before the work of Freud fostered systematized scrutiny by writers of their own thoughts and images. They reveal in the young poet, besides the craving for secrecy I have mentioned, an unquenchable energy of contemplation. He is fond of the quality of 'force', as, in later life, he would also become fond of the quality of 'centrality'. Since Frost was to dismiss Stevens as a bric-à-brac poet, it is notable that Stevens did not care for effeteness, even in 1900, when effeteness was in vogue. In that year he remarked of another poet, 'His verses occasionally have much beauty – though never any great degree of force – other than pathetic,' and commented in his journal, 'How much more vigorous was the *thought* of the old fellows than is that of any modern man.' The title he gave to one of his later poems, 'Poetry Is a Destructive Force', embodies the same view. He complains surprisingly even of Hans Arp, that whatever its emotional intensity, Arp's work 'lacks force'. His letters speak frequently of poetry as 'fury' and 'violence', as 'momentary violences', and even more purposefully, as 'letting myself go'.

Stevens no doubt manifested his youthful energy in many ways, but one way was in natural description. In 1897 Garrett Stevens remarked to his eighteen-year-old son on 'your power of painting pictures in words', as if this had been well established already, and he even noted, not just jocularly, 'eccentricities in your genius', as if this power in language had already shown itself to be phenomenal.

Garrett Stevens offers considerable assistance in deciphering what Wallace Stevens was like. The relations of the two were affectionate, and in Stevens's childhood, close. Later Stevens came to regard his father as having been the practical one, and his mother the imaginative one. But this view of them is not borne out by the letters that Stevens kept. His mother's letters – those that survive, at least – are routinely maternal, but his father's are the letters of a man interested in literature. That Stevens should characterize his father simply as practical implies a powerful and uneasy urge on his part to dissociate himself from the parent stem. Garrett Stevens wrote sketches, stories, and poems for a Reading newspaper from 1906 until his death in 1911, and the poems, whatever their defects, exhibit a propensity, of which his son was legatee, to introduce phrases in foreign languages. By profession a lawyer and businessman, Garrett Stevens was not so practical as to avoid a nervous breakdown about 1901. Stevens was aware that in some ways he had imitated his father. As he said, 'I decided to be a lawyer the same way I decided to be a Presbyterian; the same way I decided to be a Democrat. My father was a lawyer, a Presbyterian and a Democrat.' Unwittingly, Stevens disclosed deeper affinities. '[H]e was one of the most uncommunicative of men', he wrote of his father in 1943, as if he were describing someone very different from himself. And again, 'The greater part of his life was spent at his office; he wanted quiet and, in the quiet, to create a life of his own.' He forgot having acknowledged not long before about himself, 'People say that I live in a world of my own. . . .' He describes life in his father's house in Reading: 'At home, our house was rather a curious place, with all of us in different parts of it, reading.' And his daughter Holly has indicated that Wallace

Stevens's house in Hartford was inhabited in much the same way.

Garrett Stevens's letters posed questions that his son accepted as crucial ones. The father had the same pleasure in packaging wisdom into apophthegms, and one of the most beguiling is, 'A little romance is essential to ecstasy'. I suspect he wrote this in part as an admonition to his son, who was cynically mocking away romance altogether in the same fashion that Mrs. Alfred Uruguay would wipe away moonlight like mud. Wallace Stevens conceded that 'poetry is essentially romantic' but insisted that the romantic he sought would eliminate 'what people speak of as the romantic'.

Garrett Stevens liked to go into the library of his house on a Sunday afternoon and settle down with a long novel. His library also included many books of poetry, and he appears to have set the pattern for the discussion of books in the family. In an early letter to Wallace, he praises the New England writers, not for their profundity, which would be the expected thing, but for their 'suavity'. In the same way, he commends the taste for elegance among what he inelegantly calls the 'Bostonese'. This emphasis upon the high gloss of literature, upon dapperness as a mental quality and even a moral one, caught the attention of his son and seems latent in Wallace Stevens's project of confecting 'the final elegance', which he announced as a goal in 'Notes Toward a Supreme Fiction'.

I have mentioned Garrett Stevens's linguistic virtuosity. This appears quite strikingly not only in his poems but also in a letter he wrote facetiously congratulating his son on election to the Harvard literary society, the Signet:

> Just what the election to the *Signet signifies* I have no *sign*. It is *significant* that your letter is a *signal* to *sign* another check that you may *sigh* no more. I suppose you thus win the privilege to wear a seal ring or a badge with the picture of a *Cygnet* on it – to distinguish you from commoner geese, or it may be you can *consign* all studies de*signed* to cause re*signation*, to some as*signed* port where they will trouble you no more.

This fancy fooling is directly anticipatory of Stevens's 'The Comedian as the Letter C'. In that poem, he confessed long after, he had disported outrageously with the *x*, *ts*, and *z* sounds of the letter *c*, as in the line, 'Exchequering from piebald fiscs unkeyed'. Garrett Stevens's little game was still being played, if on a grander scale, after his death.

But the father's influence extended also to the discovery of topics. So far as can be determined – and of course the evidence is skimpier than one would wish – he not only joined the great internal debate of Wallace Stevens about the intercourse of the mind with reality, he also initiated it. In a letter of 27 September 1897 he writes to his son: 'When we try to picture what we see, the purely imaginary is transcended, like listening in the dark we seem to really hear what we are listening for – but describing real objects one can draw straight or curved lines and the thing may be mathematically demonstrated – but who does not prefer the sunlight – and the shadow reflected.' The expression is somewhat tortured, but Garrett Stevens is proposing, astonishingly, that when we try to say what we see, we do so through our imagination, and yet that we transcend that imagination because of the strong pressure of reality. It is the same, he says, when the sense involved is hearing: listening in the dark, we conjure up and yet really hear the sounds we imaginatively crave. ('That music is intensest which proclaims / The near . . .', his son writes in 'To the One of Fictive Music'.)

Finally, the father contrasts the abstract patterns into which imagination can turn real objects with the greater attractions of those objects in real sunlight and shadow. After all of which his letter gruffly concludes: 'Point in all this screed – Paint truth but not always in drab clothes.' This is only half of the point, the other half being: Ground the imagination in the real. Between these two poles moves his son's verse. In his poem, 'The Common Life', Wallace Stevens contrasts the reality of man and woman with 'A black line beside a white line', as, in 'The Rock', he wryly describes a meeting of two lovers as 'A theorem proposed between the two'. Or, to take another example, his poem 'So-And-So Reclining on Her Couch' allows the imagination to turn the actual woman into projections A, B, and C, but then accords the unprojected, living model a virtue that these fine inventions cannot claim:

> The arrangement contains the desire of
> The artist. But one confides in what has no
> Concealed creator. One walks easily
>
> The unpainted shore, accepts the world
> As anything but sculpture. Good-bye,
> Mrs. Pappadopoulos, and thanks.

In another exchange between father and son a month and a half later, Garrett Stevens writes: 'You have discovered I suppose, that the sun is not a ball of fire sending light and Heat – like a stove – but that radiation and reflection is the mystery – and that the higher up we get – and nearer to the sun the colder it gets. . . .' This is bad physics but good metaphysics, and as metaphor it recurs in Stevens's verse – as in 'Credences of Summer', 'Trace the gold sun.... Look at it in its essential barrenness', or in 'The Sun This March', where he says, 'Cold is our element....' The conception of the sun as surrounded by cold, a tropic conjoined to an arctic, is one that Stevens refined with enthusiasm.

His father had obscurely yet subtly glimpsed the kind of writer his son might become, an artist suave and elegant, a quizzer of both the imagination and the real, sensible of the seductions of both truth and delight. He saw him also as like himself, given over to reflection more than to action, to rumination more than to confession. Inklings of such characteristics, and others, in Wallace Stevens can be found in rare places. For example, by the time he reached high school he was demonstrating his remarkable appetite for sights and sounds and his expressive dexterity. His school friend Edwin de Turck Bechtel offers a few particulars. Bechtel is quoted by his widow as saying that ' "at high school Wallace was a whimsical, unpredictable young enthusiast, who lampooned Dido's tear-stained adventures in the cave, or wrote enigmatic couplets to gazelles" '. The recollections sound accurate. They indicate that Stevens's earliest poems involved some jollying of traditional romantic situations and some mustering of picturesque creatures. Bechtel's memory appears to be confirmed by later poems that revamp the original conceptions. In 'Le Monocle de Mon Oncle', for example, another woman – tear-stained as Dido, and saluted with regal conjurations (' "Mother of heaven, regina of the clouds, / O sceptre of the sun, crown of the moon" ' – is reproached for her gloom, which is motivated in this case by the departure not of her Virgilian lover but of her own youth, and for her gullibility to the false romanticism of pious hereafters. As for the 'enigmatic couplets to gazelles', these may well anticipate the enigmatic couplets addressed later to 'Bantams in Pine-Woods'. Bechtel saw Stevens as at once enthusiast and mocker, the poet who would offer his Crispin one integration after another, in each of which 'an ancient Crispin was dissolved'.

Bechtel's testimony is corroborated in Stevens's correspondence. By the time he began his journal at the age of nineteen, Stevens thought of himself as a poet, not so much by choice as by necessity. I suspect that he began to write out of ebullience and self-mockery and out of a disquietude over the coexistence of both qualities in his mind. In the to-and-fro of being magnified and minimized, the world might be lost; thus Stevens wrote, he said, 'to relate myself to the world'. Accordingly, he wrote poetry as if he had to, as he said of himself in contrast to another poet. He needed poetry as 'one of the sanctions of life'. The first of Stevens's letters that survives, sent to his mother when he was fifteen, indicates that he had some conception as I have said of his mixture of self-canceling qualities. Stevens had been dispatched for a holiday to the Ephrata Mountain Springs summer resort, some fifteen miles from Reading. At first he wrote to complain:

My Dear Mother –
I write this letter in depressed spirits. I have decided to come home. Ephrata as a summer resort is still extant [but] as a pleasure resort is dead, very dead, indeed, or has my cynicism embittered me. I can get along first rate but one feels the difference from home and Ephrata.

The word 'cynicism' is unexpected here. His allusion to it is at once so casual and so distinct that we may suppose it to have been a quality that he had long noted in himself, and one with which his mother was already familiar. Such a conclusion is borne out by his journal for 31 July 1899. Here is the best evidence for Stevens's intellectual crisis. One must imagine the layers of reticence that had to be cut through before he wrote these lines:

Somehow what I do seems to increase in its artificiality. Those cynical years when I was about twelve subdued natural and easy flow of feelings. I still scoff too much, analyze too much and see, perhaps, too many sides of a thing – but not always the true sides. For instance I have been here at Wily's almost a month, yet never noticed the pathos of their condition. The memory of one day's visit brought tears to Livingood's eyes. I am too cold for that.

Perhaps no one could compete with anyone named Livingood, but Stevens is severe with himself. Here his cynicism does not stand alone, as in the letter from Ephrata; it is part of a cluster of derogatory words that includes artificiality, many-sidedness carried to excess, and coldness. These are all qualities of which Stevens's critics have accused him, but what seems important is that at the age of twenty he charged himself with them.

What he meant by cynicism is presumably what Bechtel meant by mockery. It is clarified by one of Stevens's rare reminiscences about his childhood. 'When I was a boy,' he wrote Hi Simons in 1940, 'I used to think that things progressed by contrasts, that there was a law of contrasts.' The alternation, as of cynicism with enthusiasm, which in retrospect he recognized as characteristic, was at first a private habit to be reproved, as his use of the unpleasant word 'cynicism' confirms; it became – and this was the way the crisis was resolved – a response to a law that applied to things generally.

He would say later, 'North and South are an intrinsic couple', and in 'The Glass of Water' an object is 'merely a state, / One of many, between two poles'. He appears to be thinking indulgently of the same seesaw when he says of Crispin, 'Thus he conceived his voyaging to be / An up and down between two elements, ; A fluctuating between sun and moon.' So his cynicism, originally a source of guilt, was gradually transformed into just a pole of thought – a necessary one – as he proceeded through crisis into self-justifying maturity.

I am not suggesting that he accomplished this transition without paying a toll of anxiety. With Stevens, anxiety had the effect of making him aggressive in defense of qualities for which he had originally felt remorse. In the journal I have quoted he refers to his many-sidedness as perhaps excessive. The word 'many-sided' was not in itself pejorative; in fact, the term was customarily applied in the nineteenth century to Goethe, who himself liked to use it, though in *Wilhelm Meister* he said the quality was useful only if it was the prelude to single-sidedness. (G. H. Lewes, and J. S. Mill after him, gave it as Goethe's special quality, and since Stevens was studying Goethe at this time, he may well have come across it in Lewes's biography.) At first, however, Stevens allied it with his tendencies toward cynicism and artificiality and feared that the many sides he saw were not the right ones. Since he rarely admits in his journal to being bothered about anything, he was presumably bothered a good deal. Perhaps, like Yeats, he felt that he was on the path of the chameleon, and being, as he said later, at that time 'all imagination', he felt drawn in too many directions, toward too many 'jocular procreations of the dark'. Only gradually did he find 'the courage to be himself, which is, I suppose, the first necessity of any artist'.

I cannot fix the date when Stevens's remorse over many-sidedness and cynicism became an affirmation of them. His anxiety over the subject is clear in 1901; that it was followed by much mulling over and finally quelled is suggested by a letter from his father to him in November 1907, when his father replied, obviously to some expression of confidence by Wallace, 'I am glad you feel strong and self reliant.' It does not seem that Stevens ever achieved untrammeled assurance, but he had tenacity and boldness. For expression he needed to rely on his own psychic history rather than to accept what others had accumulated. The events that fostered this impulse were probably the First World War, which with its bareness questioned his profuseness, and the Armory Show of 1913, which endorsed multiple perspectives on experienced objects. By 1917 he was celebrating the Argus-eyed observer in that baker's dozen of many-sidedness, 'Thirteen Ways of Looking at a Blackbird'; a year later he wrote to his wife, 'I have always been of two minds about Tennessee'; and in 1919 the two-mindedness emerged, as Holly Stevens suggests, in 'Anecdote of the Jar'. Here pleasure in the vegetable profusion of Tennessee is cynically countered by suspicion of its artistic unkemptness, while delight in the jar's perfection is tinged with cynical regret at its un-Tennesseean aridity. Stevens's friend Bechtel would have recognized both minds.

Stevens not only looked outward to see different aspects, he also looked inward and found the same phenomenon. What in his journal in 1899 he had considered artificiality now began to seem altogether natural. For he had come to William James's conclusion, which he had perhaps heard or read at Harvard, that every self is many selves. A letter written to Elsie Moll in that period of consolidation of 1906–7 that his father had commended declares, 'After all I'm not one thing or another, but this thing today, and that, tomorrow.' He sets out the matter more amply in his journal for 27 April 1906:

> There are no end of gnomes that *might* influence people – but do not. When you first feel the truth of, say, an epigram, you feel like making it a rule of conduct. But this one is displaced by that, and thus things go on in their accustomed way. There is one pleasure in this volatile morality: the day you believe in chastity, poverty and obedience, you are charmed to discover what a monk you have always been – the monk is suddenly revealed like a spirit in a wood; the day you turn Ibsenist, you confess that, after all, you always were an Ibsenist, without knowing it. So you come to believe in yourself, and in your new creed. There is a perfect rout of characters in every man – and every man is like an actor's trunk, full of strange creatures, new + old. But an actor and his trunk are two different things.

The metaphors propose that we don't take on roles deliberately, as actors do, but simply express *seriatim* the latent possibilities or selves in our nature without premeditation. So he could write in 1935: 'To my way of thinking, there is not the slightest affectation in anything that I do.' This declaration finds a gloss in a three-line poem (published in the *Letters*) that he sent to Harriet Monroe in 1920:

Poupée de Poupées
She was not the child of religion or of science
Created by a god as by earth.
She was the creature of her own minds.

Many-sidedness, instead of being a sign of weakness, is here the controling principle. It became in fact Stevens's poetic enterprise.

But he still had to cope with the other quality for which he berates himself in his journal of 31 July 1899: coldness. Coldness is a subject to which he frequently returns. In his journal for the next day, 1 August 1899, he proposes to overcome this quality in a sonnet, for which he presents this romantic plan: 'Frost in a meadow. Is there no bird to sing despite this? No song of Love to outquench the thought of Death?' But gradually Stevens began to think of a kind of song that would affirm rather than deny coldness or frost. In fact, there is a persistent lowering of the temperature in his mind's native land. He did not abjure Livingood's capacity for pity, but other perspectives, he came to see, might also have their uses and would save him from that 'slushiness' against which Ezra Pound was later to inveigh. So, two years after he expressed such disquietude about his own coldness, Stevens began to preen himself on not yielding so readily to warmth:

> To illustrate the change that has come over me I may mention that last night I saw from an elevated train a group of girls making flowers in a dirty factory near Bleecker-st. I hardly gave it a thought. Last summer the pathos of it would have bathed me in tears. (Journal for 12 March 1901)

It is as if he were saying farewell to Florida, and treating cold as a part of experience to be valued as highly as warmth. He does not exclude the pathos, but in a palpable hit at Livingood he overcomes it 'by building his city in snow'. As he wrote to Richard Wilbur, 'The greater part of the imaginative life of people is both created and enjoyed in polar circumstances.' And in his very last poem, 'As You Leave the Room', he remarks, 'Now, here, the snow I had forgotten becomes / Part of a major reality....' (Another version of this poem, 'First Warmth', speaks of 'the warmth I had forgotten'.) By this time Stevens might well feel that he had given equal play to both temperatures. Perhaps the *locus classicus* for this defense of polar weather is 'The Snow Man', where Stevens insists that only with 'a mind of winter' can one regard the frost and the snow properly. The wind's misery has to be mentioned, just as the pathos of the factory girls had to be taken into account, but the mind must be cold to understand snow. Stevens may have been brought to this revised attitude in part because he read in G. H. Lewes's biography of Goethe that coldness was a major component of the Goethean personality. In any case, freezing temperatures played a large part in self-scrutiny. Yet the problem does not end there. Misery remains. and the snow-man's solidity is most fragile. There are sounds he cannot hear but that question his absolute authority.

This defense of coldness, which Stevens came to see as integral in his perspective, leads toward 'The Emperor of Ice-Cream'.* The succulence of ice-cream can only exist in a frame of cold. Hence the quality of coldness over which Stevens had once experienced remorse no longer seemed a defect. He became suspicious of poets, like Robert Frost (in spite of the latter's name), who kept offering up humanity in their work as though warmth were the only key to the world.

I suspect that Stevens felt increasingly that his recognition of cold, with its attendant and implicit images of death, nakedness, nothing, and saying no, was part of his original contribution to poetry. A letter of 8 April 1928 to Harriet Monroe apologizes for having talked 'gossip about death', to the dismay of Miss Monroe and other guests; evidently his at once obsessed and dispassionate consideration of the subject had given them pain. As more than the annalist of plums, he recognized an obligation to envisage plumlessness as well. ' "I have said no / To everything, in order to get at myself," ' says Mrs. Alfred Uruguay. Stevens saw more fully now the correctness of his father's insistence that the sun was surrounded by cold. The women in 'Sunday Morning' and 'Le Monocle de Mon Oncle' who talk of death and nothingness are not wrong, only one-sided; plenitude depends upon famine, as density upon blankness. The 'littering leaves' of 'Sunday Morning' connect with the 'leaflessness' of 'An Ordinary Evening in New Haven'. Poetry, being 'a destructive force', must recognize not only things of this world but also their absence. The urge to strip bare is as basic as the urge to bedeck. Affluence is joined to poverty as Oxidia to Olympia. So in his play *Carlos Among the Candles*, Stevens shows the poet lighting twelve candles in turn – a Promethean gesture – and then extinguishing them in turn, like cold yielding to abundance yielding to cold. He would speak later of a cycle from romanticism to realism to fatalism to indifferentism in a restatement of the same idea. For Stevens, reality contains and entails its own negation, just as the imagination contains and entails its own negation. As he says in 'Notes Toward a Supreme Fiction': 'it was not a choice / Between excluding things.... He chose to include the things / That in each other are included....' Hence he searches for 'a poetry divested of poetry'.

Stevens resolved his personal crisis by affirming what he had once anguished over, but some of the anguish remained. That is why his characterizations of himself or of his poetic personae seem to render them precarious, whether they are called snowman or uncle, Peter Quince or Crispin. Not only are there many selves, but self hovers

* Cf. the author's earlier essay on this poem, pp. 172–85 above.

on the edge of self-annihilation, and while death is for Stevens, as for Rilke, 'also part of the process', misery and despair are not encompassed altogether successfully by noble axiomata about being. If these components I have mentioned were essential to Stevens's view of himself and of his poetry, then his intellectual crisis of the early years of this century can have been only partially resolved. A residue of raging unhappiness clung stubbornly to even the most comprehensive poetic ordering of the world.

For an account of Stevens's dilemmas, a poem like 'Thirteen Ways of Looking at a Blackbird' may convey as much as his journal and letters. To many readers this poem is a jumble of impressions or meditations. But I suggest that this seeming discreteness masks an underlying, reticent relatedness, and that the poem came into being as a series of vignettes of his mental history. If so, it would be a covert autobiography, written, appropriately, when Stevens was getting on toward forty. It dates, in fact, from the same year, 1917, as his play *Bowl, Cat, and Broomstick*, which purports to describe a love poet, a seventeenth-century Frenchwoman, and to do so offers an obviously inadequate sketch of her life, portrays her hair, eyes and chin, and quotes from her verse. At the end her essence remains as unrecoverable as before. No biographical pigeonhole will contain the fugitive flutterings of that delicate being.

'Thirteen Ways of Looking at a Blackbird' similarly implies its own insufficiency as memoir. But Stevens makes the attempt none the less. The poem connects with another poem written in the same year and also for a time arranged in thirteen parts. This was 'Lettres d'un Soldat', which originally was a chronological sequence based upon actual entries in the journal of a French soldier. The individual 'letters' do not follow closely on one another, any more than do the thirteen ways; but Stevens begins with the soldier's resignation to his soldier's lot and ends with his disgust at digging his comrades' graves. While no close analogy can be drawn, 'Lettres d'un Soldat' discloses Stevens's dejection over the war and helps to explain why (as he told his Italian translator) the last part of 'Thirteen Ways' should have been devoted to 'despair'

In the 'Thirteen Ways', however, Stevens works more closely with the passages of spirit he had experienced in his own life. The poem begins and ends with a snow scene, but the tone in the first is quite different from that in the last, and the blackbird's eye, initial sign of animation among inanimatenesses, emerges like an infant consciousness. The effect is similar to that in Stevens's 'A Discovery of Thought', where he sees, 'in an infancy of blue snow', 'The cricket

of summer forming itself out of ice'. From this moment when consciousness, like the poem, is born. Stevens voyages through the history
of his self-identification. He could do this in only one way, not by
narrating external events, which were always for him of doubtful
solidity, but by naming those prior elements of consciousness that he
had discovered, brooded upon, and to some extent reconstituted.
The uneasiness that he continued to feel about the phases of his
intellectual crisis kept him from accepting any single formulation as
authoritative.

Accordingly, the first thing he mentions is that habit of many-
sidedness that at first had caused him so much distress. He recalls it
in stanza II lightly and even self-mockingly, as befits a memoirist
who puts no stock in memoirs:

> I was of three minds,
> Like a tree
> In which there are three blackbirds.

Nature offers its modest warrant, by the multiplicity of blackbirds,
for the multiplicity of the observer's minds. In the third stanza the
world is a pantomime in which the blackbird, like – it may be – a
child reconciled to Ephrata Mountain Springs summer resort, is
willingly whirled. When love comes in youth, with its implicit change
of climate, there is no fear that it will drown out the poetic mind,
for the creative consciousness harmonizes with love as the blackbird
with a man and woman in love. Its song is in fact a celebration, and
is welcomed as one.

These nuptial intimations lead, however, to thoughts of death,
which in Stevens are never far apart from those of love. If this
autobiography were an external chronicle, the deaths of his father
and mother in 1911 and 1912, not long after his marriage, would be
referred to, but in this internal voyage there is no place for exact
allusions. In several of his early poems Stevens insists that love derives
its savor from perishability, that without death, love could not exist.
Now the sudden intrusion of icicles upon the long glass – the window
that suggests warm, civilized life – reminds one not only of winter
but also of a cold beyond that of winter, an ultimate cold. The
blackbird, as it moves across the ice, seems to denote some indecipherable first principle, as if it were the mark of creation across
chaos.

Then follows the reproof of the 'thin men of Haddam'. In *Har-
monium* the principal reproofs are addressed to women – to 'A High-
Toned Old Christian Woman', to the dishevelled companion in 'Le
Monocle de Mon Oncle', and to the distraught companion in

'Sunday Morning'. These three are admonished by the poet for much the same failing, that they insist upon finding the actual world to be 'nothing' and upon seeking surcease for that nothing in heaven. The urgency and frequency with which the subject is pursued in these poems may well signal a recurrent effort by Stevens to cope with his wife's gloom. But in the seventh way of looking at a blackbird he makes his target the thin men of Haddam, who also fall into the heresies of rejecting the beauty of this world as if it were nothing and of attending only to the heavenly esoteric. He insists that the vital, simple, basic imagination, which in 'The Rock' he calls 'the main of things, the mind', and for which the blackbird in nature mostly stands model, is involved in everything, both the visible reality and the highest art. Even when the mind enters, as in stanza IX, into regions beyond its compassing, it delimits and marks them as, in 'The Idea of Order at Key West', the maker's words order the chaos of the sea. Poetasters, whom in stanza X he describes as 'the bawds of euphony', cannot deny, must indeed admit this essential vitality.

Yet the imagination, like being, embraces death with life, and in those unaware of its dual character, can still provoke terror, however much they try to shelter behind reality-proof glass. Having misconstrued appearances, they misconceive implications. That imaginative life has a less benevolent aspect is, however, conceded and recorded in the last two sections. Stanza XII indicates, Stevens said, 'The compulsion frequently back of the things that we do'. His explanation confirms that the blackbird, while retaining its place in nature, stands for human qualities. The mind is subject, at least sporadically, to blind forces it cannot direct. The final section, the luckless thirteenth, pictures the immobilization of the creative consciousness in a nature in which time is askew – 'It was evening all afternoon' – like a poet in his prime brooding on death. The snow, which in the first section had offered a handsome white backdrop, is now disagreeable, the world is dark. Do what it will, the mind, like the blackbird, must at moments amalgamate with cold, which is death's climate. No imaginative recovery of the world, such as in happier moments Stevens devised, could lead to continuous warmth. 'But time will not relent'. Yet the blackbird, still animate even if inert, seems to testify that despair, with its motionlessness, is as much a part of the pantomime as the earlier euphoric whirling. In this recognition the poem finds a place to stop, for one cycle is over, and yet all the elements necessary for a new cycle are already gathered. The eye of the blackbird will move again.

The individual life is a parable of all life. Hence 'Twenty men crossing a bridge, / Into a village', as he wrote the following year in

'Metaphors of a Magnifico', are also 'one man / Crossing a single bridge into a village'. With his thirteen phases of the blackbird Wallace Stevens had attempted something like Yeats's description of consciousness in terms of phases of the moon. (His earliest mature lyrics were called 'Phases', as if the discovery of this world had liberated him.) In Stevens's verse the oscillation between cold and warmth is like Yeats's gyres alternating between primary and antithetical. As did Yeats, Stevens presented a mode of apprehending reality that is also a reflection of the inner mechanism of that reality. The process by which worsted becomes silk is then not simply a record of evolution, it is a definition of consciousness. The progressive recognition of those elements that constitute being is the only true model for autobiography.

If this account of Stevens's conception of himself is valid, then the familiar separation of life and work, on which biography often rests, is inapplicable to him. The intellectual crisis shadowed forth in his letters and journal and in his poems antedates any such bifurcation. Stevens is as much concerned with his possible limitations as mortal man as with his possible limitations as immortal poet. Perfection of the work as opposed to perfection of the life is not, whatever Yeats's poem says, a genuine choice, for the opposites interpenetrate. The images that Stevens had formed of his internal being, of its needs and gratifications, its appetites, its shortcomings, its extenuations, are prior to major acts, whether of life or of literature, and yet determinant upon them. How he saw himself, how he valued and then revalued what he saw, provided the impetus to write that poetry in which he was both actor and spectator. In this sense he was right to consider that his poetry was personal. He was right to identify himself not with Shakespeare, whom he described as 'a nonentity about which cluster a great many supreme plays and poems', but with Goethe, who was 'a nucleus for his productions'. Stevens could say, in 'Thirteen Ways' and in his work generally, as Goethe said, that his poems are fragments of the grand confession of his life.

1980

Getting to Know You

'A SHILLING life will give you all the facts,' Auden said mockingly in one of his imaginary portraits. The facts could never encompass the workings of the impetuous heart. Charles Osborne's *W. H. Auden: The Life of a Poet* (1980), the first biography in the field, offers chiefly facts; most are not new, unfortunately, and some, as Stephen Spender and others have complained, are not accurate. Except where Auden's autobiographical remarks come to Osborne's aid, the context in which a being might move connectedly from incident to incident is either absent or impoverished. Auden is dangled about on a long line, dipped into one pool after another: always bait and never fish.

Some of the facts are undoubtedly of use. We want to know when Auden experienced *agape* (1933), when he married Erika Mann (1935), when he went to the United States (January 1939), when he returned to Oxford (June 1972). Our curiosity about his lovers, including one woman – Rhoda Jaffe – is satisfied. But at the end of Osborne's book we are a little farther from understanding Auden than at the beginning. Auden had warned of his biographer's probable failure when he declared, in an essay on Shakespeare's sonnets, with his usual propensity to foreclose alternative views: 'The relation between [a poet's] life and his works is at one and the same time too self-evident to require comment – every work of art is, in one sense, a self-disclosure – and too complicated ever to unravel.' The springs of any act are complicated, and perhaps especially of acts of writing; still this intricate relation tempts explorers as surely as F.6. Peaks are for climbing.

Auden's antipathy to biography seems telltale because it is so inconsistently maintained. No anti-biographer has been more biographical in his interests than he. His delight in gossip extended into the past, so that he could announce that Shakespeare, along with Eisenhower, belonged to the 'homintern', and that such pairs as Falstaff and Prince Hal could only be understood as lovers. He wanted to know, and if he could not know, to surmise, all about his contemporaries' private lives. As he wrote in 'Heavy Dates',

> Who when looking over
> Faces in the subway,
> Each with its uniqueness,
>   Would not, did he dare,
> Ask what forms exactly
> Suited to their weakness
> Love and desperation
>   Take to govern there.

He complained that J. R. Ackerley had never been 'quite explicit about what he *really* preferred to do in bed', and justified his inquisitiveness by saying, 'All "abnormal" sex-acts are rites of symbolic magic, and one can only properly understand the actual personal relation if one knows the symbolic role each expects the other to play.' About Housman he declared he was 'pretty sure' that Housman was 'an anal passive'.

He was eager, too, to detect and name psychological states and patterns. A whole series of poems is overtly biographical: Auden describes Yeats's lifelong dependence upon women, Matthew Arnold's filial upbraiding of an age that pretended to take on his father's authority, Edward Lear's fleeing to fantasy from his ugly nose, Rimbaud's abjuring verse as if it were 'a special disease of the ear', the aged Melville sailing 'into an extraordinary mildness', Pascal 'doubt by doubt' restoring 'the ruined château of his faith'. Most of these characterizations suggest states that Auden himself had experienced, and so do his imaginary portraits, which aim to catch their subjects in some giveaway moment when unconscious or secret impulse turns to act. Both types aim to uncover that relation between life and work which Auden had said could not be unraveled. He delighted in the idea that we are secret agents, with guilts – our own and others' – that we had best divulge. In youth he liked simplifications of Freud which could demonstrate by such diseases as 'the liar's quinsy' that the body offered the mind a way to expose itself.

Charles Osborne has assembled some important details about Auden's childhood. Auden was at that time bent on becoming a scientist, and won a prize for collecting and classifying shells and insects. This taxonomic urge made him say on his arrival at St. Edmund's School when he was eight, 'I look forward to studying the different psychological types.' He was never happier than when he could put matters into tabular form, as when, in an extraordinary *New Yorker* review, he compared the stages of life of Leonard Woolf,

Evelyn Waugh and himself. That the comparison was not illuminating did not bother him. He also devoted his childhood to fantasizing about lead mining:

> From my sixth until my sixteenth year
> I thought myself a mining engineer,

and to adoring large pieces of machinery. In later life he would admit, with that slightly abashed effrontery of his, that these interests had obvious symbolic meanings. Since Osborne shirks their interpretation, it may be suggested that Auden regarded mining as connected with orality, and dynamos (strength to his weakness) with passivity. He also mischievously recalled how at the age of six he sang Tristan to his mother's Iseult, as if to encourage his readers to trace his homosexuality to her influence in the routine Freudian way. Whether she instilled his homosexuality is doubtful, but it is certain that she greatly advanced his musical knowledge.

Osborne thinks that Auden did not really object to biography, but only seemed to. I suspect that he is wrong. For various reasons Auden felt uneasy about having anyone else manipulate the entrails of his experience. Of course they would not get it right. But besides that, he had a well-developed sense of guilt. He did not feel that he had spent his life in the way he ought to have done, and was conscious of much that might be revealed to his discredit. He disliked evasion, but he had evaded. He disliked pretenses, but he had pretended. He disliked imperfection, but was conscious of having too often 'slubbered through / With slip and slapdash what I do', and his excuse, that the Muse 'doesn't like slavish devotion', did not save him from feeling compunction. He had grown up in the days when poems were thought to be, at least potentially, perfect artifacts, and had some sense of having satisfied himself with imperfect results.

As befitted a lyric poet, Auden's sexual life was the center of his verse. His inclination was to disclose his own frailties and to force others to do the same. It was a risk but he took it. 'I can't help feeling you are too afraid of making a fool of yourself,' he wrote to a young poet. 'For God's sake don't try to be posh.' But in shying away from playing subject for future biographical anatomizing, Auden was conscious of having practiced the caution against which he had preached. By early adolescence he knew that he loved boys and not girls. His father found a poem addressed to another schoolboy, Robert Medley, and in a funny-awful scene, called both boys in to say that romantic friendship between young males was fine – he had experienced it himself – provided it had not gone 'that' far. Had it? Both boys were able to reassure him. Dr. Auden and his wife became increasingly worried about their son Wystan, and that son increasingly prided himself on loving, as at school on walking, 'out of bounds'. Yet he could not tell his parents, and the resultant equivocation mixes with his desired candor in his poetry as well. It encouraged him to write his love poems with their sexual direction indistinct. Readers, like his parents, were 'heters' (his word) and needed to be indulged a little. He recognized that evasion to be in a way a virtue, and in later life refused to have his poems included in a gay anthology because they were not intended to be read that way.

In his review of Ackerley Auden remarked that most homosexuals lead unhappy lives. His own stood as model. He confessed to Isherwood in 1938 that he was 'a sexual failure'. And yet there had been and would continue to be a series of sexual encounters. One reason for disheartenment may have been that, when he was twenty-three, he incurred, as the result of a pickup, an anal fissure. Osborne does not comment on it except to say that it necessitated an operation in February 1930 and caused Auden trouble for some years thereafter. The psychic effect was perhaps more serious than the physical. 'The discontinuity seems absolute,' Auden wrote in 'Letter to a Wound', a work which shows the encroachment of life upon art better than any precept:

> The maid has just cleared away tea and I shall not be disturbed until supper. I shall be quite alone in this room, free to think of you if I choose, and believe me, my dear, I do choose. For a long time now I have been aware that you are taking up more of my life every day, but I am always being surprised to find how far this has gone. ... Looking back now to that time before I lost my 'health' (Was that really only last February?) I can't recognize myself.

His wound seems to have fostered Auden's feelings of erotic insufficiency, of being finally perhaps not lovable. Osborne recalls, again without comment, the one dream in his life which Auden thought worth writing down:

> I was in hospital for an appendectomy. There was somebody there with green eyes and a terrifying affection for me. He cut off the arm of an old lady who was going to do me an injury. I explained to the doctors about him, but they were inattentive, though, presently, I realized that they were very concerned about his bad influence over me. I decide to escape from the hospital, and do so, after looking in a cupboard for something, I don't know what. I get to a station, squeeze between the carriages of a train, down a corkscrew staircase and out under the legs of some boys and girls. Now my companion has turned up with his three brothers (there may have been only

two). One, a smooth-faced, fine-fingernailed blond, is more reassuring. They tell me that they never leave anyone they like and that they often choose the timid. The name of the frightening one is Giga (in Icelandic *Gigur* is a crater), which I associate with the name Marigold and have a vision of pursuit like a book illustration and, I think, related to the long red-legged Scissor Man in *Shockheaded Peter* [*Struwwelpeter*]. The scene changes to a derelict factory by moonlight. The brothers are there, and my father. There is a great banging going on which, they tell me, is caused by the ghost of an old aunt who lives in a tin in the factory. Sure enough, the tin, which resembles my mess tin, comes bouncing along and stops at our feet, falling open. It is full of hard-boiled eggs. The brothers are very selfish and seize them, and only my father gives me half his.

As one of the first English poets schooled in Freud, Auden preserved this dream because he could not fail to recognize in its oneiric shorthand basic elements in his history: his threateningly different (because heterosexual) brothers, the hospital which was the scene of his operation, but which also was connected with his father's profession; the anal-oral imagery of squeezing and corkscrew. That the eggs given him by his father should be hardboiled seems an ironical allusion to Auden's necessarily sterile relationships, a sterility which is reiterated in the collation of appendectomy, amputation and scissors, as well as in the fact that the factory at which he eventually arrives is derelict. His conscious picture of himself was not unlike the unconscious one. He would later disparage himself to friends as 'just an old queen' and say he had 'put on my widow's cap'. In a letter to Rhoda Jaffe he remarks, 'Miss God appears to have decided that I am to be a writer, but have no other fun,' and he sums himself up as just 'a neurotic middle-aged butterball'.

A third matter that Auden was uncomfortable about was his having spent the war years in the United States. He did not acknowledge his regret ('The scrupuland is a nasty specimen') just as he did not offer confessions ('Confession is like undressing in public; everyone knows what he is going to see'), and later he brazened it out. Here was one of the subjects which he knew a biographer might easily misunderstand. Probably he had not so much decided to stay in America as to postpone his return to England, though he later claimed a much firmer resolve for his act. Then he met Chester Kallman, on 8 April 1939, fell in love, and knew he could not leave. But following the outbreak of war, as he told me soon after, he offered his services to the British Consulate-General in New York, only to be informed that at present they were not required. The loss of many

English poets in the First World War may have affected this official decision, though it was also true that Auden, flatfooted and queer, did not fit the soldier's image (Chaeronea to the contrary).

He was again rejected for service when, after having registered in 1940 for the American draft, he was examined in 1942. Meanwhile he had done something else, seemingly but only seemingly unrelated: in October 1940 he returned to the Anglican Church, from which he had separated himself in 1922. His loss of faith had been approximately simultaneous with his beginning to write verse. Auden attributed his return to the death of his mother, but Osborne helpfully points out that his mother did not die until ten months later. It must have been rather an attempt to recover something of what he had abandoned, to return to his basic English loyalty in spirit while he refused to do so in body.

The thirty-four-year attachment to Kallman may in its early phases have somewhat assuaged Auden's guilt feelings about expatriation. It was not, however, an easy relationship. The difficulty was patent: Auden was a stay-at-home, Kallman an inveterate cruiser, prone to dart off after someone else at any impulse. From the age of about fifty-five until his death, Auden was often unhappy over Kallman except when they were together, and sometimes then too.

A sequel, if not necessarily a consequence, of the attachment was that Auden, living in America remote from the war, was distracted from one of his principal subjects, politics. The pressure of events which had encouraged that interest in him was reduced by absence from his own country. In his youth he had justified, in a letter to E. R. Dodds, his traveling to war zones on the ground that the poet 'must have direct knowledge of the major political events'. His verse had gained strength from this political absorption, however deliberate it had been, and he had written under its prompting many of his best poems, such as 'Our Hunting Fathers' and various warnings of impending catastrophe.

But in America his center had shifted, and his poem 'September 1, 1939' registers a bewilderment accentuated by his being displaced. The poem declares that everyone is responsible for Nazism, a view so cosmic that Auden later decided it was 'dishonest' and left it out of later editions of his collected poems. This attitude has the same mistaken ingenuousness that led him to defend Pound's having been awarded the Bollingen prize on the grounds that 'anti-Semitism is, unfortunately, not only a feeling which all gentiles at times feel but also, and this is what matters, a feeling of which the majority are not ashamed. Until they are, they must be regarded as children. ...' In trying to rip off masks Auden can take some of the skin away.

A good deal of his exasperation with Yeats – the stalking horse of Auden's later years – came from his recognition that Yeats had responded to public, contemporary challenges in a way that Auden, for all his downrightness, found increasingly difficult. The notion that poetry might affect events, promulgated by Shelley and demonstrated by Yeats, was inconsistent with Auden's voluntary exile from his closest political concerns. His gradual insistence that poetry had value as recreation rather than as revelation seemed at least in part a rationalizing of his having expatriated himself. As if afraid that he has become ineffectual, he urges that poetry always is. Fortunately, his theory did not prevent his occasionally returning to his old subject, as when the Russians occupied Czechoslovakia and he wrote 'August, 1968':

> The Ogre does what ogres can,
> Deeds quite impossible for Man,
> But one prize is beyond his reach,
> The Ogre cannot master Speech:
> About a subjugated plain,
> Among its desperate and slain,
> The Ogre stalks with hands on hips,
> While drivel gushes from his lips.

But this, like 'The Shield of Achilles', was exceptional among the relatively private subjects that he more frequently chose.

From the beginning Auden had shown a certain inclination to miss out. Oliver Sacks writes in *W. H. Auden, a Tribute*, edited by Stephen Spender (1975), that Auden had once told him of a recurrent dream he had had:

He was speeding to catch a train, in a state of extreme agitation, he felt his life, everything, depended on catching the train. Obstacles arose, one after the other, reducing him to a silently screaming panic. And then, suddenly, he realized that it was too late, that he had missed the train, and that it didn't matter in the least; at this point there would come over him a sense of release amounting to bliss, and he would ejaculate and wake up with a smile on his face.

The pleasure in realizing he has missed out appears to be in keeping with Auden's inner wishes. Something of this attribute appears in his waking life in his fondness for words beginning in 'un-', as if unfulfillments were the law of life. One of his earliest poems, 'The Traction Engine', quoted by Osborne, is built of such words. The poem with which he started the Modern Library selection of his verse, 'The Letter', shows him to be already the poet of sour grapes.

'An artist with certain imaginative ideas in his head may then involve himself in relationships which are congenial to them,' he wrote in *Forewords and Afterwords* (1972). His examples were from Wagner, but they might have been from his own life – examples of exclusion and dismissal. His friends thought of him as laying down the law, but he thought of himself as pushed around: 'Hunt the lion, climb the peak, / No one guesses you are weak.'

His life with Chester Kallman may well have been a final cause of Auden's uneasiness about biography. Kallman was a clever man, with a deep understanding of music; Auden always maintained that his friend's poetic contribution to their collaborative opera libretti was greater than his own. But at moments he clearly protests too much. The effect of intermingling a major talent with a much smaller one is not easy to measure, but cannot have been optimal. If Auden had doubts on this score, he never thought of expressing them; his commitment to Kallman was come what come may: he preferred being saintly in his affections to being saintly, like Flaubert, in his absolute devotion to literature.

From the preceding sketch of Auden's interior drama, it seems clear that he was beleaguered. He was a great poet but fell off in his later work for reasons which seem half-consciously sought after. To some extent the trimming of his literary sails, as of his dreams of love, must have been a response to underlying forces in his character at least as much as to external accidents. Happily, even in decline he remained witty, brilliant sporadically, and always readable.

1980

The Life of Sim Botchit

OF ALL modern writers, the one presumed to be least likely to permit a biography of himself to be written has been Samuel Beckett. Addicted to silences, prone to despair and panic, suffering Job-like boils on his neck and cysts in his anus, practicing what he calls 'baroque solipsism', no more unwilling subject than Beckett could have been imagined. His aversion to public ceremonies itself became public when, in refuge from the Nobel Prize, he hid out in a Tunisian village, vainly hoping that the press would never track him there. Stomping over his desire for privacy, an American scholar, Deirdre Bair, has managed a scoop which in literary history is like that of Bernstein and Woodward in political history.

It all began in 1971. Deirdre Bair was looking for a subject for a Columbia dissertation. There in the shooting gallery was a big duck, or drake, named Beckett; she took aim and brought him down. More specifically, she wrote a letter and another letter and another, and to each Beckett replied courteously, in his best mixture of self-effacement and unwillingness to interfere. His life, he said, was 'dull and without interest. The professors know more about it than I do.' The next letter repeated that he was 'a very dull dog'. But that the correspondence continued at all was a highly favorable sign, as Deirdre Bair understood. She arranged to meet Beckett in November, and at this encounter was given one of his famous noncommitments, 'I will neither help nor hinder.'

Seven years passed during which Beckett's neither helping nor hindering proved supportive. Whenever Deirdre Bair needed a grant, or an entrée to a friend of his unwilling to suffer an interview by her, she asked Beckett, and he obliged with the information that he was neither helping nor hindering, and that the foundation or friend might be well advised to do likewise, that is, by according a grant or an interview. 'And all the while', her preface admits in a matter-of-fact way, 'I am sure he did not want this book to be written and would have been grateful if I had abandoned it.' Instead of abandoning it, she interviewed a great many people, including some anonymous Deep Throats, and secured access to correspondence.

The most important cache of material is the 300 and more letters written by Beckett to Thomas McGreevy, who was also a principal correspondent of Wallace Stevens. To the young McGreevy, a talented critic and a delightful companion, Beckett wrote with great candor; and even later, when McGreevy withered into success as director of the National Gallery of Ireland, Beckett out of loyalty continued to write to him. These letters are as revelatory as those of Joyce, and since Beckett is quoted by Deirdre Bair as expressing dismay over the publication of Joyce's letters, he can scarcely feel less at the divulging of his own.

Whatever its defects, and it has many, *Samuel Beckett: A Biography* (1978), the book that Deirdre Bair has put together, is staggeringly full of surprises. There are long melancholy stretches: his illnesses are recorded groan by groan, as if to bear out his contention to a doctor that 'All life is a disease'. Flashes of intense and unexplained physical pain forced him to undergo a two-year psychoanalysis in London. Miss Bair presents an intimate portrait of his life with his family in Foxrock, a well-heeled suburb of Dublin. She traces in some detail his love affairs, which seem to have occupied him a good deal in spite of his later remark to a young poet, 'This thing called love, there's none of it, you know, it's only fucking.' Like others before her, she summarizes his unpublished novel, 'Dream of Fair to Middling Women', from which several published works have been quarried. She also describes his unfinished early play about Dr. Johnson and Mrs. Thrale, which shows Beckett identifying closely with Johnson's diseases and depressions. He interprets Johnson's attitude to Mrs. Thrale as desire checked by unwillingness and compounded with impotence:

> It becomes more interesting, the false rage to cover his retreat from her, then the real rage when he realizes that no retreat was necessary, and beneath all, the despair of the lover with nothing to love with. . . .

Deirdre Bair describes what has been known but never before spelled out, Beckett's steady unsuccess with publishers, and his gradual convergence with publishers obscure or courageous enough to risk his work, usually at moments when he had almost ceased to care. There is a long and detailed account of his marriage – for Beckett has let himself marry – which is remarkable for containing so many elements of non-marriage. Deirdre Bair is especially interesting about Beckett's wartime activities, an account gleaned by her from fellow-members of his *réseau* in the Resistance. Beckett was recruited early to serve as a translator, and at his own suggestion soon began to microfilm as well. There were several hairbreadth escapes which culminated in his walking out of his Paris flat with his wife just before a Gestapo raid. From Paris he made his way with her to Roussillon, where he joined the Maquis as a dynamitard. Beckett told Miss Bair nothing of all this, and of course never mentioned that in 1945 General de Gaulle decorated him with the Croix de Guerre. The last part of Miss Bair's book is a close-up picture of Beckett's activity as untitled director of his own plays.

The publication of this biography, which Beckett has disdained to avert and apparently to read, is a new disaster for a man who sees his life thus far as a prolonged disaster. All his priceless things, as Yeats said after George Moore's *Hail and Farewell* appeared, are now a post that passing dogs can defile. Beckett has not always been so tolerant. When an earlier scholar, Laurence Harvey, ventured into biographical areas, Beckett insisted upon the suppression of all but the most skeletal details. Why then did he allow Deirdre Bair to proceed? The question is quite as interesting as any problem propounded by the book, and answers may be guessed at. To some extent his experience of playing censor with Harvey had revolted him more than disclosure would have done. His urge for self-protection must have grown fainter as Miss Bair turned up one new lead after another. He cannot have anticipated how much her tireless efforts would discover, and since he had tolerated her beginning the task, where to cut her off became increasingly difficult to say. More than this, he saw besmirchment as the human condition. What right had he to exempt himself from it? Might not his claim to privacy be the last rag of egotism? After all, he had himself once printed in a story some sentences from a woman's letter to him, and having violated another's privacy he could scarcely be hoity-toity about his own.

Beckett's tolerance of his biographer had another cause as well. Deirdre Bair reports, though not in relation to herself, that toward women Beckett has been almost habitually passive. There was first his mother, whose domination he accepted, though he subverted it. Some of their difficulties arose from his repeated struggle to live with her, at an age (as late as thirty or more) when lesser men than Beckett have found a filial role impossible to discharge. He was to nurse her in her last illness, and for three years thereafter, as he once told me, he wrote nothing, bogged down in grief and guilt.

Among women he knew as a lover, such as Peggy Guggenheim, Beckett is represented as having been more seduced than seducing. Giving rather than taking has been his usual tendency. His pliancy, which Deirdre Bair does not highly regard, contains an element of secularized saintliness. The principal example of female domination offered by Miss Bair is that of the woman Beckett eventually married, Suzanne Deschevaux-Dumesnil. One day in 1937 this talented pianist saw a man lying on a Paris street with a knife wound, and called an ambulance. The man was Beckett, stabbed motivelessly by a pimp. She paid visits to him in hospital, and after some further acquaintance decided to move in with him. According to Deirdre Bair, Beckett was unresisting if unrequesting. The great Nay-Sayer has never been able to say no. He seems to have accepted the situation then, and made no effort to terminate it later.

Miss Bair speaks of Mme Beckett as a substitute mother, but the attachment, which she claims to know has ceased to be sexual, is clearly not to be encompassed by such a term. During the war Beckett and his wife were joined in the intimacy of subversion, and their eventual escape from the Nazis necessitated walking hundreds of miles by night and hiding out by day. There were conflicts later, which Miss Bair describes on the testimony of their obliging friends, for at least on this subject Beckett has held his tongue, and Mme Beckett appears not to have uttered a word to her husband's biographer. To judge from the fact that they continue to live in the same flat, though not necessarily in the same rooms in it, and that they travel together on vacations, the area of disagreement may be more confined than chatterbox friends recognize. If they indeed have separate telephones in their flat, and sometimes communicate by them, this is to facilitate the exchange of messages without the obligation of meeting each other's guests. It seems clear that husband and wife (they were officially married in 1961) regard their marriage as an absolute commitment, beyond sexual trivia.

Deirdre Bair has profited from Beckett's apathy, indifference, self-destructiveness, guilt, and another quality which is the one he has exhibited in his life more steadily than any of the others – sheer kindness. This is the one about which psychoanalysis has least to say, but it is the one by which Beckett is known to hundreds of people – scholars, brothel-keepers, actors, nondescripts. It would be wrong to assume, as Miss Bair appears to do, that his passivities are directed only toward women. His relations with men often exhibit the same character. Early in his life he read Schopenhauer, and there confirmed what presumably he had already come to feel, that most people lived in an unremitting exercise of will, expressed by rapacity in love as in business. It was all push and shove, and Beckett decided that he wanted as little of it as he could manage. He is quoted as saying early on, 'All I want is to sit on my ass and fart and think of Dante.' The only form of competitiveness he has sanctioned is that involved in sports: a never surrendered ambition was to play cricket for Ireland. Chess also has been allowed. Otherwise he has stood aside. The Antwerp philosopher Arnold Geulinex, also a Beckett enthusiasm, reinforced Schopenhauer by separating will from act. We cannot claim to control what our minds do, let alone our bodies, those 'ungainly, unlovely, and unintelligent instruments'. We are only 'naked spectators' of a psychophysical machine – our mind-body and by extension the universe – which is operated in disregard of our wishes.

Against this background, Beckett could scarcely have said to the eager Deirdre Bair, when she proposed a biography, 'Don't!' To forbid others to act involves the pretense that one can forbid oneself, and that one knows what to forbid and what not. Beckett makes no such claim. For his public exposure in this book he is to blame, yet in Beckett's world blame has an uncertain status. And then, why make such a pother about what is basically of no consequence? The only secrets to which Beckett has clung are the writer's *secrets d'état*, and in the midst of meetings with Miss Bair and letters to her he has always maintained that his writing is the only thing that matters. In another mood, when like his character Belacqua he searches for 'the best method to attain nullity of being', he is not so sure that the writing matters either, though he is a little like other writers in not enjoying derogatory reviews.

The relation of Beckett's writings to his life is problem-ridden. Deirdre Bair says she wants to illuminate it, but she clouds it further. One might suppose from his apparent pliancy before the willful that Beckett is doughlike. Actually he is anything but. He is fearless in taking risks, whether on motorcycles or in the Deux Chevaux that he drives recklessly around Paris, or in his writings, the acceptance of which demanded no less than a total upheaval in his readers' habits and expectations. Miss Bair does not recognize that the passiveness she observes in his outward conduct cannot be reconciled with his absolute integrity as a writer – an integrity that he says he learned from Joyce.

She does acknowledge that in his behavior as a play director he is anything but all-accepting; here he terrifies actors with his punctilio. He has exerted increasing authority over his plays, holding like Yeats that there should be an author's not an actor's theater. Budding Stanislavskys have had to learn that they are not to act, only to do what he tells them. They may contribute to the image he has in mind, nothing more. Upstaging each other, or the author, belongs to that world of will which the play aspires to hold in check. Beckett was pleased to hear some years ago that Yeats had once thought of inserting actors in barrels so as to keep them from 'expression'. One of his more recent dramatic achievements was to realize in his play *Not I* a long ambition of having visible only 'a pair of blubbering lips', though in fact Billie Whitelaw's lips did not blubber.

This passion for exact detail in play production is strong enough to prompt the surmise that all Beckett's works are composed with the same strictness. Deirdre Bair prefers to consider that his fictional work is confessional, with *The Unnamable* as the ultimate confession. Yet the facts she has herself gathered defy this view. Beckett's first published work is written with fanatical precision. Nor can his novels be considered mere outpourings. A letter from Beckett to McGreevy about *Murphy*, for example, defends the ending of the book so eloquently and with so much awareness of other possibilities that any notion of uncontrol is scouted. When she takes up Beckett's trilogy, Miss Bair assures us without example that whole paragraphs are lifted from Beckett's confessional letter to McGreevy. If they are, other questions follow. Did Beckett remember the paragraphs, did he make copies of personal letters? In either case, the words remained in his mind as words, not drool. For Beckett the form of literature he most abominates is what he has called 'Bloody Veronicism'. That any of his works should just soak the napkin in the bloody actual would never content him.

Beckett's trilogy has its beginnings in his sense of alienation from his body, from most of his mind, and from the outside world. The old distinction of subject and object crumbles, yet a powerful narrative consciousness remains at work. When in the last volume the Unnamable feels compelled to describe life, he ultimately tries to do so in terms of subverbal sounds – 'heart-rending cries' and 'inarticulate murmurs'. 'I'll practice,' he says, and then offers, 'nyum, plop, psss, nothing but emotion, bing bang, that's blows, ugh, pooh, what else, oooh, aaah, that's love, enough, it's tiring, hee hee, that's the Abderite, no, the other. . . .' This cluster of sounds of relish, of voiding, of war, of revulsion, then in afterthought of love, and of laughter, consigns life to a ludicrous reduction. Yet the series suddenly shies off into a referential riddle: the Unnamable relates his view of life, perhaps because atomized into cries and murmurs, first to the Abderite, who is probably Democritus of Abdera (known as 'the laughing philosopher'), and then by choice to 'the other', who may well be the melancholy Heraclitus (traditionally the counterpart of Democritus), more prone to recognize how all things tire and pass.

This ponderous provenance, mockingly evoked, is proof that literacy will not be put down, and that the reduction to subverbalism sends us, as so often in Beckett's works, back to the dictionary. The mind, its part in experience disparaged, revenges itself by image- and word-making, by joking and source-hunting. If Beckett is auto-biographical in the trilogy, he is not so by denominating actual events or relationships, but by seeking, as he attributes his own qualities to his creatures, to analyze and objectify them. Grief and silence are pitted against humor and language, and never defeat them. The trilogy ends, the voice of the Unnamable goes on.

Miss Bair quotes without comment that Beckett was deeply offended by a psychiatrist friend who thought the trilogy could be regarded as photographic realism applied to Beckett's mind. She herself commits the same offense. To judge from what she quotes of the letters to McGreevy, they are written with care, and for Beckett to write is to connect or disconnect, not to vomit. Anguish described is anguish altered. Hence throughout this history, moments of dejection are given tongue quite beyond the necessities of wailing. As someone says in *Murphy*, after a depressing summary of existence, 'Very prettily put!'

To what extent then may Beckett's negativism, since it is couched with such perfection, be considered a stay against itself? The Nobel Prize committee thought he had 'transmuted the destitution of modern man into his exaltation', and awarded him the prize for literature, though literature was exactly what Beckett, like Verlaine, never wanted to write. Deirdre Bair has an opportunity here to comment on the total implications of his work. Lacking a general theory, she is more silent than Beckett. She persists in saying that his writings are autobiographical, though in what way is never specified except in passing details. For example, she quotes (twice) a sentence from a letter in which Beckett says, 'My memories began on the eve of my birth, under the table, when my father gave a dinner party and my mother presided,' but this sounds more like *Tristram Shandy* than like Beckett's autobiography. When she feels compelled to deal with Beckett's mental history, she follows passages in Laing or Jung which skirt the central difficulty, that Beckett is an inveterate writer rather than just an inveterate sufferer.

When she does offer to generalize, she cannot sustain her own generalizations. Beckett remarked, 'My father did not beat me, nor did my mother run away from home,' and she asserts that the opposite is true. His mother may have beaten him, but Deirdre Bair's own evidence indicates that his father never ran away. In fact she almost at once admits that the father was very much there, and that 'his homecoming each evening was the special event of the day'. Miss Bair feels she has caught Beckett out in petty deceptions over the date of his birth, which he claims to be Good Friday, 13 April, and over the denial of authorship of a sophomoric piece in the Portora school magazine. But these deceptions imply a useless vanity at odds with the self-accusation she represents as his usual burden, and no one who knows Beckett will impute to him gratuitous lies.

Such details may appear unimportant, but they suggest that continuous slight distortion which Miss Bair performs on Beckett in the absence of interpretation. With so amorphous a conception of him, the biography often seems to be a collection of learned gossip. So she speaks more than once of his considering people to be inferior to him because he, unlike them, was born an Anglo-Irishman and attended Trinity College. This is to attribute to Beckett an order of experience utterly foreign to him. Even Joyce comes in for this sort of treatment, as Miss Bair says Joyce took 'a snobbish pleasure' in having Beckett help him because Beckett was a Trinity man and other helpers were mostly from University College. But Joyce recognized Beckett as the most gifted of his entourage, and had no need of snobbery to value assistance from him. Miss Bair, contemplating a relationship between geniuses, might well forbear to diminish it with tidbits indiscriminately gathered. She seems needlessly offensive to Eugene and Maria Jolas, especially since Maria Jolas helped her, when she speaks of them as having 'insinuated themselves' among Joyce's friends. Some other term might have been found for two of Joyce's solidest friendships. Or she will say, some time after Beckett received the Nobel Prize, that 'he was unshakably confident that ... there would be nothing in his future that he could not handle'. Beckett has suffered too much to be subjected to such banalities.

These distortions become more lamentable when Deirdre Bair describes a trip Beckett made to Nazi Germany in 1937. To prove he was apolitical (a point she insists upon in spite of evidence that he has been a lifelong rebel), she says he was oblivious to the Nazi control of the country, and then two pages later reports Beckett's amazement at two German graduate students who were working on subjects the Nazis disapproved of. Miss Bair hangs on to wrong views even while amassing information that discredits them.

When she discusses Beckett's writing, she is liable to get things wrong. His piercing essay on Joyce's *Work in Progress* she patronizes as 'showing promise', for example, and she insists that *Krapp's Last Tape* ends on 'a note of self-realization' which was Beckett's own:

> Perhaps my best years are gone. When there was a chance of happiness. But I wouldn't want them back. Not with the fire in me now. No, I wouldn't want them back.

But the 'fire' which Krapp feels among his banana peels, as he listens to this bit from Spool 3, dictated when he was thirty-nine, is not to be taken in so Wordsworthian a fashion.

Miss Bair's writing is occasionally well turned, but she lacks the fastidiousness of her subject, and is quite oblivious to such clichés as 'crass roots of commercialism', and can say with a straight face that Peggy Guggenheim 'had him in her thrall'. Sometimes there are meaningless subtleties: 'Irony is undercut by wit.' There is a good deal of flat and thoughtless summary: 'Beckett regarded himself as equally at home in the disciplines of poetry and criticism.' It is not possible to ascertain, since many of her sources are unavailable, how accurately she is rendering them, but certain mistakes, such as placing La Baule in Switzerland, or making Nora Joyce alive in 1953, are disquieting. Beckett must know of many errors, and his tacit toleration of them is not so much a comment on Miss Bair as on the universe.

Yet if Deirdre Bair offers no interpretation in a book which demands one, she provides details which must some day be marshaled from multiplicity. One constant element is the depth of Beckett's convictions and of his loyalties. Among the convictions is a steady hostility to his native country. He has that anti-Irish quality which only Irishmen can display. Ireland is for him a *côte de misère*, 'the land of my unsuccessful abortion'. Not that he regards his nationality as anything but determining. When a Frenchman enquired if he were English, on an occasion unrecorded in this book, Beckett responded, '*Au contraire.*' Asked how it happened that so many Irish writers have written so well in this century, Beckett offered (as Miss Bair recounts) a simple explanation, 'It's the priests and the British. They have buggered us into existence. After all, when you're in the last bloody ditch, there is nothing left but to sing.' The wanton puritanism of suppressing his books, of which the Irish government was guilty, aroused him to say also that Ireland while banning all forms of contraception had legislated 'sterilization of the mind'.

In his loyalties Beckett has shown absolute steadfastness. When he talks even today of the deaths of Paul Léon and Alfred Péron at the hands of the Nazis, he clearly has the same feelings of pain and hatred that he had at the time. Miss Bair says he participated in the Resistance not to help the French but because the Nazis were killing his friends, and says this confirms her view that he is apolitical. It would seem to confirm the opposite. One related aspect of his life which she fails to handle is that Beckett in all his loneliness has always been gregarious. At a certain stage of his life, she says, 'With few exceptions, Beckett was without friends.' He has always had such exceptions, probably more than most people. Friendship is a bright spot that relieves and perhaps throws into doubt his melancholy.

As an artist Beckett has demonstrated a relentless perfectionism. His works appear, each more forbidding than the last, stern and inevitable. 'My work is a matter of fundamental sounds (no joke intended) made as fully as possible,' he has said. No one but Joyce has offered as little concession to popularity. Perfection for Beckett has meant a renunciation of small ambitions: his models have been Joyce and Jack Yeats. Early on he denounced most Irish writers for being antiquarians, and he has insisted that any insight into the present age requires a recognition of the 'breakdown of the object' and 'the rupture of the lines of communication'. These in turn are suited to the lowering metabolism of his characters, and the grotesquerie which he finds to be an indispensable component of the tragic.

He has sought the liberation from family and nationality first by foreign residence and then by writing in a different language. The shift from English to French was an achievement that coloured everything that followed it. Henri Michaux remarked, at the time that *En Attendant Godot* was being performed, that Beckett was one of the few living persons who could write French. The larger number of Beckett's experiences have occurred in English; to recast them in French has been a source of a second life for him. This was not altogether voluntary. As he has said of his books, or as he sometimes calls them, his 'miseries', 'It was not as though I wanted to write them.'

Beckett is quoted by Deirdre Bair as saying, 'I'm not interested in stories of success, only failure.' His own success has been a new sadness, and his ultimate reason for permitting her biography is to let his infirmities become public knowledge and so challenge that success. Yet the success is real and deserved. What Miss Bair has presented, in an account that is crowded with stumbles and thwarts and mischances, is a simulacrum, Sim Botchit rather than Sam Beckett. Happily Beckett exists somewhere else.

1978

At the Yeatses'

IN THE summer of 1945 the fortunes of the Second World War had propelled me to England, where I was serving in the Navy with a temporary assignment to the Office of Strategic Services. After V-E Day the neutral Irish government relaxed its restriction on visits by American servicemen, and the moment seemed propitious for me to write to George Yeats, asking if she would see me about a study of her late husband which I had begun three years previously. Fortunately I knew nothing of that distinguished woman's well-earned reputation for never replying to letters. She answered yes.

At 46 Palmerston Road, Rathmines, the first sight of Mrs. Yeats's study, which had been her husband's, was astonishing. There in the bookcases was his working library, often heavily annotated, and in cabinets and file cases were all his manuscripts, arranged with care by his widow. She was very good at turning up at once some early draft of a poem or play or prose work, or a letter Yeats had received or written. When complimented, she said she was just a hen picking up scraps. Among the scraps were all Yeats's letters to Lady Gregory, done up in innumerable small bundles according to year, with ribbons to hold them together. I asked her about Yeats's first meeting with Joyce, and she showed me an unpublished preface to *Ideas of Good and Evil* (1903) in which Yeats described that singular occasion. I evinced a perhaps unexpected interest in the magical order to which Yeats belonged, the Golden Dawn; she opened a chest and took out his implements and regalia and rituals. Agape at such profusion, I could only say that I would like to return after the war, and she replied, 'I hope you will.' So it came about that I spent the year 1946–7 in Dublin, working with these books and papers.

It was obviously impossible for me to knock every day at her door, but Mrs. Yeats was equal to the problem of logistics. She produced an old suitcase and filled it with the manuscripts that I wanted to examine. At the beginning she was anxious about one of them, the unpublished first draft of Yeats's autobiography, and asked me to return it speedily. I felt that I must make a copy of it at once, but found Yeats's handwriting very difficult to decipher. There was nothing for it but to stay up all night, and towards dawn I discovered that during this vigil I had begun to sense his rhythm and to recognize his characteristic turns of phrase, so that I was able to allay her disquiet by returning the manuscript on time.

Mrs. Yeats's kindness extended not only to the loan of the manuscripts, but sometimes to their interpretation. For example, I once suggested to her that the 'Old Rocky Face' in Yeats's poem, 'The Gyres', might be the moon, presiding there over the ages of human history. But she remembeed that, at the time he composed the poem, her husband had been reading up on the Delphic oracle, and was excited by the image of the oracle speaking through a cleft in the rock. She felt sure that it was the oracle who was being described, and not the moon. No doubt she was right. Another day, I asked her with some embarrassment whether she thought that the outburst of blood, which in several poems Yeats associated with the end of each 28-phase lunar cycle, might not be based on the menstrual cycle. After all, Freud had for a time indulged his friend Fliess in the theory that the basic numbers of the universe were for the same reason 23 and 28. But on this matter Mrs. Yeats was firm. 'W. B. knew very little about all that when we married,' she said, 'and in fact until well after that part of *A Vision* had been settled.' This many years later, I can see that Yeats had in mind a blood-letting like sexual violation rather than the habitual process I had proposed.

I came to know Mrs. Yeats well during this year, and to apprehend that, with all her self-effacement, she had played a great role with aplomb. Once I quoted to her a remark in a letter from Yeats's father, written while she was ill with influenza and in danger of death in 1918. J. B. Yeats said that if she died, Willie would fall to pieces. 'I haven't read the letter,' she said, 'and anyway, it wasn't true.' All she would admit was that it was useful for Yeats to have someone so much younger than he with whom he could converse. But he himself wrote, with greater accuracy, 'For how could I forget / The wisdom that you brought, the comfort that you gave?' She provided him with a tranquil house, she understood his poems, and she liked him as a man. She could also offer help. For example, it was she who suggested that the medium in his play, *The Words upon the Window-Pane*, should count the money paid her for the seance – just the realistic scrap that he needed.

She talked to me with candor about 'the marriage', as – to her amusement – I pedantically found myself calling it, perhaps in unconscious response to her own objectivity about it. She had met Yeats in 1911, when she was eighteen, having been born on 17 October 1892. If he noticed her then, it was simply as 'a girl / Perched in some window of her mother's house'. By that time she had already spurned her mother's wish for her to lead an upper-middle-class life of balls and parties, on the grounds that she wished to become an artist. Her artistic career did not get far, but she used her freedom to look into subjects her mother considered unwomanly, such as philosophy and occultism, just as earlier she had read the 'forbidden' novels of George Moore. The interest in occultism was one she shared with Yeats; he encouraged her to join the Golden Dawn in 1914, and at her initiation acted as her Hiereus or sponsor. She quickly passed through the early stages and was initiated into the Inner Order, which he himself had reached only a little time before. Then, with the outbreak of war, she had to shift her interests, and became first a hospital cook – which she enjoyed – and then a nurse, which she liked less.

Yeats was well acquainted with her mother and their friends, but some years passed before he took a stronger interest in her. It was known that one of his reasons for attending seances so diligently at this time had to do with matrimonial plans: he would ask the mediums first the secrets of life after death, and then the likelihood of his marrying his old sweetheart Maud Gonne during his present life. Since Maud Gonne was already married, and had been converted to Catholicism, this question was academic until 1916. Then the Easter Rebellion brought about her widowhood: her husband John MacBride, from whom she had long been separated, was one of those executed. To Yeats that husband had appeared to be 'a drunken vainglorious lout,' and when he heard that MacBride had refused a blindfold, saying, 'I've been staring down rifle butts all my life,' he remarked that he might better have said that he had been staring down pintpots all his life. His antipathy to MacBride at first made him see the rebellion as all wrong, and he and Maud Gonne had – according to her daughter Iseult – a furious argument on the subject. Then he brought himself to recognize the importance of the blood sacrifice that had been made, and even MacBride's part in it. The poem he wrote, 'Easter 1916', did not give up his reasons for opposing the rebellion, or his dislike of MacBride, but he now attributed the rebels' 'bewilderment' to 'excess of love', a malady with which he could thoroughly sympathize, and one appropriate to Easter in any year.

Yeats seems to have felt honor-bound to propose marriage to Maud Gonne, though he knew well enough the difficulties that might ensue. As Iseult Gonne Stuart remarked to me, 'My mother is not a woman of much discernment, but she had enough to know better than to marry Yeats, to whom she wasn't suited.' It was then that

Yeats considered for a time the possibility of marriage to Iseult, whom he had known since childhood, and whose severe beauty he greatly admired. (In the characterology of *A Vision*, she is one of the denizens of the 16th phase, where beautiful women forgather.) Iseult was quite different from her mother. At that period of her life she was bored by Maud Gonne's politics, though she came to share them; many years later she would harbor a Nazi espionage agent at her house in Glendalough. As a young woman, her interests were literary and artistic. She and Yeats read some French writers such as Péguy together, and she took great interest in what he was composing. In 1916 he remarked to her, as she recalled to me, that he had been rereading Keats and Shelley, and now thought it strange that he had ever seen anything in them. The poem which he wrote to her, entitled 'To a Young Beauty', bids her attend not to these poets but to Landor and Donne. At the age of fifteen, she confided to her diary (as she told me) that she was in love with Yeats, and asked him to marry her, only to be rejected. Now he bethought himself, and said to her that he would take her away from her mother's atmosphere of extremist politics; though he was an old man, he would give her a life among agreeable people. 'You wouldn't say you loved me, would you?' she asked. Being uncertain, he would not. Iseult Stuart told me that she had thought to keep Yeats about as her mother had done, but he became very decisive. They met by arrangement at a Lyons Corner House in London, to discuss the matter. She tried to equivocate, but he said, 'Yes or no?' At this she could only say no. Years afterwards he said to her nostalgically, 'If only you and I had married,' and she caught him up with, 'Why, we wouldn't have stayed together a year.'

At this time Yeats began to think seriously about Georgie Hyde-Lees. She was more intelligent than Maud Gonne or Iseult, and more companionable, with a sense of humor that was lacking in them. If she had not the 'beauty to make a stranger's eye distraught', she was attractive, with bright, searching eyes and a high colour which gave her, as he described her to a friend, a barbaric beauty. She was interested in his subjects; she had the virtue of being in love with him. Yeats had felt for some years that he must marry. An incident in 1914, when a woman with whom he had been having an affair thought she was pregnant, had alarmed him, and though the woman proved to be mistaken, Lady Gregory advised that marriage would be a good idea. (Dorothy Shakespear Pound told Mrs. Yeats that at one time Yeats and Lady Gregory herself had planned to marry, but Mrs. Yeats never had the courage to ask him if this were true.) To Lady Gregory the best candidate was Iseult: she liked Iseult's unworldliness, and thought she would be easier to control because of it. But Dorothy Pound's mother, Yeats's friend Olivia Shakespear, preferred Georgie Hyde-Lees, in part because she saw a wildness or strangeness in her. Yeats was open with Miss Hyde-Lees about his previous attachments; he described himelf as a Sindbad who after many misadventures had at last found port. Their intimacy blossomed. In August 1917 she gave up her job as a nurse. When he confided to Lady Gregory that he and Georgie (whom he would soon rechristen George) were to be married, he asked if he should bring her to Coole for a visit. Lady Gregory replied, 'I'd rather you didn't come till you were married and nothing could be done about it.'

Under such unpropitious auspices Yeats and Miss Hyde-Lees were married on 17 October 1917. But during the first days following the ceremony, Mrs. Yeats saw, as she told me, that her husband was 'blue'. They were staying at the Ashdown Forest Hotel. She knew his situation and understood that he felt he might have done the wrong thing in marrying her rather than Iseult, whose resistance might have weakened in time. Mrs. Yeats wondered whether to leave him. Casting about for some means of distraction, she thought of attempting automatic writing. Yeats was familiar with this procedure although it was disapproved of by the Golden Dawn. Her idea was to fake a sentence or two that would allay his anxieties over Iseult and herself, and after the session to own up to what she had done. Accordingly on 21 October, four days after their marriage, she encouraged a pencil to write a sentence which I remember as saying, approximately, 'What you have done is right for both the cat and the hare.' She was confident that he would decipher the cat as her watchful and timid self, and the hare as Iseult – a fleet runner. ('Two Songs of a Fool' offers a similar bestiary.) Yeats was at once captured, and relieved. His misgivings disappeared, and it did not occur to him that his wife might have divined his cause of anxiety without preternatural assistance.

Then a strange thing happened. Her own emotional involvement – her love for this extraordinary husband; and her fears for her marriage – must have made for unusual receptivity, as she told me later, for she suddenly felt her hand grasped and driven irresistibly. The pencil began to write sentences which she had never intended or thought, which seemed to come as from another world. As images and ideas took pencilled form, Yeats went beyond his initial relief about his marriage. Here were more potent revelations: he had married into Delphi. To Maud Gonne and her daughter he appeared to be buried in what they always referred to as 'the prosaic marriage'. But nothing could have been less prosaic than what he was experiencing. His excitement entered into a long epithalamion he now wrote, 'The Gift of Harun Al-Rashid'. In it he continued the Arabian imagery initiated by his image of Sindbad, this time casting himself as the court poet Kusta Ben Luka.

Sultan Harun Al-Rashid is exhilarated because with spring he has as usual taken a new bride, and he urges the aging and celibate Kusta Ben Luka to marry too. Kusta is anything but eager. For him, he says, if not for the sultan, love is not a matter of seasons, and he despairs of finding a lasting love. The sultan – who represents Yeats's more worldly and promiscuous aspect – maintains that an unlasting love is the better, something transitory and animal, because it is man's mockery of the changeless soul. Knowing Kusta's opposite mind, however, he has found for the poet a woman who shares the 'thirst for those old crabbed mysteries',

> And yet herself can seem youth's very fountain,
> Being all brimmed with life . . .

If that be true, says Kusta, 'I would have found the best that life can give.' He marries her and soon after the marriage she sits bolt upright in bed and speaks of mysteries, not so much in her own person as in the voice of a Djinn.

He is at once delighted yet anxious, as Yeats must have been, for fear that she should suppose he loves her only because of 'that midnight voice' – like the automatic script – and all it reveals. No, he insists,

> The voice has drawn
> A quality of wisdom from her love's
> Particular quality. The signs and shapes;
>
>   . . . . . .
>
> All, all those gyres and cubes and midnight things
> Are but a new expression of her body
> Drunk with the bitter sweetness of her youth.

The preternatural drew its power from the natural and affirmed that.

Along with intellectual excitement and emotional involvement there came to Yeats a great serenity of spirit, which lasted until the Irish Civil War broke out five years later. He liked being husband, and he liked being father; they soon had a girl and then a boy. The volume he published in 1919, *The Wild Swans at Coole*, contained a number of poems about his new life and thought, and in 1921 another

volume, *Michael Robartes and the Dancer*, formed an elaborate tribute
to his wife. The title poem and the one that followed it, 'Solomon and
the Witch', celebrated with urbanity their matrimonial conflation of
wisdom and love. Several of the poems following these dealt in one
way or another with gleanings from the automatic script. The birth
of Anne Yeats was heralded in 'A Poem for My Daughter'. The
final poem, 'To Be Carved on a Stone at Thoor Ballylee', proudly
associated husband and wife,

> I, the poet William Yeats,
> With old mill boards and sea-green slates,
> And smithy work from the Gort forge,
> Restored this tower for my wife George . . .

Changing her name had been rewarded with this magnificent line.

In the meantime he had an opportunity to demonstrate his
freedom from his old life. Maud Gonne had rented her house at
73 Stephen's Green in Dublin to him in 1918. She herself had
been forbidden by the British authorities to enter Ireland. But she
smuggled herself in, disguised as a beggar woman, and presented
herself at Yeats's door asking to be taken in. At this point George
Yeats was extremely ill with influenza. Yeats knew that Maud
Gonne's presence in the house was bound to create turmoil, and he
refused to admit her. She refused to leave, it being her own house,
even when the doctor advised her that her presence might endanger
his patient. Yeats became quite fierce until Maud Gonne gave in
and decamped. He knew where his true loyalty lay.

He worked passionately to embody in systematic form, for which
A Vision offered an appropriate title, the fragmentary revelations in
the automatic script. He was in hot pursuit of a much more complete
symbology than he had achieved in his earlier efforts to compound
the poetic and mystical traditions. He asked his wife about the
books she had read before their marriage – William James, Hegel's
Philosophy of History, Croce – and read them himself to see if the
automatic writing unconsciously reflected them. Happily it was
independent of them:

> Truths without father came, truths that no book
> Of all the uncounted books that I have read,
> Nor thought out of her mind or mine begot,
> Self-born, high-born, and solitary truths,
> Those terrible implacable straight lines
> Drawn through the wandering vegetative dream . . .

The vocabulary of the script included unusual words for grand discourse, such as 'funnel' and 'spiral' (which he altered to gyre) and names of household pets (the Yeatses had a great many) that the communicating voices took over for themselves. He insisted that his wife keep up the automatic writing for two or three hours a day, usually from three to six in the afternooon. It was a great strain for her. She feared as well that it might become simply a new obsession for him, like the obsession with 'spooks' that he had had before his marriage. That one had alienated old friends from coming to his Monday evenings at Woburn Buildings. A reluctant Sybil, she therefore broke off the communication several times, and insisted that he return to writing verse. Yet the verse began to register its effect, too. Not only were there explicitly symbological poems like 'The Phases of the Moon', but he would scarcely have conceived of 'The Second Coming' as the extinction of rationality, she felt, if it had not been for the automatic script. His daily behavior was also affected: to place people in their appropriate phases of the moon, as the script required, entailed listening to what they said and watching the way they behaved, and for the purpose he took a much greater interest in the outside world. This interest proved surprisingly congenial to him.

For a time he accepted without qualification the messages that came through the automatic writing. The fact that his wife could answer during sleep by word of mouth, without the need of writing, made him try that method of communication as well, though much less frequently than the other. Some matters did not seem capable of resolution by either method. For example, as Mrs. Yeats informed me, he was never sure how much control the daimon had of the self; and while he sometimes thought of the anti-self as a spirit, at other times he did not.

That all this revelation must some day come to an end in a book was Yeats's idea from the start. The method of presentation worried him. Mrs. Yeats wished him to present the material directly, without introduction, but Yeats's mind was too modulated and subtle for that. After all, he had spent most of his writing life couching in gracious terms conceptions that would otherwise have made his audience recoil. He therefore began within weeks of the start of the automatic script to concoct a transmission myth. This was the elaborate fable in which Giraldus Cambrensis, the historian of England, joined forces with Kusta Ben Luka. (Two characters from the early stories, Michael Robartes and Owen Aherne, were also incorporated.) To Giraldus he attributed – much to the amusement of better Latinists – the *Speculum Angelorum et Hominorum* (for *Hominum*), to Kusta the dance which choreographed the principal

symbols of the automatic script. He got his friend Edmund Dulac to
carve a woodcut portrait cf Giraldus, obviously modelled on Yeats's
face, and since this was completed by January 1918, the primary
fable must have been constituted in the first two months of his
marriage.

The first edition of *A Vision* did not appear until early 1926. Soon
after, Yeats realized that much of it was too close to the original
automatic writing, and that further elucidation was necessary. He
decided to do a second edition of the book, and this time to tell about
the automatic writing. Mrs. Yeats was absolutely opposed to this,
and they had then, as she told me, the first and only serious quarrel
of their marriage. Yeats prevailed, but included his mythical variations as well as his realistic account. The second edition of 1937
made room for many second thoughts and also many doubts. When
Allan Wade asked him if he believed in *A Vision*, he said evasively –
though accurately, 'Oh, I draw from it images for my poetry.' The
book hovered between philosophy and fiction, bread and cake.

Once Yeats had revised *A Vision*, he was free to do other work,
though a surviving document called 'Seven Propositions' indicates
that during his last decade he pushed his speculations about final
matters even further. He also did a good deal of reading in philosophy
with the hope of confirming and enlarging his theories. Sometimes
he joked about mysticism, but as his wife pointed out, one can do
that and still be serious about it. My own attitude toward automatic
writing, and indeed toward spiritualist phenomena in general,
seemed too skeptical to Mrs. Yeats. 'Do you not believe in ghosts at
all?' she asked me. 'Only in those inside me,' I replied. 'That's the
trouble with you,' she said with unexpected severity.

I still know very little about ghosts. But I can see that the metaphysical urge in Yeats was inseparable from his greatness as a poet.
Were it removed, there would be few poems left. He regarded as
metaphysical certain experiences which others might regard as
within merely human compass: moments when memory offers bitterness or sweetness like a taste, or when, for no mere reason, the
being becomes radiant. He wrote about one such experience in
'Stream and Sun at Glendalough':

> What motion of the sun or stream
> Or eyelid shot the gleam
> That pierced my body through?
> What made me live like those that seem
> Self-born, born anew?

Besides these accesses of feeling, there were others (possibly less certain in provenance) in which it seemed that two worlds converged, offering totality of being, insight into the heart of things, foreknowledge of what was to come.

I learned from Mrs. Yeats, in fragments of recollection, something of what Yeats was like. One day she spoke about his hands, for example. His palm was very large in relation to the hand's outer surface; the fingers were tapered to very thin, square edges, with rounded nails. (In Sean O'Sullivan's portrait of him at the Abbey Theatre, Yeats is shown, inaccurately, with pointed nails on round fingers.) She told me how before their marriage he had been investigated by the Inland Revenue, because his reported income was so small. Until well after 1900 it was only a few hundred pounds a year. George Russell was invoked as a character witness. The officials ended up apologizing and explaining that they had not supposed it possible that someone so much in the newspapers could be making so little money. She talked of his late preference for blue shirts, and of how people wrongly assumed that he wore them in sympathy with the Irish fascist organization, the Blue Shirts, when in fact blue went well with his white hair. It was true that he had met with General Eoin O'Duffy, the Blue Shirt leader, but she noticed that 'they spoke on different lines and neither listened to the other'. In describing O'Duffy to friends, Yeats always called him 'the swashbuckler', a label derisory enough to indicate the labeller's unenthusiasm. For, notwithstanding such parleying, Yeats never ceased to advocate 'the right of every man to see the world in his own way', as he wrote to John Quinn in 1905. He was always ready to denounce authority when this right was impinged upon, and so could never have accepted an authoritarian regime.

She told me of Yeats's sense of humor. Sometimes this took the form of prankishness, as when he allowed his wife, on their first visit together to Coole, to bring their cat along. Lady Gregory's life was made up of prohibitions; when she was twenty-four she had given up hunting because she enjoyed it too much. She had an absolute rule against animals in the house. So Yeats had to wait until their hostess was asleep to bring the cat in, and to take it out early in the morning before she woke up. Mrs. Yeats asked why he had not forewarned her, and he replied, 'I wanted to see what she'd say.' He liked to force his friend George Russell to play croquet with him, and then spent all his time keeping Russell from getting his ball beyond the first wicket. Russell's only recourse was to pay his calls at 9.30 in the morning, a time when Yeats would not impose recreation.

A story of her husband that gave his wife less pleasure was one he told with Tory irony to Frank O'Connor: it seemed that Mrs. Yeats, who was as far to the left in politics as he was to the right, disliked their next-door neighbors as fascist sympathizers. On a certain day she went out and discovered that one of her democratic hens was missing, and assumed it had been devoured by the neighbors' police dog. She wrote them a letter. A prompt reply came back, 'Dog killed.' She was still reeling from this message when the democratic hen reappeared. She wanted to write to the neighbors, but Yeats said, 'You won't be able to bring back the fascist dog.' On a milder note, Yeats always addressed her in letters as 'My dear Dobbs', Dobbs being the name of a round man, and she being a bit round herself. But he never used this epithet in conversation.

Mrs. Yeats found her husband to be very 'human' The description he gives of himself in 'Coole Parke, 1929', 'There one that ruffled in a manly pose / For all his timid heart', was true, as she assured me: he *was* shy. She once remarked to Frank O'Connor, on rescuing him as he came into a party of unfamiliar people, that she had seen him to be shy because he had put his hand through his hair with the same gesture as her husband in the same state. To tide him over such situations, she told me, Yeats evolved a patter. He had to, because, as he complained to her, people looked at him as if he were the zoo. Lady Gregory, he said to his wife, was very sensitive, but had no idea that he was sensitive too.

When his children were born he was perhaps too old to respond intimately to them, though there are accounts of his romping with them when they were very small. He was inclined to be partial to Anne over Michael; and once when he refused to take anyone but Anne on some errand, Michael gazed at his retreating back climbing the stairs and amid sobs asked his mother, 'Who is that man?' But Yeats's later letters indicate that he did have pride and affection for them; he describes in one how Michael, 'tall and elegant', had come in fresh from winning a mathematics prize, and in another how Anne, attired in a new dress, had shown it off to him. In 1937, during the takeover of Czechoslovakia, Yeats explained the situation to Michael, then sixteen. When he had finished, the boy suddenly said, 'Well, that's not quite right,' and he proceeded to tell it correctly. Yeats was dumbfounded.

Because Yeats's poetry and life were pervaded by Maud Gonne, I paid a number of visits to that grand vestige of an ancient flame. Madame MacBride, as she was always called (in my ignorance I called her 'Mrs.' until her friend Ethel Mannin sternly reproved me), was then eighty-two, six feet tall, majestic in her skin and bones. She received me as a young man come to call, and I too regarded it as a courtly visit. I can see more clearly now that she had many mysteries. In the annals of Irish emancipation from British rule, she had a peculiar status. Her family and birthplace were English, yet she claimed Irishness for reasons which, though creditable, remain puzzling. Her passion for her adopted country was in many ways admirable, but it was adulterated by a fanatical quality which led her from the time of the Dreyfus case to anti-Semitism, and from the time of Hitler to pro-Nazi sympathy. Hitler was to carry out the attack on Britain for which she had always longed. To consecrate her work she would have to have been martyred, like Madame Roland, but she lived on, habited in black, not mourning the executed husband from whom she had been separated after two years of marriage, but an Ireland similarly partitioned. Longevity brought its grandeur. Yeats had conferred upon her an immortality which she had perhaps not earned. Gradually young men, like those who had once adored her for her beauty, came as I did to visit because they adored Yeats's images of her; and she died, rather unwillingly, into his poems, which she had never greatly liked. John Sparrow told me he owned a copy of one of Yeats's books, inscribed to her by the poet, in which the only pages that she had troubled to cut were the ones that contained poems written to her.

Maud Gonne said that all her letters from Yeats had been destroyed during the Irish 'troubles', though some late ones, at least, lie unimpaired in a Dublin bank vault. She did not agree with Yeats's version of their relationship. He thought she had never decisively discouraged him, she thought she had never given him reason for hope. Probably she had forgotten the 'spiritual marriage' that, according to his first autobiographical draft, she had contracted with him. He said in verse,

> Others because you did not keep
> That deep-sworn vow have been friends of mine.

When she wrote to inform him of her marriage to John MacBride, Yeats felt that she had betrayed that vow. He overcame his initial shock and anguish, however. He was too good a poet, and too generous a man, not to understand that beauty has its privileges, including cruelty, and many of his poems, while making clear the injury suffered, are elaborate acts of forgiveness.

I had always assumed that Yeats remained an unrequited lover, an impression fostered in Maud Gonne's writings. But one day in Dublin, reading an occult journal kept by Yeats in 1908, I came across a passage written late in the year while he was staying with

Maud Gonne at Colleville, her house in the Norman countryside. There was an obscure reference to her feeling that they could not continue. I asked Mrs. Yeats what was meant, and she said, 'I wouldn't have volunteered the information, but since you have found it out for yourself, I can confirm that W. B. and Maud Gonne were lovers at that time.' Subsequently I heard the same thing from a woman whom Yeats loved late in life, Edith Shackleton Heald, to whom he had also confided it. I realized the meaning of the reference in 'A Man Young and Old', where he wrote in one section, 'His Memories', the lines ending:

> My arms are like the twisted thorn
> And yet there beauty lay;
>
> The first of all the tribe lay there
> And did such pleasure take –
> She who had brought great Hector down
> And put all Troy to wreck –
> That she cried into this ear,
> 'Strike me if I shriek.'

For Yeats, at least, this autumnal flowering of a springtime passion had an importance out of proportion to its brevity. It made him feel he had vindicated his earlier fleshless pursuit of her.

As I try to imagine Maud Gonne's relationship with Yeats from her point of view, I can now comprehend it somewhat better. At the time when she paid her momentous first visit to the Yeats household in 1889, she was already, unbeknownst to him, deeply in love with a Frenchman. A year later, in January 1890, she became the mother of a small boy (not girl) named Georgette. The father was Lucien Millevoye, a newspaper editor and a married man, whose political extremism was a point of affinity with her. Millevoye had ardently supported the political ambitions of General Boulanger, and Maud Gonne carried secret messages about Europe to promote the cause. But in 1889, Boulanger, his oven having cooled, fled from France. Maud Gonne turned to the Irish independence movement. Yeats, instantly enamored of her, gathered her into his own activities and found some new ones that they could engage in together. Oblivious of Millevoye's existence, he felt that the spiritual marriage to which she had acceded might eventually become material too.

To Maud Gonne's grief, Georgette died, I think late in 1893. She questioned Yeats and his friend George Russell on what might happen to the soul of a dead child, and Russell pronounced that it was often reborn in the same family. Yeats noticed her emotion, and in his autobiography says he wanted to tell her that what Russell spoke of as a likelihood was only a speculation. It actuated her to descend with Millevoy to the dead child's vault in the hope of there re-conceiving the soul of the lost child in another body. A daughter, Iseult, was in fact evoked. The theatricality is less than the pathos. In many ways, as Yeats knew and said, Maud Gonne had a kind of hapless innocence in her experiences. He speaks in 'A Bronze Head' of murmuring at the thought of her, 'My child, my child!' As for her lover Millevoye, he treated her badly, but she did not break with him until he appeared one day in 1896 to see Iseult, in the company of a more recent mistress.

Iseult was born on 6 August 1894, and for a year or more Maud Gonne occupied herself with her daughter's care and stayed in France. During that time Yeats met Lionel Johnson's cousin, Olivia Shakespear. Mrs. Shakespear was a solicitor's wife, unhappy in her marriage. She had already borne the daughter, Dorothy, who was later to marry Ezra Pound. In his autobiography Yeats always called this charming woman by the *Rob Roy* name of Diana Vernon. The affair with Mrs. Shakespear, which was straightforward, was one for which Yeats always remained grateful. She had disburdened him, he wrote in the poem 'Friends', of 'youth's dreamy load'. Unfortunately, after a few months Maud Gonne wrote to say she had had a dream about him; Yeats's resultant agitation was patent to Mrs. Shakespear, who thereupon broke off their affair. They resumed it later, more casually, and remained good friends for life.

Yeats did not really obtain his sexual freedom until Maud Gonne was married in 1903. Then he took up with a number of women, including the actress Florence Farr and a masseuse named Mabel Dickinson, about whom he had his pregnancy scare. His evident sexual interest in another woman caused a falling-out with his friend John Quinn, the New York lawyer and collector. Quinn accused him of making overtures to Quinn's mistress, Dorothy Coates, while Miss Coates was in Paris. Yeats denied it in Edwardian style: 'If it had been your wife, yes,' he said to Quinn, 'but your mistress – never!' Quinn, unmarried and unamused, did not speak to him again for several years.

In Yeats's later years, and especially after a long period of illnesses culminating in Malta fever, from 1927 to 1928, he felt keenly his regret over his celibate youth. He wrote the poems of sexual reminiscence in the volume, *The Winding Stair*. Then in 1934, feeling his powers diminished, he submitted to a Steinach operation, the physical results of which were less dramatic than the imaginative ones. For several years, until the illnesses which were to bring him to his grave developed, Yeats had a 'marvellous' renewal of sexual and poetic fervor, which he had always regarded as allied. Towards the end of his life he had several late love affairs. Mrs. Yeats knew how important they were to him and, conscious of her role as a poet's wife, she countenanced more than she discountenanced them. 'After your death,' she once said to him, 'people will write of your love affairs, but I shall say nothing, because I will remember how proud you were.'

She sometimes talked to me about another burden, besides Maud Gonne, which Yeats had brought with him to their marriage. This was his lifelong tension with his father. Yeats considered that his father's influence upon him was incalculable. It had begun in childhood, when J. B. Yeats, suddenly taking note that William could not read, taught him himself, often by physical coercion. The other children, Lily, Lollie, and Jack, were permitted to go their own ways, though J. B. Yeats always took over the young men who came to visit, and the daughters never had a chance to get married. He made Willie his special concern. He knew his son through and through, and could pierce his self-protective armor with a word. The pressure included much physical pushing around, at least until early youth. Jack Yeats, observing one scene of paternal belligerence in the bedroom he shared with his brother, cried out to William, 'Mind, not a word until he apologizes.' J. B. Yeats would rag his son into the night about his marks in high school, or about not going to Trinity College, or about wasting his talent in occult activities, or even about his decision in 1903 to change publishers and go to Fisher Unwin. Their quarrels only ceased when J. B. Yeats went to America in 1908 and remained there until his death in 1922. He and George Yeats, who met in New York in 1920, got along well, and he greatly admired the poems that emerged from his son's marriage. They accorded with his theory of the necessity of grounding art in experience.

J. B. Yeats always insisted that his son's stubbornness was due to his Pollexfen genes – his mother's side, as though such a quality had never been heard of among the Yeatses. Yet no one was ever more stubborn than himself, whether in his resolution to become an artist or in his determination to defuse William's inveterate metaphysical urge. In later life he took more relaxed pleasure in his son's achievement: 'Old Priam was not much in himself, but then Hector was his son,' he would say. What he did for his son was to make available for twentieth-century use ideas that had been prematurely discredited in the Nineties. One was that poetry and art were forms of truth superior to all others, which J. B. Yeats improved by making clear that they were in no way separated from life. The other was that the individual should not, like Pater, value experience for its own sake, nor should he subordinate experience to moral or religious principle. Rather he should search for what J. B. Yeats called Unity of Being, in which all the qualities of the personality could chime together.

In these theories his son followed him, though with much additional complexity. J. B. Yeats had worried excessively that his son would put occult theory upon everything. He need not have concerned himself. The system which William evolved in *A Vision* was one that had a sort of anti-system built into it. Ostensibly deterministic, it had many elements of free will. While in favor of totality of being, it recognized that the saint's annihilation of selfhood had a place in the world too. It trembled throughout on the edge which separated a doctrinal account of personality and history from a myth with an uncertain epistemological status. As Mrs. Yeats said to me, sometimes he believed it, sometimes he didn't. In one section of it, phase 17, Yeats described people like himself who were always outgrowing their own systems like bursting pods.

The history of Yeats's last years is a sad one, with illness challenging his constant desire to renew himself. Three years before his death, he told his wife that it was harder to live than to die. He revealed, closer to the end, 'I must be buried in Italy, because in Dublin there would be a procession, with Lennox Robinson as chief mourner.' She told me that it would have taken him a hundred years to complete his work. I surmise that he was roughening the edges of the two forces he had always seen at work in the world, the one regarding reality as temporary, provisional, tidal; the other regarding it as hive- or nest-like, tenacious, lasting. 'Let all things pass away,' says a world-conqueror in 'Vacillation', while in *A Vision* Yeats quotes with approval an impromptu song of Iseult Stuart, 'O Lord, let something remain.' These were related to the two forms of love he had contrasted in 'The Gift of Harun Al-Rashid', the one mocking the permanence which the other sought. In May 1938 he wrote a quatrain for Edith Shackleton Heald in which he offered, as 'the explanation of it all', that 'From nowhere into nowhere nothing's run.' The same word resounds in two of his last plays: the old man in *Purgatory* says at the end, 'Twice a murderer and all for nothing,' and the last speech of *The Herne's Egg* includes the line, 'All that trouble and nothing to show for it . . .' Yet in another late work, the poem entitled 'The Gyres', Yeats insisted that out of 'any rich dark nothing' the whole gazebo would be built up once again. He could conceive of nothing as empty and also as pregnant. I think he saw with increasing rawness the clash between the urge to have done with fine distinctions, subtle passions, and differentiated matter, and the urge to keep them at all costs. In his last play, *The Death of Cuchulain*, the final chorus asks:

> Are those things that men adore and loathe
> Their sole reality?

Yeats had begun to evolve a theory beyond *A Vision*, of how the varying panoply of the material world is really the reflection of spirits and their changing relations to each other. This was perhaps one of the explorations he did not live to complete. With a bow to skepticism, and yet a last rebellion against it, he said in one of his final letters, 'Man can embody the truth but he cannot know it.'

Mrs. Yeats held views sufficiently at odds with his own to protect him from complacency. Mostly she tried to make possible his last poems. She knew his agitated spirit, knew also that he could be absurd and difficult as well as witty and sympathetic. She knew as well how he could overstate and then have second thoughts, and had helped him save himself from many follies. She had made it possible for him to shape the symbology and ideology of his major poetry. One quality in her husband never ceased to astonish her. This was his extraordinary sense of the way things would look to people later on. Very possibly he knew that she would be at the center of his story. If she bore his impress, he also bore hers.

When I had completed my book on Yeats, of which she did not disapprove, I wrote, after the passage of some years, a biography of Yeats's friend James Joyce. I asked Mrs. Yeats if I might dedicate it to her, and she acquiesced. Should I say, 'To Mrs. W. B. Yeats', 'To Mrs. George Yeats', or 'To George Yeats'? I asked her. 'That's for you to decide,' she said. I settled on 'To George Yeats', to make explicit what I hope I have represented here, her independence, her astuteness, her humor. Marriage to Yeats was as problem-ridden as it was magnificent. She lived through it with self-possession, with generosity, with something like nobility.

1979

Freud and Literary Biography

ALTHOUGH many writers today find fault with Freud, I should maintain that we are all still under his long shadow. Not long ago in the United States I read in the press of a dreadful crime: a young man, egged on by his mother, murdered his father. The newspapers helpfully explained that the young man had a very prominent Oedipus complex. If we dismiss this as just a journalistic excess, and an American one to boot, we would do well to remember how hard it is to open our own mouths without registering the effect of Freud upon the language. We converse casually about the sexual proclivities of infants, about sibling rivalries, about dependency upon the mother, about sado-masochistic impulses. When we forget things we suspect ourselves of having wanted to forget them. We may shun the technical vocabulary of Freud, words such as ego, super-ego, id, the anal, oral and genital stages, the pleasure principle and the reality principle, yet we are hardly likely to do without such words as aggression, anxiety, complex, compulsion, the conscious, defense mechanism, narcissism, death wish, erogenous zones, fixation, guilt feeling, sublimation, wish-fulfillment. Freud may not have invented most of these words, yet he connected them together and gave them a special colour and shape. And quite apart from terminology, Freud has given us the conviction that a secret life is going on within us which is only partly under our control.

Perhaps no part of society has been more disrupted by the coming of Freud than has the community of letters. During the nineteenth century, literature grew more and more in the habit of claiming autonomy as a privileged and separate subject. Words such as 'art' and 'artistic' took on an extraordinary dignity. Psychoanalysis has disrupted these pretensions in several distinct ways. First, it has argued that we are all, artists and non-artists, involved in the chronic production of symbolic fantasies, in dreams or day-dreams, in more or less directed oneirism. This being so, artists are not an élite, they are much like other people, at most Rembrandts when the rest of us are only Grandma Moseses. Second, psychoanalysis, an infant discipline, takes over from age-old literature terms such as Oedipus and Narcissus, and to some extent pre-empts them, so that their literary uses become merely illustrative of larger principles. In fact, the word 'Oedipus' now makes us think of Freud, not of Sophocles. That is because psychoanalysis lays claim to an even greater antiquity: Oedipuses were living before Sophocles wrote about him, minds expressed their basic drives before artists seized upon them for subjects. Third, literature becomes something that psychoanalysis fancies it must validate; literature cannot know what it is doing, and in spite of its verbality, cannot speak for itself. It can only offer the practice for which Freud would provide the theory. Fourth, literature, by reason of being without theoretical comprehension of its own processes, uses words in an unconsidered way: it talks of love, when it might be better advised to speak of libido; it speaks of what Byron calls 'the gentlemanly vice of avarice' when it might better talk of anal erotism. So its putative revelations are imprecise. Finally, in the nineteenth century we looked to literature, especially to the novel, for news of the human mind; now we turn to psychoanalysis for the news behind the news.

Freud himself was at once respectful and disrespectful of literature. He acknowledged and even insisted that many of his discoveries about the psyche had been anticipated by literary works. In his discussion of Jensen's *Gradiva* (1907), for example, he praised Jensen for just such an anticipation. Jensen, then still alive, was singularly ungratified by such a view of his work. But when Freud considered art at large, he was often (though not always) less laudatory. The writer sublimates his desires, or, as Freud says, 'the writer softens the egotistical character of his egoistic day-dream by altering and disguising it'. Writing becomes a pleasurable cover-up, furtive rather than open, a repression of reality at least as much as it is an expression of it. It conceals neurosis rather than freeing from it. Qualities that writers have cherished, their aesthetic power, their inspiration and exaltation, their development of previously established forms, have no psychoanalytic standing; they are demystified, or it may be, explained away as results of more basic drives and appetites. Writers fancied they were eagles, and are only clams.

Sensing a challenge, the literary community responded uneasily to the new psychology, especially in an area where it is particularly intrusive, that of biography. Traditional biography has relied upon two kinds of information: documents such as letters, and written or oral reminiscences. These being absent, biographers have often made their surmises or conjectures on the basis of written works. Shakespeare, they think, was a bit like Hamlet as a young man and like Prospero as an old one, and books have been written on such speculations. Freud himself was not inhibited by scarcity of documents or oral histories. Taking up a reminiscence of Leonardo da Vinci, of being in his cradle as an infant when a kite came and struck his mouth with its tail feathers, Freud insists that this was not a memory but a dream, mistranslates kite as vulture, and on these beginnings offers a psychological sketch which takes in not only Leonardo's childhood but his mature paintings. In the same way, he finds Dostoevsky's parricidal guilt feelings to be the cause of that writer's immediately subsequent contraction of epilepsy. It appears, however, that the epilepsy did not develop until long afterwards. Freud is equally bold with a childhood memory of Goethe, of throwing crockery out of the window. This he traces to the birth of a sibling, and does so quite plausibly, though we don't know whether the crockery was actually thrown at the time of a birth or not. No recent biographer has, I believe, followed Freud's theories of Leonardo, Dostoevsky or Goethe. But Freud was perhaps just exploring possibilities. He was more resolute about his theory of Moses, though even here he worried (in a letter to Arnold Zweig of 16 December 1934) that he 'was obliged to construct so imposing a statue upon feet of clay, so that any fool could topple it'. He was perhaps more interested in the general truth of such psychological patterns than in their accuracy in the particular instance.

Jean-Paul Sartre wrote three huge volumes on Flaubert which take off from a similarly minuscule beginning. Flaubert's niece, Mme Caroline Commanville, wrote in old age about her uncle, and recalled his having confided that he could not learn to read at the age of nine. Unfortunately, we have a letter of Flaubert written just at the beginning of his ninth year, and written very well, in which he speaks of having already written plays. Sartre might have decided that Mme Commanville, writing as an old woman, had confused her uncle with somebody else. But he wants to use her reminiscence, so he decides that she has just made a little slip, and remembered that Flaubert said nine when he must have said seven. He then postulates that someone said to the boy of seven, who could not learn his letters, 'you are the idiot of the family'. (Those familiar with Sartre's writings will recall that in his biography of Genet he imagines that someone said to the child Genet, 'you are a thief'.) So the title of Sartre's biography of Flaubert is *L'Idiot de la famille* (1971–2). Were we to object that the child Flaubert, even supposing that he had trouble learning to read, was in other ways precocious, I cannot imagine Sartre retreating. For ultimately Flaubert must be shown to fail in the eyes of his family, and I think we could say, in the eyes of Sartre. And if Sartre lacked the testimony of Mme Commanville, however unreliable that testimony may be, he is quite willing to say that by observing the effects in the mature Flaubert, we can reason back to the causes in Flaubert the child. Given a particular kind of dog's tail, we can deduce a particular kind of muzzle.

The rigorous scrutiny which psychoanalysis offers writers, depriving them of their élite status and sitting as a sort of posthumous authority to take note of their aberrations and concealments, has roused considerable misgivings among them. There has been no one response to Freud. Thomas Mann belauded him. Auden begins the Prologue to *The Orators*, 'By landscape reminded once of his mother's figure', and we realize we are in the age of Freud. T. S. Eliot's reaction was more mixed: in 'The Dry Salvages' he said that 'to explore the womb, or tomb, or dreams is among the usual / Pastimes and drugs, and features of the press', though in *The Cocktail Party* he included among the characters a benign and unworldly psychoanalyst. Joyce in *Finnegans Wake* speaks mockingly of the time 'when we were jung and easily freudened', but he was perhaps the first writer to use Freudian slips in a conscious way. Leopold Bloom speaks of 'the wife's admirers' when he consciously means 'the wife's advisers' and unconsciously thinks of his own wife's admirer; and his tongue slips again when he speaks of that admirer as his wife's 'business menagerer' instead of 'business manager'. Joyce did not subscribe to the Freud–Jones theory of *Hamlet* as Oedipal conflict, though it fascinated him, and in *Ulysses* he centered a psychological explanation of the play in the feelings of the dead king rather than of the living son, *Hamlet* without the prince almost. Joyce turned down a suggestion that he be analysed by Jung, but he allowed Jung to attempt to cure his distraught daughter. In a later generation Ernest Hemingway would revolt against the idea that his works were the result of a psychic trauma rather than of the utmost aesthetic cunning. There are of course examples of writers who have been analysed, such as H. D. and Doris Lessing, but other writers have felt that the peculiar synthesis of weakness and strength which constituted their gift would not profit by being anatomized. Erich Fromm advised Conrad Aiken not to risk it.

Of course, writers have always been dubious about putting their lives at the mercy of biographers. They could see that they had much to lose, and probably little to gain, by having their pasts reconstructed without the right of reply. Oscar Wilde remarked that biography 'adds to death a new terror, and makes one wish that all art were anonymous'. Thomas Carlyle declared that 'the biographies of men of letters are for the most part the saddest chapter in the history of the human race except the Newgate Calendar'. For while traditional biography was usually animated by a desire to be adulatory, or when necessary exculpatory, it could scarely fail to present details which were irrelevant or perhaps at odds with this motive. The lives of creative writers, as of other men, cannot consist only of moments of victorious self-transcendence and transcendence of circumstances, but must include pettinesses and humiliations. Of this Freud was well aware. In 1936 Arnold Zweig offered to write his biography. Freud responded (31 May 1936) that he was too fond of Zweig to permit it. 'To be a biographer,' he said, 'you must tie yourself up in lies, concealments, hypocrisies, false colourings, and even in hiding a lack of understanding, for biographical truth is not to be had, and if it were to be had, we could not use it.' He went on, 'truth is not feasible, mankind doesn't deserve it, and anyway isn't our prince Hamlet right when he says that if we all had our deserts, which of us would 'scape whipping?' So he offers two objections, somewhat self-contradictory: one that biographers tell lies, the other that if they told truths the truths would be unbearable. He found a discreet biographer in Ernest Jones, who skirted many of those issues that Freud would have dealt with in other men, and, though a psycho-analyst, made no effort at psychoanalysis.

Given such cogent objections, even from Freud himself, to bio-graphical undertakings, the proliferation of biography in our century is astonishing. The advance tremors that dying writers have felt have proved justified. Scarcely has their breath left them when their widows or widowers feel obliged to choose among the outstretched pens of eager memorializers. There is hardly time for mourning; the public's appetite for information must be filled as soon as the grave. This appetite is not altogether discreditable. We long to understand our world, and imagine we can do so by understanding the vivid personalities within it. We want to bring them back to life, so far as we can. With literary men this impulse is especially understandable, for while television figures – politicians or athletes or newscasters – are people we can recognize like old acquaintances, writers work in such strict privacy and are generally so secretive about their inten-tions and sources that we look at their lives with even keener interest. We wish that the biographer would explain the mainsprings of genius. Freud acknowledged that the comprehension of genius was beyond his powers, and later biographers, without disclaiming the task, have had less success at it than we hoped.

No doubt we have also, in reading or writing biography, a less noble aim, a gossipy one, to confirm through the details of a life that a gifted man or woman, though in many ways unlike us, is, like us too, subject to the same needs, smelling equally of mortality. We at once want them to present themselves on the same stage that we occupy, and yet – for we have not given up the heroic altogether – we want them undiminished.

Freud understood that his own case histories were close to biographies; he called them pathographies. Yet health and disease are so intermingled by his theory that no one can escape being a potential patient. His epoch seems based on the aphorism: one touch of kinkiness makes the whole world kin. Normality, healthy sexuality and similar terms are out of order. The ordinary is as much subject to scrutiny as the extraordinary. Freud's case histories are however biographies without heroes, as they are without villains. They are also biographies without history, for the linear past interests him less than the imaginative past, especially the mythology of childhood which may well be partially invented by the patient to suit his later needs, and which may suddenly obtrude itself quite out of regular order. There is no time in the unconscious, as Freud points out. Whether we saw the primal scene or not, he eventually decided, was irrelevant; we thought we did, we imagined we did, and that is enough. We live among feelings, to which facts may or may not adhere. Biographers have never felt so free of the necessity of distinguishing fact from fantasy.

Towards biography as practiced before his time Freud was severe. He regarded it as based on deliberate concealment. In his essay on Leonardo he said that the majority of biographers pass over in silence the subject's sexual activity or sexual individuality, and therefore cannot arrive at an understanding of the subject's mental life. On this point he was obviously right. Pre-Freudian biographers were averse to breaking taboos about sexual details. Froude had heard from a close friend of Jane Carlyle, on her deathbed, that Carlyle was impotent; but in four long volumes of biography of Carlyle he avoids mention of this point. While novelists, especially in France, were becoming increasingly open about sexuality, biographers were slow to follow, and tended to cling to notions of respectability that novelists were trying to dislodge.

Freud also declared that 'biographers are fixated on their heroes in a quite special way. In many cases,' he says in *Leonardo da Vinci* (1910),

they have chosen their hero as the subject of their studies because – for reasons of their personal emotional life – they have felt a special affection for him from the very first. They then devote their energies to a task of idealization, aimed at enrolling the great man among the class of their infant models – at reviving in him, perhaps, the child's idea of his father. To gratify this wish they obliterate the individual features of their subject's physiognomy. They smooth over the traces of his life's struggle with internal and external resistances, and they tolerate in him no vestige of human weakness or imperfection. They thus present us with what is in fact a cold, strange, ideal figure, instead of a human being to whom we might feel ourselves distantly related. That they should do this is regrettable, for they thereby sacrifice truth to an illusion, and for the sake of their infantile phantasies abandon the opportunity of penetrating the most fascinating secrets of human nature.

This is a vehement indictment that Freud makes, though now a little out of date. I should doubt that modern biographers are fixated on their subjects or look in them for father figures (or even mother figures, a possibility that Freud characteristically ignored). The modern biographer has read Freud, or even if he has not, he has absorbed him. He has come to recognize the dangers of fixation and idealization. The biography of Woodrow Wilson (1966) in which Freud purportedly collaborated with William C. Bullitt originated in what might be called counter-fixation, in active dislike, as they admit. If a modern biographer identifies himself a little with his subject, he does so reservedly, and withdraws a bit at the same time.

And it must be said that the subject of the literary biographer – the writer – has also become more wary, apprehensive of being psychoanalysed too easily. An analyst of my acquaintance tells me that he rarely sees among educated people in cities the classic symptoms of hysteria, such as paralysis of an arm or leg, inability to speak or swallow, fainting or convulsions, which were so marked when Freud began to delineate hysteria. Even hysterics know a cliché. But an Austrian analyst tells me, 'in Vienna we have still the classic symptoms'. Now that our possession of an Oedipus complex has been dinned into us from our early years, writers are much less prone to present so well acknowledged a behavior pattern. Were Sophocles alive today, he would write about someone else than Oedipus. Other discoveries of Freud, such as meaningful slips of the tongue, are grasped at once by the tongue-slipper, not to mention by his auditors, and so seem to bear a reduced significance, as if whatever was being repressed was not repressed very far down. If we have an accident, we know all about accident-proneness, though this may not stop the pain. Nor do we fall so easily into the error marked out by Freud of being too hero-orientated. The unheroic interests us too – moments of shabby conduct, or symptoms of disease – Freud's own cancer of the palate, for example. Biographers are often accused of indecorum, and reply by accusing their detractors of squeamishness.

Our conception of the creative process has undergone such an upheaval that we no longer look, as a nineteenth-century biographer would, for evidence of the taking of infinite pains that genius traditionally is said to constitute. Mere gumption does not impress us. In the last century it was assumed that literary works came into being because their authors willed them to. The modern biographer would question the anatomy of that will. He would be likely to see the writer as the victim of internal compulsions or familial and extra-familial complications, bursting into literature, willy-nilly, writing not to express finesses but, it may be, to exorcize horrors. Henri Michaux, in one of his imaginary voyages, describes how a people whom he calls Les Hacs rear their artists. It might be a parable of our present conception:

The Hacs have arranged to rear every year a few child martyrs, whom they subject to harsh treatment and evident injustices, inventing reasons and deceptive complications, based on lies, for everything, in an atmosphere of terror and mystery.

Entrusted with this work are some hardhearted men, real brutes, directed by cruel and clever overseers.

In this way they have reared up great artists, great poets, but also, unfortunately, assassins and especially reformers – incredible bitterenders.

If a change is made in the customs and social institutions, it's owing to them; if, in spite of their small army, the Hacs have nothing to fear, again they owe it to them; if, in their straightforward language, lightning flashes of anger have been fixed, beside which the honeyed deviousness of foreign writers seems insipid dog food, it is again to them they owe it, to a few ragged, wretched, hopeless kids.

Art, by these lights, is not the result of virtue but of handicap. Matthew Arnold admired Sophocles for seeing life steadily and seeing it whole. We on the other hand admire our writers because they respond with fury and passion to abuse and indignity. The wise contemplative visage of Goethe is not our model, but the hurt, furtive face of Kafka. When Joyce in *Ulysses* has Stephen Dedalus offer us a portrait of Shakespeare, it is not the swan of Avon serenely regarding the human scene, but a vengeful cuckold writing out of anger and jealousy. I think we can attribute to Freud the way that our biographical attention has been directed away from the perfection of artifacts and on to the imperfection of artificers. Yeats reminds us that all the artistic ladders start in the foul rag- and bone-shop of the heart, and the rag- and bone-shop is what we want to examine – not the empyrean loft to which the ladders go. So Robert Lowell, an imperfect poet, wrote in a late poem that imperfection is the language of art. Sartre conceives of Flaubert as saying to himself, 'loser wins', as if only through defeat in life is victory in art possible. The writer gets his own back by writing.

If we try to isolate the features of modern biography, the first is its heightened sensitivity. I think we can attribute this in large part to Freud. The biographer conceives of himself not as outside but as inside the subject's mind, not as observing but as ferreting. Facts do not speak for themselves. We model ourselves on Freud, analysts without couches. What Freud instructs us, as Philip Rieff observes, is to recognize all experience as symptomatic. Trivia have as much to tell us as crises. We should all like to collect tell-tale slips of tongue or pen, for example, although these are not so easy to find as perhaps *The Psychopathology of Everyday Life* makes them seem. We live in what Paul Ricoeur in his book on Freud calls the age of suspicion; we do not so much present as arraign. Sartre, in writing of Baudelaire as in writing of Flaubert, often seems the prosecuting attorney, when an earlier biographer would have been attorney for the defense.

The conviction that everything is relevant is somewhat destructive of chronology. The nineteenth century could view a life as a progress from primitive childhood to civilized adulthood, followed perhaps by the return to primitivism in dotage. But Freud makes us recognize that linear development may not describe the psyche adequately, the *Nachträglichkeit* or deferred action may suddenly project the being into new areas, as hitherto suppressed parts of the self manifest themselves. The ahistorical unconscious is constantly obtruding into the historical layers of the mind. Moreover, the unity of the self is likely to be relinquished by the biographer in favor of a more protean entity. Like the wizened Christ child in some early Italian paintings, we are born old. Sexualized from birth, ridden by un-directed or half-directed fantasies, we have no time to grow up even if we have the will. Sartre suggests that a life is simply a childhood with the stops pulled out; but it might well be a childhood with many of the stops pushed in even further. Our seeming selves are only palimpsests under which may be dimly perceived features suc-cessfully or unsuccessfully repressed. If we persist in regarding the self as in some sense one rather than many, we have still to allow for what Sartre calls its carousel of motives moving about the pool of its central ipseity.

The lesson that Freud inculcates, of our sexual nature, has been learned almost too well. The word Freudian has become a synonym for sexual, although Freud makes clear in his essay, ' "Wild" Psychoanalysis', how wrong this is, because repression is an essential part of sexuality. The nineteenth-century reticence of which he complained is hard to discover in our contemporary behavior. We are quite prepared to make our sometimes naïve deductions from what we can find out about bedroom quirks. That Ruskin's moral fervor derived in large part from his sexual fears, and that Carlyle's pungency compensated for sexual impotence, are near-commonplaces of biographical interpretation. Recent biographies of Fitzgerald and Auden discuss not only their mating habits but the size of their genitals. We are all prepared to acknowledge what Freud called somatic compliance, the body's submission to the mind, as well as its opposite, the mind's submission to the body. Even Yeats says, 'our bodies are nearer ... to the "unconscious" than our thoughts'. On the other hand, when Sartre says that Flaubert's maternal grandfather, after the death of his wife in childbirth, took revenge upon the new-born infant by sickening and then dying himself, we become skeptical, especially when we discover that his death did not occur until ten years later. What protracted vindictiveness! Psychoanalysis may also relieve our envy of sexual athletes; their success may be as pathological as the commoner unsuccess. Don Giovanni is not sensual, he is sick; he needs a hospital, not a hell. Maybe.

The effect of our new-found methods of detection is vast and unpredictable. The unknown need not be the unknowable. To paraphrase Freud, where obscurity was, hypothesis shall be. In this sense, paucity of information may even be an advantage, as freeing the mind for conjecture. The early years, to which psychoanalysis attaches so much importance, are just those about which we know least. But there are mysteries throughout. Where direct evidence is missing, we have to rely on outside testimony. The witness of friends or relatives may or may not be helpful. Of course, there are always letters. The modern biographer is aware that the letter is itself a literary form, through which writer and recipient play a game of concealment and revealment. What we have to read in correspondence is what is not written there, as at a party we notice who has not been invited. For earlier biographers, letters were saints' relics; for biographers since Freud, they are likely to be duplicitous or at least incomplete.

In presenting his subject a biographer agrees with Freud that we must be skeptical of heroics. We have always known, even without Freud's help, or Rochefoucauld's, that our virtues are often vices in disguise. Now the existence of virtue is itself almost in question. In Eliot's *Murder in the Cathedral* the last temptation of Thomas à Becket is that of martyrdom. We cannot even die for a cause without worrying that it may be just a means of self-aggrandizement. Self-sacrifice is another virtue that has lost much of its earlier prestige. Oscar Wilde connected it with the self-mutilation of savages. The appetite for suffering is one of which Freud has made us intensely conscious. The concept of sado-masochism has put to flight many seemingly virtuous acts. For what Freud tells us, though he never said so explicitly, is that the stomach hunts the ulcer.

Just as virtues have taken on a little viciousness, so vices have lost some of theirs. The vice of extravagance is such a failing. Questionable as a method of household economy, it may be defensible when applied to literary innovation. Joyce regarded himself as guilty of both kinds. Drunkenness may be reprehensible in itself, but as a control over schizophrenia, as Jung said Joyce used it, it may have its merits. Abysses of shyness and evasion may underlie dogmatism, inner firmness may be concealed under wobbling and waffling. Lautréamont said of his fearful book *Les Chants de Maldoror* that he had indeed, like Byron, Baudelaire and others, sung the praises of evil. 'Of course I exaggerated a bit in order to make an original contribution to the kind of sublime literature that only sings of despair in order to depress the reader and make him long for goodness as a remedy.' Beckett's work proceeds somewhat differently; it undercuts despair by saving humor, and undercuts saving humor by unsalvageable despair. All that is certain is uncertainty. Contradictory impulses may coincide; as Freud tells us, there is no *no* in the unconscious. Lacan points out in *Ecrits* (1966), 'what the unconscious forces us to examine is the law according to which no utterance can ever be reduced simply to its own statement'. When Yeats asks whether he believes in that farrago of occultism and philosophy and poetry which he calls *A Vision*, he seems to reply that he both does and does not, and that the question of belief may not belong to our age, and that truth can be embodied in a poet's life but not known. George Eliot, in a sentence admired by Henry James, spoke of 'the suppressed transitions which unite all contrasts'. Freud's term, reaction-formation, indicates how we may repress a wish by doing the exact opposite of it. The modern biographer recognizes that every motive is a multiplicity of motives, many of them in conflict; as Michaux says, we are born of too many others.

We must infer that biology has plunged into a new phase. At the same time, many biographies are not written in full awareness of what has been happening. The responsibilities of this kind of subtle and devious interpretation are so manifold that few practitioners rush to take them all on. Their failure to do so is not reprehensible.

For one thing, the information they have about matters which are crucial for Freud is often scanty, and they may be reluctant, understandably, to introduce their own speculations as if they commanded equal attention with known particulars. Another is that the tracing of ultimate causes may reduce differentiation: the biographies of Woodrow Wilson by Freud and Bullitt, of Martin Luther by Erikson, and of Flaubert by Sartre, all make so much of their subjects' Oedipal complexes and their relation to God the Father, that the President, the religious reformer and the writer might almost be confused with one another. The unconscious is a great melting pot. Even Freud sometimes apologizes for the repetitiveness of certain psychological patterns, and a biographer who depends heavily upon them is likely to create a stereotype instead of a person.

It seems probable that certain patterns made available by psychoanalysis may have a blurring effect. For example, among the character traits isolated by Freud is the anal erotic. Edmund Wilson attributed this quality to Ben Jonson. It could easily be attributed to Ernest Hemingway. For Hemingway, unlike his prodigal friend Fitzgerald, was always gathering, absorbing, hoarding, withholding. He prided himself on his secrets, and his method of writing was to offer information as sparingly as possible. 'You'll lose it if you talk about it,' says Jake in *The Sun Also Rises* [*Fiesta*]. For Hemingway writing was a kind of suppression with only partial release. He behaved in life as in his art, going without food to save money, then engaging in some gush of expense, but all the time keeping a money heap in reserve. His capacity for retention extended to keeping his early notebooks in bank vaults for many years, for future exploitation. Even his method of composing a paragraph in circles around key words suggests a peristaltic movement. Though he wanted to be known as swashbuckling, his strength came from self-concealment. His well-known competitiveness was as much as anything an attempt to protect his winter stores.

A biographer of Hemingway will certainly wish to present this character trait. But the fact that it was presumably shared by Ben Jonson – so different a writer – may make us less cocky about what we have found. Could it be that anal erotism is pretty general among writers? They are usually inclined to be thrifty, to build up reserve supplies, to play ant rather than grasshopper. Whether there is any physical parallel – whether their bowels behave anally erotically – we can rarely find out. But one thing is sure: the daring innovation in style of Hemingway, its fanatical economy, like the humor and lyricism of Ben Jonson, may be disparaged by offering it in the context of anal erotism.

Another post-Freudian situation arises in biography when the biographer shapes, to the point of distortion, the facts at his disposal in accordance with Freudian theory. Henry James, as is well known and confirmed by love letters to a man, was predominantly homosexual. Freud offers several explanations of homosexuality, including a genetic one, but the one he expounds most prominently, as in his essay on Leonardo, is that the homosexual is fixated on the mother. (Freud regretted later that he had had so little to go on in this essay.) Leon Edel in his biography of James searches for evidence that James's mother 'smothered' her son Henry. Unfortunately the evidence is lacking, and almost all the testimony Edel gives – from friends, relatives, or Henry James himself – appears to differ with his conclusion. Of course, one can still say that it is true without evidence. In an area where witnesses are so hard to come by, speculation can be rife. An aphorism of our time for Freudian biography might be: if you can't see it, it must be there. Still, caution is necessary if we would persuade others.

It has required the assurance of Jean-Paul Sartre to carry out a fullscale biography of the modern kind. Though not by any means an orthodox Freudian, since he finds the unconscious to be conscious, he still keeps largely to Freudian patterns. He has little to say of the feat of Flaubert in remaking the novel, partly because he is suspicious of literature; in particular, Sartre is contemptuous of late nineteenth-century literature, which he calls an 'art-neurosis' engineered by the Knights of Nothingness, whose ideals he finds to be anti-human. Flaubert was a Knight of Nothingness, and Sartre's interest is in showing how he came to be one. I have already mentioned the slender memories to which Sartre often attaches so much weight. When questioned as to how he knows something about Flaubert, he has the assurance to reply, 'Well, I've read Flaubert'. And though he insists that life and work should not be equated, he does equate them again and again. For example, he relies heavily upon patterns he claims to find in Flaubert's early stories. When he has to allow that these stories are common ones of the period, very much to hand for Flaubert, he counters by asking why Flaubert – faced with many common stories – picked these particular ones.

The argument is conducted with great force and wit. Still, it is not quite so convincing as Sartre imagines. In the stories, for example, he is particularly eager to find instances of sibling rivalries. Usually in the stories the older brother is triumphant, thus confirming Sartre's conjecture that Flaubert felt victimized by his elder brother. But in one story the young brother is triumphant. Sartre is not fazed: he announces that this time Flaubert has 'shuffled the cards'. But of course the question then arises, why did he not shuffle the cards some more? And if shuffling the cards is to be conceded, then how do we know that the other stories, in which the older brother is triumphant, are not the ones which have been shuffled the most? I think that we know enough about the creative process to insist that the erect pen has no conscience, that Flaubert may well have imported details from other lives rather than from his own, or just tried his hand at a story which he had happened to hear or read recently. There is always the hopeful possibility, which occurs to the reader as Sartre completes his accusatory case against his subject, that Flaubert's family life was quite different from the nightmare version Sartre conjures up. Sartre offers Flaubert no liberty, keeps him on a tight leash, binds him hand and foot, fetish and phobia. With certain presuppositions about family life, largely based on Freud, Sartre can prove his case over and over again. His eloquence about the unknown is staggering. The flimsier the documentation, the more he has to say. When facts are mentioned, they come as a relief. Substitutions are everywhere: about one of Flaubert's stories Sartre insists that the father is really the mother, and the mother the father. (Later on he says that Flaubert's father mothered him after his breakdown at Pont-L'Evêque.) He has also the family romance at its most intense: not only does son murder father but father murders son. This is grand stuff, and we wish it could be confirmed.

I think that Sartre has indicated the merits and demerits of modern biographical method. On the one hand, thanks to Freud, we have been alerted to all sorts of complexities in the personality. On the other hand, these can be interpreted so variously that it is hard to establish firm footing. Where everything can stand for its opposite, where fantasies and facts intertwine, we look desperately for a position in time and space. Freud is supposed to have said that there are times when a cigar is just a cigar. But how to recognize these tranquil moments of simple identity?

That Freud makes biography difficult does not mean that he should be put aside. Biographers need a depth psychology, and Freud, with his followers and deviationists, offers one. Conceptualizing a life is different from living it; experiences cannot be simply transcribed on to paper without filtering them through an alien consciousness. Perhaps we should be gingerly in applying Freud's theories, for it is when they are most ostentatious that they awaken most uneasiness. Yet if Sartre runs too fast, not to run at all would be craven. A modern biographer is bound to attend to incursions of the irrational upon the rational, to look for unexpected connections and unsuspected motivations. For all this Freud remains a model, though no doubt a tricky one.

1984

Acknowledgements

A number of Richard Ellmann's essays included in this volume have been previously published, sometimes in somewhat different form, and we wish to thank all those who have granted us permission to include them here: "The Uses of Decadence," presented as Lecture Six in the Ben Belitt Lecture Series at Bennington College, Bennington, Vermont, was subsequently published as a Bennington Chapbook in Literature. Copyright © 1984 by Bennington College. Reprinted by permission of Ben Belitt and Bennington College; "Yeats Without Analogue" was published originally as the "Preface" to *The Identity of Yeats*, 2nd Edition, by Richard Ellmann. Copyright © 1964 by Oxford University Press, Inc. Rights outside the U.S. administered by Macmillan and Company Limited, London. Reprinted here by permission of Oxford University Press, New York, and Macmillan and Company Limited, London; "Ez and Old Billyum" and "Gazebos and Gashouses" are from *Eminent Domain* by Richard Ellmann, Oxford University Press, New York and Oxford, 1967. Rights administered by the Estate of Richard Ellmann; "'He Do the Police in Different Voices,'" "Dorothea's Husbands," and "Two Faces of Edward" are from *Golden Codgers* by Richard Ellmann, Oxford University Press, 1973. Rights in the U.S. administered by the Estate of Richard Ellmann. Reprinted here by permission of Oxford University Press, Oxford, and the Estate of Richard Ellmann; "Crab-Apple Jelly" (originally published as "O'Connor's Crab-Apple Jelly"), "Love in the Catskills," "Getting to Know You," and "The Life of Sim Botchit" were published originally in *The New York Review of Books*. Reprinted by permission of the Estate of Richard Ellmann; "Henry James Among the Aesthetes" was presented as a lecture at the British Academy, London, May 19, 1983, and subsequently published in the *Proceedings of the British Academy*. Copyright © 1984 by The British Academy. Reprinted by permission of the British Academy; "Lawrence and His Demon" was published originally in the *New Mexico Quarterly*, Winter 1952, Vol. XXII, No. 4. Reprinted by permission of the Estate of Richard Ellmann; "Wallace Steven's Ice-Cream" was published originally in *The Kenyon Review*, Winter 1957, Vol. IX, No. 1. Reprinted by permission of *The Kenyon Review* and the Estate of Richard Ellman; "The Ductile Universe of Henri Michaux" was published originally as the "Introduction" to *Henri Michaux: Selected Writings* translated by Richard Ellmann, 1952, with excerpts from the "Foreword" to the 1968 edition. Copyright © 1968 by New Directions Publishing Corporation. Reprinted by permission of New Directions Publishing Corporation; "The Hemingway Circle" was published originally in the *New Statesman*, August 15, 1969. Reprinted by permission of the Estate of Richard Ellmann; "How Wallace Stevens Saw Himself" is from *Wallace Stevens: A Celebration* edited by Frank Doggett and Robert Buttel. Copyright © 1980 by Princeton University Press. Reprinted by permission of Princeton University Press; "At the Yeatses'" was published originally as the "Preface" to the 1979 Oxford University Press edition of *Yeats: The Man and the Masks* by Richard Ellmann. Rights administered by the Estate of Richard Ellmann; and "Freud and Literary Biography" is from *Freud and the Humanities* edited by Peregrine Horden. Rights outside the U.S. and Canada administered by Gerald Duckworth & Co., Ltd. Reprinted here by permission of St. Martin's Press, Inc., and Gerald Duckworth & Co., Ltd.

Excerpts from two unpublished letters, January 1 and 3, 1913, from W.B. Yeats to Lady Gregory. Reprinted by permission of Oxford University Press, Oxford, England.

Grateful acknowledgement to the following for permission to reprint previously published material:

Harcourt Brace Jovanovich, Inc., and *Faber and Faber Limited:* Excerpts from "The Waste Land" in *Collected Poems 1909–1962* by T.S. Eliot. Copyright 1936 by Harcourt Brace Jovanovich, Inc., Copyright © 1963, 1964 by T.S. Eliot; and excerpts from *The Waste Land: A Facsimile and Transcript of the*

Acknowledgements

Original Drafts, edited by Valerie Eliot. Copyright © 1971 by Valerie Eliot. Rights outside the U.S. administered by Faber and Faber Limited, London. Reprinted by permission of Harcourt Brace Jovanovich, Inc. and Faber and Faber Limited.

David Higham Associates Limited: Excerpt from a poem by Louis MacNeice from *Letters from Iceland*, 1937; and an excerpt from the poem "Last Will and Testament" written jointly by Louis MacNeice and W.H. Auden. Reprinted by permission of David Higham Associates Limited for the Estate of Louis MacNeice.

Alfred A. Knopf, Inc.: Excerpts from "Three Travellers Watch a Sunrise," "Cortege for Rosenbloom," "The Emperor of Ice-Cream," "Sunday Morning," "Le Monocle de Mon Oncle," "Esthetique de Mal," "Peter Quince at the Clavier," "Thirteen Ways of Looking at a Blackbird," "So-and-So Reclining on Her Couch," and "Poupee des Poupees" by Wallace Stevens from *The Collected Poems of Wallace Stevens*. Copyright 1954 by Wallace Stevens. Copyright renewed 1982 by Holly Stevens; and excerpts from *Letters of Wallace Stevens*, edited by Holly Stevens. Copyright © 1966 by Holly Stevens. Reprinted by permission of Alfred A. Knopf, Inc.

Macmillan Publishing Company and *A.P. Watt Ltd.*: Excerpts from various poems from *The Poems of W.B. Yeats: A New Edition*, edited by Richard J. Finneran. Copyright 1916, 1919, 1924, 1928, 1933 by Macmillan Publishing Company, renewed 1944, 1947, 1952, 1956, 1961 by Bertha Georgie Yeats. Copyright 1940 by Georgie Yeats, renewed 1968 by Bertha Georgie Yeats, Michael Butler Yeats, and Anne Yeats. Rights outside the U.S. administered by A.P. Watt Ltd. Reprinted by permission of Macmillan Publishing Company and A.P. Watt Ltd. on behalf of Michael B. Yeats and Macmillan London Ltd.

New Directions Publishing Corporation: Excerpt from *Henri Michaux: Selected Writings*. Copyright © 1968 by New Directions Publishing Corporation; excerpts from "La Fraisne," "Hugh Selwyn Mauberly," "Plotinus," "Alf's Eighth Bit," and "Under Ben Bulben" from *Ezra Pound: Personae*. Copyright 1926 by Ezra Pound; and excerpts from Canto LXXXII, Canto LXXXIII, Canto LXXXI, Canto LXVIII, Canto 116, and Cantos from *The Cantos of Ezra Pound*. Copyright 1948, © 1959, 1962 by Ezra Pound. Reprinted by permission of New Directions Publishing Corporation.

W.W. Norton & Company, Inc. and *Routledge and Kegan Paul Ltd.*: Excerpt from *Leonardo da Vinci and a Memory of His Childhood* by Sigmund Freud, translated by Alan Tyson. First American Edition, 1964. Reprinted by permission of W.W. Norton & Company, Inc. and Routledge and Kegan Paul Ltd. (in *Selected Essays of Sigmund Freud*, Vol. 11.) All rights reserved.

Random House, Inc., and *Faber and Faber Limited*: Excerpts from various poems by W.H. Auden including "August 1968," "Heavy Date," "In Schraft's," "The Letter," and "Letter to Lord Byron" from *W.H. Auden: Collected Poems*, edited by Edward Mendelson. Copyright © 1976 by Edward Mendelson, William Meredith, and Monroe K. Spears, Executors of the Estate of W.H. Auden; and an excerpt from "Letter to a Wound" by W.H. Auden from *The English Auden: Poems, Essays, and Dramatic Writings, 1927–1939*, edited by Edward Mendelson. Copyright © 1977 by Edward Mendelson, William Meredith, and Monroe K. Spears, Executors of the Estate of W.H. Auden. Reprinted by permission of Random House, Inc., and Faber and Faber Limited.

Unwin Hyman Limited: Excerpt from July 1915 letter by Bertrand Russell from *Autobiography of Bertrand Russell*. Reprinted by permission of Unwin Hyman Limited, London.

Viking Penguin, Inc.: Excerpts from "Lightning," "The Wild Common," "The Enkindled Spring," "Last Words to Miriam," "Snake," and "Hymn to Priapus" from *The Complete Poems of D.H. Lawrence*, collected and edited by Vivian de Sola Pinto and F. Warren Roberts. Copyright © 1964, 1971 by Angelo Ravagli and C.M. Weekley, Executors of the Estate of Frieda Lawrence Ravagli. All rights reserved. Reprinted by permission of Viking Penguin, Inc.

Index

273

Index

Index

Index

ABOUT THE AUTHOR

Richard Ellmann died on May 13, 1987, of amyotrophic lateral sclerosis ("Lou Gehrig's disease") in Oxford, England, where he was retired Goldsmith's Professor of English Literature and Fellow of New College. He was sixty-nine years old. His distinguished career as a scholar and teacher included studies at Yale and at Trinity College, Dublin, and teaching positions at Harvard, Yale, Northwestern, Emory, the University of Chicago, Indiana, and Oxford. His great biography of James Joyce won the National Book Award in 1959. Other widely praised books included two on Yeats, two volumes of Joyce letters, several collections of essays and last years' definitive—and best-selling—biography of Oscar Wilde, completed just before his death.

Also by

Richard Ellmann

Oscar Wilde

"Magnificent . . . Biography on the grand scale . . . a lasting monument
to both Oscar Wilde and Richard Ellmann."
—Robert E. Kuehn, <u>Chicago Tribune</u>

"A master of the biographer's art . . . a distinguished book . . . Ellmann
has the first, indispensable virtue of telling his story well—not just the
big story but the lesser stories that lie coiled inside it."
—<u>The New York Review of Books</u>

"It is difficult to imagine a more comprehensive, measured and
fascinating account."
—<u>Time</u>

"A great book . . . the second of his masterpieces . . . a product of long
and meticulous labour, which is also an expression of Ellmann's exquisite critical sense, wide and deep learning, and profound humanity."
—Anthony Burgess

"A brilliant life . . . capacious, deeply sympathetic and vastly entertaining."
—<u>Washington Post Book World</u>

VINTAGE BOOKS

AVAILABLE AT YOUR LOCAL BOOKSTORE OR CALL
TOLL-FREE TO ORDER 1-800-733-3000
(CREDIT CARDS ONLY).